MW01286421

LITTLEJOHN'S POLITICAL MEMOIRS

(1934-1988)

By
Bruce Littlejohn

Spartanburg, South Carolina

Library of Congress Catalog Card Number 89-92715
ISBN 0-9625077-0-9

Published by
Bruce Littlejohn
P.O. Box 2526
450 Connecticut Avenue
Spartanburg, South Carolina 29304

PRINTED IN THE UNITED STATES OF AMERICA

First Edition

Dedicated to my eighteen law clerks,
who served me well while I was a member of
The Supreme Court of South Carolina,
in order of their service
commencing in 1967:

Jackson V. Gregory
Robert L. Wynn III
William C. Stork
William Youngblood
A. Camden Lewis
James W. Hudgens
Sidney Riggs
Richard Rhodes
Glen Baldwin
Steve Cannon
James W. Shaw
P. Townsend McChesney
Reginald L. Foster
Alan M. Tewkesbury Jr.
David White
Daryl Hawkins
Frank Grimball
Jane Matthews

ACKNOWLEDGEMENTS

I am indebted to Miss Suzanne Wilson, my secretary, for many hours devoted to helping me with the creation of this book, to Beth Littlejohn for copy editing, and to Robert P. Wilkins for much timely advice.

INTRODUCTION

As a rule, political science is no more relevant to a South Carolina politician than ornithology is relevant to a bird. That is to say: it would be as unlikely to find a Pee Dee precinct president persuing W.J. Cash's *Mind of the South* as it would be to find a bluejay with his beak stuck in Roger Tory Peterson's *Field Guide to the Birds*. This book by Bruce Littlejohn is the exception to the rule, and only he could have written it.

A good case can be made for the proposition that the two most important public offices in South Carolina have been those of the Chief Justice of the Supreme Court and the Speaker of the House of Representatives. To be sure, the President Pro Tempore of the Senate and the Governor have, from time to time, emerged as worthy challengers. But, at least from the historical perspective, the Chief Justice and the Speaker have most often reigned preeminent in this state.

In the half-century of 1936-1986, only nine people have served as Chief Justice: John Stabler, Milledge Bonham, Gordon Baker, Taylor Stukes, Claude Taylor, Joseph Moss, Woodrow Lewis, J.B. Ness and Bruce Littlejohn. During this period, only seven people have served as Speaker of the House: Claude Taylor, Solomon Blatt, Thomas Pope, Rex Carter, Raymond Schwartz, Robert Sheheen and Bruce Littlejohn.

In the entire history of South Carolina, only three people have served as both Chief Justice of the Supreme Court and Speaker of the House of Representatives: Ira Jones, Claude Taylor and Bruce Littlejohn. Of these three, only one has written a book: Bruce Littlejohn.

In addition, Bruce Littlejohn has served as an officer in the Army during World War II, a prosecutor of Japanese war criminals after the war, a member of the House of Representatives, a Circuit Court Judge and, after his retirement as Chief Justice, an Acting Judge of the South Carolina Court of Appeals.

Bruce Littlejohn, therefore, has been uniquely situated to bring to this book of history, not the oompah of the academic, but the

intimacy of the eye witness. He has written the history of fifty
years of South Carolina politics from the perspective of one who
has seen it happen—indeed, one who has, more often than not,
caused it to happen.

This single volume chronicles the political history of this State
from the election of Olin Johnston to the election of Carroll Campbell, from the triumphant return of Jimmy Byrnes to the almost
triumphant return of Pug Ravenel, from Strom Thurmond of the
1940s to Strom Thurmond of the 1980s. Included are such quintes-
sential South Carolina political stories as the time the Highway
Department was declared to be in a state of insurrection, the role of
the State in the effort by Franklin Delano Roosevelt to pack the
United States Supreme Court, and the rebirth of the Republican
Party in this century. Separate chapters are devoted to all the
political campaigns in this state, 1936 through 1988.

When he asked me to write this introduction, Chief Justice
Littlejohn made only one request: that I include a poem in it. (Why
he did so is another story, best left untold for now.) The lines which
most immediately come to mind are those of Kipling:

Recessional

God of our fathers, known of old
    Lord of our far-flung battle-line—
Beneath whose awful hand we hold
    Dominion over palm and pine—
Lord God of Hosts, be with us yet,
Lest we forget—lest we forget!

The tumult and the shouting dies—
    The captains and the king depart—
Still stands Thine ancient sacrifice,
    An humble and a contrite heart.
Lord God of Hosts, be with us yet,
Lest we forget—lest we forget!

Of course, the Spanish philosopher, George Santayana, said es-
sentially the same thing, more ominously. "Those who cannot
remember the past," he warned, "are condemned to repeat it." I
have observed over the years that virtually everyone in South
Carolina who has heard this quotation is condemned to repeat it.
Nevertheless, despite the high regard South Carolinians appear to

have for things historic, South Carolina politicians seem far more adept at repeating history than remembering it. Perhaps this is because, up until now, there has never been a book like this one.

ALEXANDER M. SANDERS, JR.
Chief Judge, South Carolina Court of Appeals

CONTENTS

Part I: Potpourri

Part II: The Political Campaigns

Part I
POTPOURRI

1

WHY THIS BOOK

In 1974 I wrote and published a book entitled *Laugh With the Judge*, a collection of 180 humorous anecdotes. It is owned by the Sandlapper Publishing Company of Orangeburg, South Carolina, and they continue to reprint and market it.

In 1987 I wrote a book entitled *Littlejohn's Half Century at the Bench and Bar (1936-1986)*. It is a history of the developments at the Bench and Bar, in the court system and in the administration of justice in South Carolina during the fifty years I have pursued the law since graduating in 1936 from the University of South Carolina Law School. The manuscript, royalties and profits therefrom have been given to the South Carolina Bar Foundation, which published the book and used the proceeds for good causes consistent with the purposes for which the Foundation was formed.

That book is a combination of my memoirs, biography and history as they relate to legal and court developments, with emphasis on the history.

Initially it was my intention to include some political history in my second book—history from the same half century as gleaned by me, either by actual participation in several political campaigns or from observations after I became a member of the judiciary and was no longer permitted to participate in political matters. It soon became obvious that the combination of what I term my "legal book" and what I call my "political book" had become more voluminous than was desirable. And so I pulled out all the political chapters from the 1987 book—and here they are now.

A history teacher about sixty-five years old was asked by one of her students, "Teacher, did you study history in college or do you just remember what happened?" While this book has involved substantial research, I have in large measure merely called upon my memory because in most cases I recall what happened.

Politics in 1936 was as different from politics in 1988 as day is from night. To me the changes are of interest, and so I have recorded many of them with explanations as to how and why they came about. Similar great changes have occurred in the practice of

1

medicine, in the manufacture of textile goods, in the agricultural world, and so on down the line.

Over the years I have accumulated many files which relate to political campaigns and political matters. These have been highly helpful. In addition, I have had my memory refreshed by reviewing once again such books as *The Bishop of Barnwell* by W.D. Workman (relative to the late Senator Edgar Brown), *His Challenges Were Greater* by John Cauthen (about the late Solomon Blatt), *All In One Lifetime* (a biographical work) by the late James F. Byrnes, *South Carolina: One of the Fifty States* (a history) by Lewis Jones of Wofford College, and *The Primary State* by Frank E. Jordan Jr.

I have elected to arrange my political memoirs in two parts. Part one relates to miscellaneous incidents of interest which have come to my attention over the years. Part two relates to the twenty-seven elections I have either participated in or been an interested observer of from 1936 to 1988.

2

WHY POLITICS

Sometimes I am asked why I decided in 1933 to study law and why I decided in 1936 to run for public office. I don't suppose I have a real good answer, except to offer the explanation given by a drunk at a bar after he threw a bottle and shattered a mirror behind the bartender. "Why did you do that?" the bartender asked.

"It seemed," the drunk replied, "the appropriate thing to do at the moment."

No member of my family had ever pursued the study of law or sought public office. My older brother Boyd loved politics and enjoyed talking about governmental matters, largely because of his friendship at Wofford College with Olin D. Johnston, who later served as governor and United States Senator. The two became bosom friends by reason of the fact that they read proofs on alternating nights at the *Spartanburg Herald* while working their way through college. While I was in high school and college, Boyd, who was a teacher, was at home a great part of the summer months; we would discuss the law and political matters. He gave me advice which was highly helpful and, I might add, influential in making important determinations.

My interest in politics commenced at Wofford. At that time it was not exactly considered gentlemanly for students to seek office on campus. In that Methodist institution, one was supposed to be more reserved. The result was that fraternity men usually got elected, since their fraternity brothers would take care of the campaigning for their candidate who could not personally seek votes with dignity.

When I was at Wofford, the fraternities could not sponsor dances in their own names. Dances were held, but the fraternity alumni (ostensibly at least), did the sponsoring.

About two years before I entered Wofford College, a young man from Pacolet named Charlie Wood was attending the college on a baseball scholarship. He was an excellent pitcher and later made it to the big league. One Sunday night Wood and three of his buddies were playing bridge in Snyder Hall and Wood was dealt a hand containing thirteen spades. It was such an unusual hand that he

3

could not withstand the temptation to advertise. Wood and his friends called the Spartanburg paper, which ran the story the following morning. Dr. Henry Nelson Snyder, the president of Wofford, promptly shipped Charlie Wood for playing cards on Sunday. It is my observation that students on campus today do nothing so tame or harmless as playing bridge on Sunday.

When I came to the University of South Carolina, the political situation was quite different. Unlike students at Wofford, students at the University announced their candidacies, made speeches, swapped votes and did everything that candidates for public office normally do to get elected. This suited me much better. I became involved, and during my three-year stay at the University Law School sought and was elected president of the senior law class, chairman of the student board of publications, chairman of the debate council and chairman of the Pettigru Law Club. People at the University, and particularly at the law school, generally were interested in political matters both on and off campus. Columbia, where the campus is located, is a political town. It is the capitol of the state and political matters are in the news constantly, especially while the General Assembly is in session.

Some law students did not wait until they were graduated and admitted to the Bar to pursue a political career. In 1934 six were elected to serve in the House of Representatives while continuing to study law.

One of my roommates, T.S. Watt of Due West, was not a member of the General Assembly but worked on the desk for Speaker Claude A. Taylor in the House of Representatives. He would regularly tell me of the interesting things that were taking place in and about the House. I yearned to be there.

People who are interested in and want to be a party to whatever is going on are more likely to end up in politics than others. Even in high school I always wanted to be a party to whatever was taking place and participated in the declamation contest, acted in plays and played on two teams—baseball and basketball. At Wofford I commuted from home most of the time and inasmuch as I was not living on the campus did not participate in extracurricular activities as I might have if living in a dormitory. Even so, I was on the tennis team, belonged to a literary society and was a member of the dramatic club. In all of these activities one might detect a political leaning.

Back home at Pacolet I worked on the farm during high school and before college. My father, who was a rural letter carrier, always said he needed to farm on the side so his five sons would have something to do which would keep them out of devilment. I am not at all sure he succeeded in keeping us out of devilment, but he did succeed in keeping us on the farm, at least part time. There is one thing for sure. I did not want to pursue a career at farming. I have, however, always been glad I had the experience of plowing a mule, hoeing cotton, pulling fodder, shucking corn, picking cotton and taking it to the gin. Broad experiences in different types of endeavors are helpful to a lawyer, who must attempt to understand everybody's problems. I was always sorry that I did not have the experience of working in a textile plant. During the summer months at Wofford I applied for employment at the Pacolet Manufacturing Company, but that was during the deep Depression when jobs were hard to find and accordingly, my application was not approved. Instead, during one summer vacation I pursued a temporary career as a Fuller Brush man. While at the University I was employed part time at the State Highway Department during the fall of the year, when about 125,000 license plates were issued. Today the Department issues a million licenses every year.

The first case in court which I ever observed was held at Pacolet while I was a student in high school. I recall going upstairs over Brown's Store Warehouse to an improvised courtroom where the mayor of the town, sitting as judge, with the help of a jury, was trying an accused person for assault and battery. Lawyer Lawrence Southard of Spartanburg was there representing the defendant. When all the testimony was in, Southard demanded that the mayor charge the law to the jury. The mayor was not a lawyer and knew nothing about what should be included in a charge. He requested the defendant's lawyer to charge the law for him. Mr. Southard obliged and the defendant was found not guilty. I have never in any other case heard of a lawyer substituting for a judge in his charge.

At Wofford College I would sometimes go to the Spartanburg County Courthouse to listen to cases in trial. It was on such an occasion that I first came to see Judge Donald Russell in action. He was arguing a case to the jury. At the time he had just come to Spartanburg from Union and joined forces with Lawyers Sam Nicholls, C.C. Wyche and James F. Byrnes.

At the law school we had looked upon those law students who were already in the Legislature with much admiration. I had visited in the House and Senate from time to time, and growing out of these experiences, I suppose, politics just got in my blood. And once politics gets in the blood, it is not easy to eliminate it.

Upon graduating from the law school and being admitted to the Bar in early June of 1936, I was ready for two things—some good paying clients and the pursuit of a seat in the House of Representatives.

3

THE DEPRESSION WE KNEW

As this book goes to press in 1989, it is not easy for people who did not experience the Great Depression of the 1930s to understand how most people lived during that era. Today the great majority of people enjoy, and take for granted, many of the luxuries of life such as good roads, automobiles, radios, television sets, telephones, computers, air conditioning and travel by air. During the Depression, we did not miss the luxuries of life because we had never been introduced to them. While a few people enjoyed wealth during those years, most people truly suffered for lack of such basic things as adequate housing, wholesome food and medical care. Even before the Depression, the masses lived hard by modern standards. Accordingly, the Depression did not cause them to change gears greatly. In most instances they merely tightened their belts, grinned and suffered difficult living conditions. Governmental aid to the poor was practically unknown.

Herbert Hoover, as President of the United States from 1928 to 1933, has been given much blame for the Depression we knew. Actually, he was not as bad a president as history records him to have been. Franklin Roosevelt, upon being elected in the fall of 1932, had great vision, and the time had come when people were ready to venture with his new ideas relative to government. The economy had hit rock bottom; the people were ready for a change, and Roosevelt was ready to lead them to it. His ideas were roundly approved, and at the end of his first four years in office he was re-elected, in 1936, by a landslide. Those congressmen and senators who agreed with Roosevelt were generally re-elected, and many who opposed his new ideas were defeated in 1936. The economy was definitely improving.

During the Depression, the dollar was king. It would buy something. A hot dog sold for a nickel and a hamburger for a dime. A man's suit of clothing could be bought for fifteen to twenty dollars and the best shirt in town could be procured for $1.95. Schoolteachers made from sixty to seventy dollars per month, but room and board could be had for twenty-five dollars a month. The state of South Carolina was unable to pay teachers in cash and issued to

7

them what was called "script." This was the equivalent of a note to be paid at a future date. Merchants would accept "script" but at a discount. In 1937 the Legislature took pride in raising a beginning teacher's salary to seventy-five dollars per month for the first year, eighty dollars per month for the second year, eighty-five dollars per month for the third year and ninety dollars per month for the fourth year. A new car could be bought for $600, but few teachers could afford one.

Many common items which most people enjoy today were not available to the average person during the Depression. For example, bathroom scales were not to be had. There were penny scales in the front of most department stores and ten-cent stores. By dropping a penny into a slot, you could learn your weight and sometimes get a fortune-telling card as well.

Only city people enjoyed plumbing facilities. Rural people normally drew water from the well and bathed as best they could. Electricity for rural residents was to come years later. Good barber shops provided a shower with a cake of soap and a rented towel for twenty-five cents. Small towns had taxicabs. Today most small towns have few, or more likely no taxis, because practically every household today has at least one automobile.

Hitchhiking was also in vogue. When I was at Wofford, only four students there owned cars. College students lined the highways on weekends and motorists willingly gave them a lift. At that time there was little fear of being robbed by hitchhikers.

There was a lot of fuss about the fact that the price of a stamp on a first-class letter had gone from two to three cents. Penny postal cards were still available at every post office.

The entertainment world was considerably different. While records were available and provided good music, not every family could afford a record player. Radio was coming into use, and Spartanburg's WSPA-AM in 1930 provided the Palmetto State with its first radio station. Today there must be some 300 radio stations in operation in South Carolina. Television, of course, was unknown; people went to the "picture show" instead. The first movie I can recall seeing was at the Criterion Theatre in Spartanburg; and the admission fee was ten cents for everyone—child and adult, night and day. There being no air conditioning, theaters were less popular in the summer months; in the winter they fared better.

As a boy I well remember attending fiddlers' conventions at the high school, which served as a means of raising funds for worthy school and community projects. Entertainers from nearby areas took much pride in participating in these events. Admission was fifteen cents for children and a quarter for grownups. High school plays also were popular as a means of raising funds. The churches sponsored all-day singings with dinner on the church grounds. All these events gave local talent a forum for developing skills. Television, among other things, has caused such events to become obsolete as a means of entertainment. Now that people can stay home and enjoy the most skilled entertainers in the world for free, they need no longer be content with local third-rate actors.

At Pacolet, my home town, Southern Railway operated four passenger trains bound north and four passenger trains bound south every day. A ticket from Pacolet to Spartanburg (eleven miles) cost forty-two cents. In that day the train was the popular way to travel. The efficiency and comfort of automobiles and the development of acceptable roads for travel were yet to come, and plane travel was in its infancy. The way to travel any appreciable distance was by train. One by one over the years, the passenger train service was diminished, until today there is no passenger train service for Pacolet. At Spartanburg only one train goes south and one train goes north each day. In the meantime, the comparatively new Greenville-Spartanburg Airport serves thousands and thousands of people every week. This mode of travel, plus modern automobiles and interstate highways, have changed the habits of moving around on the face of the globe.

By describing conditions as they existed prior to my graduation from law school and my entry into politics, I have attempted to depict the conditions with which people in government were confronted in 1936. There was a general feeling among the people that government should, and could, do things to improve the economy. Until that time most people had been content with the doctrine of laissez-faire. They were now ready and anxious to try something new, and those candidates who held out hopes for a change were looked upon with great favor.

4

AS THE ECONOMY WAS IN 1936

In 1936 we were on the tail end of the Great Depression. We had experienced the Wall Street crash in 1929. In the early 1930s the banks were going broke by the dozens. Franklin Roosevelt, upon assuming office as President in 1933, declared a bank holiday and closed all of them. Then the government permitted the banks to open by degrees as (and if) they could prove their stability; but some of them could not and those were closed permanently after the bank examiners completed their audits. Lawyers frequently were engaged in the foreclosure of mortgages and in defending the foreclosure actions. They represented bankrupt individuals and trustees in bankruptcy. There were also many lawyers who made good money representing bootleggers. In those days there were many worthless checks and a great deal of embezzlement—not to mention robberies, burglaries and an occasional murder.

There was little real estate business for lawyers because real estate simply was not moving. As I came to the law, the banks were becoming stable and the savings and loan associations were coming into being. These associations paid their depositors two percent on their deposits. They provided loans and helped the builders to get going again.

The practice of law in 1936 was tremendously different from the practice of law in 1988. This is not big news because the practice of medicine is different; merchandising is different; manufacturing is different; and nearly everything else is different too. Throughout this book I hope to point out some of the changes that have come about in the practice of law and in politics as well as changes brought about in the economic system.

In 1936 there was no social security, there was no unemployment compensation insurance and workers' compensation was only one year old.

There were, however, what we refer to as poorhouses. Almost every county had its own poorhouse, where people who were elderly and indigent could live. The poorhouse in Spartanburg, which came to be known as the county farm, occupied several hundred acres and was located where Interstate 85 is today, near Hearon Circle but more specifically where Beverage Air is now located. So far as I know, there are no poorhouses in South Carolina today.

There was no wage and hour law in 1936. In order to get the economy going, Roosevelt initiated many programs. Among them was the Works Project Administration or WPA. Another was the Civilian Conservation Corps, known as the CCC, for young men who were unemployed. They lived somewhat like troops in barracks, and their basic task was to work in the forest, planting trees, harvesting timber and preventing soil erosion. The CCC lasted for several years but was phased out about the time the United States entered World War II in 1941.

The size of state government in the 1930s was indicated in a speech by Speaker Sol Blatt in the House of Representatives in 1957. The occasion was the unveiling of his portrait in the House chamber. Blatt had come to the State House as a member of the House in 1933. He was contrasting the appropriations bill of that year with that of 1957. I quote from the speech. He said:

> In 1932, the Legislature had appropriated $9,500,000 for general purposes and the Highway Department whose funds were separately accounted, had received $9,900,000 in revenues, a grand total of $19,400,000 for all state purposes as compared to the current year's total of $178,300,000 or roughly one-ninth of what we are now spending.
>
> We were concerned only with the $9,500,000 for general purposes, and the state had, mind you, a deficit of $9,000,000. We were running, therefore, almost exactly a year behind in finances. Our credit had been exhausted, and we could not borrow a dime.

Spartanburg in 1936 was greatly different from Spartanburg in 1988. At that time the voting population of Spartanburg County was approximately one-third city, one-third textile mill communities and one-third agricultural. The county had a population of 116,000 and the city approximately 30,000. Lawyer Ben Hill Brown, originally of Cowpens, was serving his twelfth year as mayor. The city was typical of urban areas of its time. Street cars had been phased out and people who did not own automobiles were dependent upon taxi cabs or city buses. One could call a taxi and be taken anywhere within the city limits for ten cents, but if two or more people were transported, each would have to pay a dime. Most Spartanburg lawyers, of whom there were about sixty, had offices on Morgan Square. Nearly all of them were upstairs, and none dared have a truly luxurious office for fear that clients would rationalize that the fee would have to be too high. In the city,

Wofford College and Converse College were each serving about 500 students. In 1986 Wofford had approximately 1,000 students; Converse College had nearly as many. The University of South Carolina at Spartanburg serves far more.

At the turn of the century, textile plants were moving away from the North, particularly out of Massachusetts, and into the South. Spartanburg County and South Carolina got a lion's share. In 1936 there were approximately 220 mills in South Carolina, of which 40 were located in Spartanburg.

When the mills came to Spartanburg County in about 1900, it was necessary for management to build enough residences within walking distance of a plant to house the employees. These houses were poorly built—usually averaging about four, and not more than five, rooms. There was no modern plumbing and few had electricity. Management continued to own the houses until the late 1930s. The rent was cheap, running anywhere from fifteen to fifty cents per room per week. The average wage of textile workers for a fifty-five hour week was about $700 per year. Child labor had been phased out a few years before, and labor unions were attempting to make inroads throughout the South. Few textile employees owned automobiles. A community center, maintained by management, was the gathering place for all sorts of activities. Telephones were pretty well unknown at the textile worker's house. Many, but not all, had radios, but television was ten or fifteen years away.

The wage scale and standard of living was such that few children of textile workers could go to college. Grants and scholarships as we know them today simply did not exist.

Textile workers were traditionally the victims of loan sharks. At that time it was permissible for employees to borrow money and assign their wages to a lender, at ridiculously high interest rates. Assignment of wages was made unlawful a few years later.

It was not until about 1936 that mill companies decided to go out of the house renting business. I remember young Victor Montgomery, who was connected with Whitney Mills, alerting me for the first time that mill houses would be sold. My first reaction was that the deed must include a provision that if the purchaser ceased to work for the mill, the house could be retrieved. Mr. Montgomery told me that the time had come when the plants were no longer dependent upon local labor and that people were driving to work from adjoining towns. One mill company after another placed its houses on the market, until today few, if any, textile plants control housing of their employees.

So long as the company owned the houses there was sort of a caste system within the mill community. The overseers lived on "boss line." This distinguished them from other employees, somewhat the way that being an officer in the Army distinguished one from an enlisted man.

The mill company was always interested in helping the community to build and maintain churches. It seemed to be thought that church people made better employees than the unchurched. It was not unusual for a church group to be the recipient of substantial contributions from the mill. In like fashion, substantial contributions were traditionally made to the schools. Having good schools available made recruitment of good employees more feasible.

Many years prior to 1936, textile interests in and about Spartanburg had brought into being the Textile Industrial Institute, which was located near Saxon and Arcadia. At this school, adults could attend classes for a week and work in the mill for a week. This plan enabled underprivileged persons to get an education and prepare themselves for college. One of the most distinguished students who attended this school was Olin D. Johnston. The school produced many other well-known professional people. It was not until 1941 that the Textile Institute as such was phased out and converted into what was called Spartanburg Junior College (later named Spartanburg Methodist College).

In 1936 the farmers in and about Spartanburg produced mostly cotton and corn. Ben Gramling Sr. at the town of Gramling was beginning to experiment with growing peaches commercially. Machinery was pretty much unknown to agriculture in Spartanburg County, even though it was fairly well known to farms in the Pee Dee section of the state. We farmed in Spartanburg County with horses and mules, and the size of a farm would be indicated as "a two-horse farm" or "a three-horse farm," etc. A multitude of people operated small farms and gardens. A great many people worked for wages but farmed on the side. Cotton was the main money crop, and it was my recollection that 80,000 bales were produced in Spartanburg County in 1936. There were three cotton gins within three miles of my home at Pacolet. Today there are probably not more than three in the entire county.

Traditionally, farmers needed financing, and nearly every community had an outstanding merchant who supplied the farmer and his family with the necessities of life through the summer and until his crop could be gathered and sold in the fall. Large landowners did a substantial part of their farming with the use of sharecroppers. Under this arrangement, the farmer would finance a tenant and in the fall they would split up the profits of the year.

Spartanburg County as of 1986 had a population of 201,000 with approximately 45,000 in the city. About 25,000 or 30,000 people live just outside the city limits, refusing to vote themselves in because of additional taxes which might be required. Between 1970 and 1980 the county gained 28,000 in population. The county budget today far exceeds that of the entire state in 1936. While Spartanburg has not experienced growth comparable to Greenville, Columbia and Charleston, we take pride in the fact that ours has been a rather well-balanced economy. While our agricultural undertakings are far less than before, our manufacturing and industrial undertakings have multiplied tremendously. Elsewhere I have commented that in 1936 Spartanburg had approximately 60 lawyers. In 1986 there were 241. In the meantime, throughout the state, the lawyer population had increased from about 800 to approximately 7,000. It is my observation that the 7,000 are generally more prosperous than the 800. Certainly they enjoy more of the abundant life.

5

THE JOHNSTON-SAWYER HIGHWAY FEUD

The Olin D. Johnston-Ben Sawyer feud played an important part in the election of legislators in 1936, which was the first year I offered for public office. In many counties during that year, the issue was: "Are you for Olin or against him?" Johnston was at the time in the middle of his first four-year term as governor of the state.

Johnston had come to Spartanburg to attend the Textile Institute and Wofford College just prior to World War I. He was originally from Anderson County and had served in the Legislature as one of that county's delegates to the House. Later he moved to Spartanburg and served as a member of the Spartanburg County delegation.

While the governor had been elected by a substantial margin in the summer of 1934 and assumed his duties as a very popular officeholder, his stock fell considerably during his first two years in office by reason of his aborted efforts to oust Chief Highway Commissioner Ben Sawyer. The story of this feud depicts the background of my first campaign.

After the Legislature in the late 1920s had authorized the issuance of $65 million in bonds for the repair and construction of highways, several actions were brought to contest the constitutionality of the statute. These actions were consolidated and the State Supreme Court heard the matter in 1929, filing an opinion in October of that year.

The Constitution, as of that time, allowed the Supreme Court to sit *en banc*. When important matters were involved, the Court could call in all of the circuit judges to participate in the decision. It was an unusual procedure used in this case. If the Court has held an *en banc* session since that time, it has not come to my attention.

This was an extremely important issue of the day, and so the fourteen circuit judges were invited to form a court of nineteen judges—which, of course, included the five members of the Supreme Court. A majority of the Supreme Court said the act was unconstitutional, but two members held that the act was constitutional. Joining Associate Justices Stabler and Carter were Circuit Court Judges Wilson, Shipp, Sease, Rice, Mauldin, Dennis, Johnson, Grimball, Ramage, Featherstone and Mann. The dissenting opinions were written by Chief Justice Watts and Associate Justices Cothran and Blease, joined by Circuit Court Judges Bonham, Townsend and Henry.

Thus, if the Court had not been *en banc*, the act would have been declared unconstitutional. In my view, this chilled the inclination of the Supreme Court to order *en banc* sessions. Members simply did not like the idea of a majority of the Supreme Court being outvoted by invited interlopers of a lower rank.

Courthouse rumor had it that the circuit judges looked charitably upon the legislation because they had to travel the state's roads regularly to get to the forty-six courthouses where trials were held. They wanted and needed better roads. On the other hand, the members of the Supreme Court traveled good roads to Columbia nine times a year and so were not as conscious of the fact that other roads needed repair and construction. For this reason they were said to have looked with less charity upon the statute and the act's validity.

Without concern to the constitutionality of the act, I would say that this was most important legislation. It would have been tragic if the road program had not gone forward. The roads built with funds from this bond issue have been one of the state's most valuable assets. In addition, this legislation and this decision of the Court paved the way for incidents which made political history.

Olin D. Johnston, as a candidate for governor in 1930, made his opposition to the bonds one of the main planks in his platform. He was almost elected, and many people were of the opinion that the election was actually stolen from him. This can never be proved or disproved. But in 1934 he ran again and was elected. Two planks in his platform in the latter race were: first, to institute a three dollar license plate for all motor vehicles and second, to break up the highway ring headed by Ben Sawyer, the Chief Highway Commissioner.

A ring is hard to define, but oldtimers can remember that Ben Sawyer was one of the most astute politicians the state has ever known. As Chief Highway Commissioner he called the shots when highway monies were involved. His influence in the South Carolina Senate was tremendous. He wielded his influence by looking out for senators from the small counties. At that time each county had one senator. There were thirty-five small counties and eleven larger counties. It was well known that Sawyer could get anything he needed enacted in the Senate. His influence in the House was great but not always prevailing.

At that time, the governor appointed the highway commissioners subject to confirmation by the Senate. The terms of four members expired in the spring of 1935, during Governor Johnston's first year as chief executive. Instead of making new appointments in the winter or spring while the Senate was in session, Johnston, realizing that Sawyer could and would block his appointments in the Senate, waited until the Senate had adjourned and then designated the four successors in office. These appointees appeared at the next Highway Commission meeting on October 9, 1935 and were denied a seat by the chairman because they had not been confirmed by the Senate.

On October 28, 1935, Governor Johnston issued a proclamation by which he declared a state of "rebellion, insurrection, resistance and insurgency" to be in existence against the laws of the state of South Carolina "in connection with the operation, policing, management and general control" of the highways of the state coming under the jurisdiction and control of the State Highway Department. He ordered the militia to immediately take charge of "all highways of the state coming under the management, control, supervision or jurisdiction" of the highway department or its commission.

On that date Johnston designated his friends Joe Calus, Wade Sanders, Frances Drake, Robert Gregory, W.M. Smoak and Walter Stilley Jr. to take possession of the offices and properties of the Highway Commission—which they did. These five were to carry on the business of the department. Major Frank Barnwell, in control of the militia, took possession of the state office building wherein the highway department operated. Machine guns were planted at the principal entrances of the building.

The governor's appointees to the Commission were J.C. Long, Louis Richardson, W.L. Rhodes and Frampton Toole. They had been designated to replace E.T. Heyward, R.J. Ramer, W. Fred Lightsey and C.F. Riser, who were incumbents. After the governor's proclamation, the incumbents commenced an action in the original jurisdiction of the Supreme Court against the four new appointees. On October 30, 1935, the Chief Justice issued a temporary injunction enjoining the new appointees from assuming duties incident to their offices. Simultaneously, he issued a Rule to Show Cause why the temporary injunction should not be made permanent.

About the same time, the members of the Highway Commission brought an action in the original jurisdiction of the Supreme Court against those persons designated to operate the highway department until the rebellion was ended. The plaintiffs requested the Court to review the actions of the governor and to hold his actions unlawful.

Both cases came to be argued in the Supreme Court in November 1935, and many of us who were in attendance at the law school cut classes to attend. This was my first visit to the Supreme Court of South Carolina, and this was the first case I ever heard argued.

On December 5, 1935 the Supreme Court filed opinions in both cases. In essence it ruled that the new appointees were not entitled to assume office and enjoined and restrained them from interfering with highway department activities.

In the Commission's action against those designated to operate the highway department (Calus and others), the Court held that the action of the governor was subject to review by the Court, and inasmuch as courts were open to the governor and his designees and inasmuch as ". . . all was as calm, quiet and peaceful as a May morn . . ." no insurrection or rebellion existed to warrant his proclamation.

The Court perpetually enjoined and restrained Calus, Sanders, Drake, Gregory, Smoak and Stilley from performing or attempting to perform any duties for the department.

Following the Court's rulings, Governor Johnston promptly called a special session of the General Assembly to meet in Columbia on December 10. He declared that an emergency had arisen as a result of the Court's actions and that a special term of the Legislature was necessary in order to deal with the situation.

In his message to the General Assembly, Johnston stated that he would have a bill introduced to provide for the sinking fund commission of the state to temporarily operate the highway department and to provide that an election by the people be held the following summer to select highway commissioners for the respective congressional districts. He also proposed to support a bill which would reduce motor vehicle license fees to three dollars per year.

It was well known that a majority of the senators was hostile to the governor. Appointees of his would have difficulty in procuring confirmation in the Senate. The governor had substantial support in the House but was short of a majority upon which he could depend.

The House and Senate members came to Columbia reluctantly. It was just before Christmas, and the session presented difficult political issues with which the Assembly was not in a mood to deal. Several resolutions were introduced—some favorable and some unfavorable to the governor. Some assemblymen quarrelled with the fact that machine guns encircled the highway department building. Some would have refused to act until the militia was withdrawn.

After much haggling over a period of two weeks, the Legislature passed an act in the form of a bob-tailed bill providing that for a period of sixty days the duties and powers of Ben Sawyer and the State Highway Commission were devolved upon Highway Engineer T.S. Williamson and O.P. Burke, Secretary and Treasurer of the Highway Commission. During that time the state treasurer and secretary to the Commission of the sinking fund were to act as a supervisory board. This was worked out as a compromise with the approval of the governor, in order that the legislators might go home for Christmas. The militia was withdrawn. All were to return on the second Monday of January for the regular 1936 session, at which time further legislation would be in order.

At that 1936 session, a bill was introduced and approved which provided for the three dollar license tag for which the governor was anxious to claim credit; the legislation also provided for a new method of selecting the highway commissioners. It took the appointive authority from the governor and stipulated that highway commissioners would be elected by the legislative delegations of the respective fourteen judicial circuits. It further provided that the office of commissioner within each judicial circuit would be rotated from county to county, so that each county would be assured of having a highway commissioner periodically. Many counties had never had a resident commissioner, and every member of the House and Senate cherished the idea of having a commissioner at some time from his own county. The temptation was too great. The House members swallowed the bait and approved the legislation.

In order to claim credit for the three dollar license plate, Governor Johnston, with much reluctance, signed the bill. The three dollar license tag was short-lived but this method of electing highway commissioners has remained with little change for the last fifty years. Although there is some agitation today for changing the number of highway commissioners and the method of selection, I seriously doubt that any change will be made in the foreseeable future.

Under this system of selecting highway commissioners, a member is rotated off the commission at about the time he or she has learned enough about the Department's operation to give meaningful service. Under the old system, members occasionally would serve for several appointments over a period of ten or fifteen years. Each system of selecting commissioners has its advantages and disadvantages. The method of selecting the commissioner is not as important as the chore of selecting the chief commissioner. Sawyer died suddenly of a heart attack about three years after this controversy, and no chief commissioner since has been so powerful— which is as it should be.

The 1936 session of the Assembly was a difficult one for all members, since there was, in effect, a two-party system. We might call them the Johnstonites and the anti-Johnstonites. The governor was to be a big issue in the elections of the summer of 1936. Several people were defeated because they were supporters of Governor Johnston, and several were elected because they were his supporters. In most counties, the people gave substantial consideration to the positions which the incumbents had taken at the previous session. In some areas where Johnston was strong, House members simply did not run again because of their opposition to him. It would be a fair summary to say that Johnston's supporters did not fare well in the 1936 elections. The two-party system was to continue into subsequent meetings of the General Assembly.

6

HOUSE MEMBERS ARRESTED

For more than a hundred years the Constitution of South Carolina has provided that members of the General Assembly could not be arrested while attending, going to or returning from sessions of the Assembly, nor for ten days before or after those sessions, unless charged with treason, a felony or breach of the peace. The Constitution also protects electors on election day and provides that they may not be arrested during their attendance at polls for voting or while going to and returning therefrom.

An incident growing out of this law made much news in 1935 while I was a student at the University Law School. It involved the arrest of two members of the Spartanburg House delegation who were returning home over the weekend and passing through Fairfield County. At that time the conventional way to travel from Spartanburg to Columbia and back was by way of Union, Santuc Carlisle and Salem Crossroads.

This was at a time when many law enforcement officers had little training and little knowledge of the law. Certainly they had little understanding of constitutional law. It was not unusual for the sheriff or mayor of a town to give a citizen a badge and a gun and tell him to enforce the law. It was also about this time that legal whiskey came to be purchasable in South Carolina, but there was still a great deal of moonshine being distilled and consumed.

As William Fred Ponder and C.B. Kendrick, members of the Spartanburg House Delegation, were motoring through Fairfield County in the Salem Crossroad area, they were apprehended by Deputy Sheriff J.M. Feaster and W.C. Weir, a rural policeman. Apparently the officers suspected that these two members of the House of Representatives had illegal liquor in their car. Identifying license plates for assemblymen were not in vogue at that time; even though the House members identified themselves and claimed immunity, they were taken some twenty miles distance and brought before Magistrate D.L. Stevenson, who issued a warrant permitting the search of the automobile. Nothing unlawful was found.

When the House convened the next week, on March 19, 1935, Messrs. M.M. Brown and Phil Huff introduced a resolution directing the Sergeant-at-Arms "... to at once apprehend and bring before the House of Representatives of the State of South Carolina to be dealt with according to law, the said W.C. Weir, J.M. Feaster and D.L. Stevenson." The Sergeant-at-Arms complied and on March 20, 1935, these frightened individuals were brought before the House of Representatives and tried. Each of the three filed a plea of guilty. Then the House resolved itself into a committee of the whole. When the committee arose and reported to the House, it recommended that the Speaker deliver a reprimand to each of the accused persons and they then be discharged.

There were members who preferred to ignore the recommendation and favored either confinement in jail for a period of twenty-four hours of confinement until *sine die* adjournment of the legislature. In the last analysis, however, the House agreed to administer a public reprimand by the Speaker. The House journals reflect the following:

> J.M. Feaster then made a statement to the House in which he admitted that he had acted wrongly and apologized to the House.

> W.C. Weir then likewise apologized to the House.

> D.L. Stevenson stated that he had made a mistake and was sorry for it and apologized to the House.

The public reprimand, among other things, included:

> It may not be amiss to advert to some of the reasons which we now think compelled the framers of the Constitution to insert certain provisions in the fundamental law of our land. I call your especial attention to Section 14 of Article III of the Constitution which in part provides that the members of both houses shall be protected in their persons and their estates during their attendance on, going to and returning from the General Assembly. You appreciate the fact that no man under our form of Government can hold a higher commission than that which is held by members of the General Assembly. They are entrusted with the solemn and responsible duty of making the laws under which the citizens of this state are to live and carry on their respective avocations. I imagine that one of the reasons which compelled the incorporation of this provision was that in the event that any important measures were pending before the General Assembly, the decisions of which would likely be close, conspiring members of our society could by arresting and detaining certain members

of the General Assembly bring about a determination of legislation in accordance with their views. . . .

I am convinced that what you did was with full knowledge of the identity of the gentlemen you arrested. This makes your conduct in exercising the powers of officers more reprehensible. Your deliberate acts were and are unbecoming officers of the law and deserve the most severe censure.

I am unaware of any law, statutory or otherwise, that spells out appropriate procedure when a person violates the Constitution by arresting a member of the General Assembly. Many of us wondered whether the House was the proper forum for such a case. Three frightened individuals raised no issue of authority to try them and were happy to return to Winnsboro reprimanded. Conceivably, a sentence to confinement by the House of Representatives might have brought about a court contest.

In my fifty years at the Bench and Bar, I know of no other instance in which a member of the General Assembly of South Carolina has been arrested in violation of the constitutional provision. I doubt that punishment could legally be ordered by the House of Representatives and am more inclined to think that guilty parties should be answerable to a court and given traditional due process.

7

SECRETARY TO THE CONGRESSMAN

Little quirks of fate sometimes make or break one. Certainly decisions made today, though seemingly unimportant, may point one's destiny.

I have sometimes wondered what my fate would have been had I accepted employment as secretary to Congressman-elect Joseph R. Bryson in 1938.

After leaving law school in June 1936, I entered upon a campaign seeking one of Spartanburg's eight seats in the House of Representatives. Upon being elected, I learned that newly elected Congressman Heyward Mahon of the Fourth Congressional District of South Carolina was seeking a secretary from Spartanburg. Since Mahon was not an attorney, he particularly wanted to employ someone who was.

The district at that time was composed of Greenville, Spartanburg, Union and Laurens counties. Inasmuch as Congressman Mahon was from Greenville, he understandably preferred to have his secretary from another county. Spartanburg was the county next highest in population to Mahon's home county of Greenville.

I had just turned twenty-three and was a bachelor. Although I had opened an office in Spartanburg for the practice of law, I had accumulated no clients of consequence and most of my time since law school had been spent in the campaign for public office.

At that time Congress met for only about five months a year. Going to Washington was particularly attractive to me, so I applied for the job. In retrospect, I do not know how I could have justified giving up my newly acquired seat in the General Assembly, which would have necessitated a special election to fill the vacancy. I guess my eagerness to go to Washington outweighed my common sense.

Congressman Mahon selected attorney Thomas W. Whiteside, a very good lawyer who graduated about one or two years before I did, for his secretary. Whiteside was at that time associated with former Governor Ibra C. Blackwood and Charles M. Pace in the practice of law.

24

In the summer of 1936 Mahon had defeated Bryson, Claude A. Taylor and J.G. Leatherwood. The runoff race was a hotly contested one between Mahon and Bryson.

Two years later Bryson entered the race again in an effort to unseat Mahon. The vote count was contested and the race was so close, with Bryson barely leading by eight votes, that Bryson suggested the victory should be more pronounced. He challenged Mahon to repeat the contest in a rematch. This time Bryson won by a fairly substantial vote.

Bryson was aware that I had sought to be secretary of the Fourth District Congressman in 1936 and offered me the position in 1938. By this time I had run two successful campaigns and had just led the ticket among twenty-eight candidates. In addition, I was making a fairly good living at the law. I thanked the newly elected congressman and declined the employment offer.

At that time congressmen had a $5,000 appropriation for secretarial help. Bryson himself drew $7,500. He proposed to pay me $2,500 and split the other $2,500 between two other persons who would perform stenographer-type services.

The activities of a congressional office today are to be contrasted rather than compared with those in 1938. In lieu of the $5,000 appropriation for office help, the figure is now $406,560. The congressman (or I should say congresswoman) from our district has eighteen full-time and four part-time staff members, with at least one representative in each of the district's three counties.

It is also interesting to note that the office of congressman from the Fourth Congressional District was occupied by a Greenville resident from 1921 until 1987—a period of sixty-five years. On several occasions the incumbent congressman was challenged by a resident of Spartanburg—among the challengers being Miller C. Foster, Claude A. Taylor, Charles C. Moore, Virgil Evans, Matthew Poliakoff and E.C. Burnett Jr. Greenville County had the most votes, and no Spartanburgan was elected until 1986, when Elizabeth Johnston Patterson was elected to succeed Carroll Campbell when he was elevated to the office of governor. Representative Patterson is the daughter of former Governor Olin D. Johnston and had served on Spartanburg County Council and as a member of the State Senate from Spartanburg County. A Democrat, she is well versed in politics and defeated Greenville Mayor William D. Workman Jr., a Republican, in that race. Greenville residents who served from 1921 to 1986 were John McSwain, Heyward Mahon, Joseph

Bryson, Robert Ashmore, James Mann and Carroll Campbell. All were Democrats except Campbell.

Forty-four years after my first two opportunities in that direction, I was again offered employment in Washington. In the fall of 1982 Senator Strom Thurmond suggested that if I would retire as a member of the Supreme Court he would appoint me to a prestigious legal position incident to his work with the Senate Judiciary Committee. The offer was quite a compliment. By that time I was sixty-nine and going to Washington at that age would have been quite different from going to Washington as a twenty-three year old bachelor. I did not accept for two basic reasons: First, I thought I would not be happy living in Washington. Secondly, and perhaps more important, I wanted to stay in the Supreme Court and hoped to serve as Chief Justice.

When a lawyer settles a law suit out of court, he has a conviction that the settlement is good. He never knows whether he would have fared better at the hands of a jury. By a similar token, I will never know what fate would have had in store for me had I gone to Washington in 1936 or 1982. But I have never regretted my decisions to remain in South Carolina.

8

PACKING THE SUPREME COURT

Upon his election as President of the United States, Franklin D. Roosevelt inherited a nation laden with a deep Depression. He assumed a leadership greatly needed and did a very good job of proposing legislation which put the country on the way to prosperity again.

Much of the legislation Roosevelt proposed was drastic by the constitutional standards to which we had previously adhered. The President advocated and brought into being such things as the NRA, the CCC and the WPA—which were the National Recovery Act, the Civilian Conservation Corps and the Works Project Administration. Several of his programs came into contest before the Supreme Court of the United States and were declared unconstitutional.

By 1936 the people had enjoyed enough of Roosevelt's prosperity to send him back to the presidency with a landslide vote. He lost only the states of Maine and Vermont, which were won by Alf Landon. Fortified with the people's support, in February of 1937 Roosevelt sent to Congress a "court packing plan" by which he proposed that the Supreme Court of the United States be increased to fifteen—which would, of course, give him the authority to remake the court through his appointive power.

The South Carolina Bar Association met in Columbia the following month, and Roosevelt's proposal was the main matter for discussion. Even as the country was divided on this issue, the Bar was also split. A resolution was offered by Attorney S.M. Wolfe as follows:

> RESOLVED, that it is the sense of the South Carolina Bar Association, that the text of the Bill, proposed by the President of the United States in his message to Congress on February 5th, 1937, would, if enacted into law, destroy in effect, the integrity of the Supreme Court of the United States and thus, necessarily break down the American system of Government; that it would not only constitute a dangerous precedent but would result in incalculable possibilities for the abuse of power in the legislative, and the executive branches of the government and the inevitable abrogation of Constitutional rights, immunities, privileges and liberties of the American People.

That it would in effect, amount to a reprimand of those members of the Supreme Court, who, because of their honesty and high character, have shown themselves capable of independent judgment in the face of stress and political brow-beating; that it would result in a serious blow, if not the ultimate death of popular government and would tend strongly to supplant this form of government by an oligarchy or absolute dictatorship; that for the sake of the preservation of our Government and of our Nation founded upon this government, and all that has come to the American people by virtue of their hopes, their prayers and their sacrifices of war, it is the earnest desire of this body, that this radical departure and drastic proposal be defeated at the hands of the Congress now assembled.

That a copy of this resolution be sent by the Secretary of the South Carolina Bar Association, to each of the Members of Congress, and to each of the Senators from South Carolina, and that a copy be sent to the Chief Justice of the Supreme Court of the United States.

Similar issues were being debated throughout the country, and newspaper editors were busy with their typewriters.

At that time there were approximately 800 members of the South Carolina Bar, but comparatively few of these were members of the South Carolina Bar Association. The Association was a purely voluntary organization and was composed largely of senior lawyers whose main clients were corporations. After much heated debate, the resolution was adopted by a vote of 86 to 37. An analysis of the roll-call vote which was recorded would indicate that the opposition was composed largely of young attorneys with political inclinations.

The matter also became an issue for debate in the General Assembly. Senator Edgar Brown and others introduced a concurrent resolution endorsing the Roosevelt plan as set forth in his message to Congress. The resolution was adopted in the Senate with comparatively little opposition. In the House of Representatives the resolution was hotly debated and amended, the vote being 78 in favor of the resolution as amended with 24 voting in opposition.

The resolution, as finally adopted, read in pertinent part as follows:

Be it further resolved, that the General Assembly of the State of South Carolina does hereby approve and endorse the recommendations of the President of the United States for the reformation and reorganization of the Federal Judiciary in the particulars specified in his message to the Congress on February 5, 1937.

Be it further resolved, that the General Assembly of the State of South Carolina does hereby commend the Representatives and Senators from South Carolina in the Congress of the United States, who have given assurance of their support of the said recommendation of the President.

In retrospect, it is fortunate that the President's plan was not adopted by Congress. What he advocated did not need a constitutional amendment; a statutory enactment would have been sufficient to change the number of justices who sit on the Supreme Court of the United States.

The debate which Roosevelt's proposal brought about probably had an impact on the thinking of the Supreme Court. It has been said that the judiciary follows the election. We can never prove or disprove the impact of the people's reaction upon the thinking of the members of the court. It followed, however, that the court began to take a more liberal view of the programs which President Roosevelt was advocating, most of which were thereafter ruled constitutional.

There is an old proverb which says "A stitch in time saves nine." The Supreme Court began switching its views, and there came into popular parlance a revised version of the proverb, "A switch in time saved nine." Congress did not ride with the President's views, and the act did not pass.

No president and, so far as I can recall, no member of Congress has since that time advocated what was commonly referred to as "packing the court."

9

JAMES F. BYRNES LEAVES THE SENATE (1941)

By 1941 James F. Byrnes had been a member of the United States Senate for a decade. After unseating Senator Cole L. Blease in 1930, he was re-elected in 1936 to a term which normally would have ended in 1942. On July 8, 1941 President Franklin D. Roosevelt appointed Byrnes a Justice of the Supreme Court of the United States. Byrnes resigned, leaving the Senate seat vacant.

It became the duty of Governor Burnett R. Maybank first to appoint an interim senator and second to call an election to choose Byrnes' successor. Maybank appointed Federal Judge Alva M. Lumpkin, who took office July 22 but died ten days later. The governor then named Roger C. Peace, editor of *The Greenville News*, who served until November 1941.

Maybank then announced that he himself would be a candidate in a special Democratic primary, the results of which would be the equivalent of election.

Former Governor Olin D. Johnston had been out of office for three years but had been mending fences with a view to seek statewide office again. Congressman Joseph R. Bryson of the Fourth Congressional District had an ambition to move from the lower house to the upper house of Congress. Johnston and Bryson announced their candidacies for the Senate, which gave the people three choices.

Maybank led the ticket with 59,000 votes to 40,000 for Johnston and 25,000 for Bryson. The voting once again proved that it is difficult for a Congressman to attain a higher office. Many have failed to be elected governor or United States senator over the years, both in South Carolina and throughout the country. There are, of course, a few exceptions. At the same time, incumbent Congressmen are almost impossible to defeat for re-election.

In the second balloting, Maybank bested Johnston by a vote of 92,000 to 70,000. To some degree it was a contest of the Up Country against the Low Country, but Maybank of the Low Country was rapidly ingratiating himself to the Piedmont counties. This was Johnston's second defeat since leaving the office of governor in 1938, but it did not chill his enthusiasm for statewide public office. He kept on campaigning and mending fences, with a view to seek the governor's office in 1942, which he did, successfully.

10

WAR AND POLITICS

Happenings at Pearl Harbor on December 7, 1941, changed the destiny of multitudes of people all over the world. At that time the Hawaiian Islands were not one of the United States, but relationship of our country to the Islands was such that an attack by the Japanese on American ships anchored at Pearl Harbor was equivalent to war on the United States.

On the following day, President Franklin D. Roosevelt addressed Congress and it declared war on Japan. The war was to extend over a period of some four years, ending after President Harry S. Truman ordered the dropping of atom bombs on two of Japan's major cities.

The United States had already been in a state of preparing itself for military activities in 1941 by reason of the war being fought in Europe. Camp Croft had been established at Spartanburg, and a law providing for a general draft of young men into the Army had been enacted sometime previously.

The declaration of war called into service not only young men and women of the United States, but industries as well. Time was of the essence, and many factories were quickly built throughout the country to provide for the manufacture of machines of war. In addition, many conventional industries, such as the automobile factories, were converted to build implements of war.

The Great Depression of the 1930s was pretty well winding down, and a reasonable degree of prosperity was returning to the country. Military activities and money spent in preparing for hostilities activated business undertakings and brought an end to the Depression.

In 1941 I was a member of the Spartanburg County Legislative Delegation. The Chamber of Commerce advocated the bringing of a military camp (Croft) to our county. With the help of Senator James F. Byrnes, who was influential in Washington at the time, Spartanburg was able to procure an infantry training installation in the Cedar Springs-White Stone area, to which would be sent some 45,000 trainees.

The building of Camp Croft brought much money to Spartanburg County. I was among those who cooperated in the procuring of the camp. Under similar circumstances again, I would not take the same position. Instead I would say to my government, "If you need our area for the training of soldiers, we will make it available to you." While a military installation brings money to your area, that is about the only good thing you can say about it. Along with a military camp comes inflation, crowded facilities, overloaded traffic conditions, prostitution and many other criminal activities. In retrospect, I would not bear these burdens for the monetary profit Spartanburgans came to enjoy.

At the time of Pearl Harbor, I had been serving as a member of the House of Representatives for some five years. Like many other House members and some Senators, I was of draft age. Quite a few legislators had commissions growing out of ROTC and other military service. I had been in ROTC at Wofford College for three years but had left Wofford to attend the University of South Carolina Law School, where there was no ROTC. I did not get a commission because I did not participate in ROTC for the entire four years.

In the House of Representatives in Columbia, there is a plaque on the wall commemorating the service of "The Members of the South Carolina House of Representatives Who Answered the Call of Their Country 1941-1945." They are as follows: James Clator Arrants, Lemuel George Benjamin Jr., George Andrew Brown, George Preston Callison, Stratton Christensen, George Henry Davis, Samuel Woodrow Hamlet, S. Rhea Haskell, Harold Bleckley King, Thomas Wilson Lemmon, James Woodrow Lewis, Bruce Littlejohn, Leonard Lawrence Long, P. Bradley Morrah Jr., Charlie Cowan Murdock, Jack Howard Page, Ernest Edward Richardson, Charles E. Simons Jr., James Park Sloan, Robert Edward Vandiver and Jacob Henry Woodward Jr.

Christensen, Hamlet, Lemmon and Woodward made the supreme sacrifice and did not return. The rest of us were more fortunate, and several came to serve again in the General Assembly and in other important South Carolina political offices.

From 1941 to 1945, the average age of men serving in the General Assembly was substantially higher than the average age both before and after that time. The younger men were in the service. At the end of the war, the average age dropped as many young men returned to political activities.

During 1940, while I was practicing law on Morgan Square in Spartanburg, I was appointed by the governor as a member of the "Advisory Board to Registrants." The duty of this board's membership was merely to help young men fill out complicated registration forms which would serve as a basis of determining who would be drafted into service and the order of such drafting. The Draft Board was located at the corner of Dunbar and North Converse streets, and it was easy for the Draft Board to tell registrants how to get to my office.

The time came when I was filling out forms all day instead of practicing law, so I went to the Draft Board to ask them to route some of the applicants to the offices of other persons serving on the Advisory Board. It was a quirk of fate that I met a lovely young lady, Inell Smith, who was clerk of one of the boards. Some fifteen months later she became my wife.

It had first appeared that this would be a short war, and I had in 1942 run for re-election to the House of Representatives. By 1943 it became apparent that the war would not be a short one. I waived my 4B classification (given to legislators), resigned from the House and volunteered for service.

On September 30, 1943, I was inducted at Camp Croft and became "Pvt. Cameron B. Littlejohn Serial Number 34892642." Obviously, this necessitated my giving up the practice of the law as well as the political base I had developed. Along with about thirty other Spartanburg County registrants, I was ordered to the Fort Jackson reception center, where I was issued my first uniform. It was handed to me by my cousin Frank Mayfield of Greenville, who took particular pains to see that I got a good fit.

My salary as a private was $50 per month. I allocated $22 a month to my wife and the government supplemented that amount with $28, giving to her a total of $50 per month. The remaining $28 of my $50 salary was mine to spend as I chose.

The Army didn't need many lawyers. Most of us would have preferred to become a part of the Judge Advocate General's Department, which deals with military legal matters. Since the Army needed only a few lawyers, they were routed to the infantry, signal corp, quartermaster, engineers, etc. It became my lot to go to Camp Lee, Virginia, a quartermaster installation, which was charged with the duty of providing equipment, food and services to Army personnel.

After seventeen weeks of intense basic training, I applied for a commission and was sent to Officer's Candidate School at Camp

Lee. On March 14, 1944, on entering the school, I quit being a private and came to enjoy corporal's pay ($66) but was, during my schooling, called "Cadet Littlejohn." No allowance was made for the fact that I was three-fourths of a lieutenant already by reason of being in the Wofford College ROTC for three of the required four years.

On July 14, 1944, I received my commission as a second lieutenant and traded my serial number 34892642 for 01593169 and a lieutenant's gold bar. I was then entitled to about $150 per month salary and came to enjoy certain benefits not available to enlisted men.

During their military service, most lawyers lost connection with the legal world. I was more fortunate. Upon graduation from OCS, I was retained at the school to teach military law and court martial proceedings to other officer candidates. Upon being commissioned a second lieutenant, one would normally be in charge of a platoon or sometimes a company and would need a little bit of education relative to dealing with troops who violated either military or civilian law. We undertook in an eighteen-hour course to give to each officer candidate a little understanding of the court martial system.

The court martial manual which we taught has since been superseded. At the time there were (and may still be) three court martials. We referred to them as (1) a general court martial, (2) a special court martial and (3) a summary court martial. In addition to teaching military law, I served on occasion as assistant trial judge advocate, which is a prosecuting officer, and as assistant defense counsel, whose chore it was to defend persons charged with violating military law.

In the early summer of 1945, there was much rejoicing at all military installations. The war with Germany was over and all of us began thinking of the day when we might return to civilian life. In August of that year the atom bombs were dropped on Japan, and this brought an end to hostilities in the Pacific.

It had been determined long before the end of the war that when the United States was victorious, those persons responsible for the war and those persons guilty of war crimes would be prosecuted. At the Pentagon they began looking for young lawyers with comparatively short periods of service. The computer spit out my card, and I was assigned to the War Department Investigating Attachment in Manila, capital of the Philippines, and to the Judge Advocate General's Department. I was ordered to Camp Beale in California for shipment to Manila. On the plane with me were quite a few other attorneys given the same assignment. I was elated that

I received a promotion to first lieutenant because that gave me a salary of $166 per month.

Our lawyer group arrived in Manila on December 3, 1945. Half the young lawyers arriving with me were appointed defense counsel. I was fortunate to be appointed one of the prosecuting attorneys. Captain Arnold Fein, an excellent lawyer from New York, and I formed a team for the purpose of presenting cases to military commissions. These commissions were normally composed of five senior officers, including one law officer who ruled on evidentiary matters. This commission was not a part of the court martial system but operated in large measure similar thereto. All of us were under the direction of General Douglas MacArthur, who by this time had moved his headquarters to Tokyo.

There was nothing formal about the operation of a military commission trying accused Japanese war criminals. Most of them were Japanese officers who had been responsible for the mistreatment of Filipino natives during the occupation from which General MacArthur had freed the Filipino people. The spirit of the law, as developed over the years in the trial of cases in both military and civilian courts, was generally respected, but the commission was given great latitude in determining what evidence would and would not be relevant in the trial of cases.

It can easily be seen that there were many problems incident to American officers and other military personnel moving into a country and establishing a court system. There was no courthouse, no clerk of court, no process servers and no established rules of evidence, not to mention many of the other things which we enjoy in the United States. Many of these problems had been solved prior to our arrival in December, and at least one important case had already been tried which resulted in a penalty of death by hanging.

Some of the attorneys defending one of the first accused persons filed an appeal from the commission's ruling with the Supreme Court of the United States. This made much news in and about the investigating detachment; we always rationalized that the appeal was filed for the purpose of getting a trip back to the United States so the attorneys could visit their families. In summary, the United States Supreme Court refused to intervene and in essence held that what was taking place in Manila and Nuremberg was not unlawful. Among other things, the Justices ruled that accused war criminals were not entitled to the protection of the Constitution of the United States.

Top: The author at his desk in the House of Representatives, 1941. Left: The author and his wife Inell at Camp Lee, Virginia. Above: The author with monkey while prosecuting Japanese war criminals in the Philippine Islands, 1946.

It was not possible to prosecute and try all of those who were guilty of war crimes in either the Pacific or European theatres of operation. Trials were held simultaneously in Manila and in Nuremberg. The purpose of the trials was mostly to deter similar activities, should there be future wars. After trying symbolic cases in both Manila and Nuremberg, the prosecutions were discontinued. One can only speculate on the effect these trials may have to deter similar crimes in the future. Although we can say that hopefully some good will result, it can never be proved or disproved.

Service in the Philippines was a great experience which gave me an opportunity to learn how people live in other countries. We found that Manila was torn by the ravages of war when the Japanese came to occupy it early in the war and when General MacArthur's forces retook it at the end of the war.

There are about 7,000 Philippine Islands. Only a few of them are relatively civilized. Most of them are primitive. Manila was a town of approximately one million people. There were only a few roads and streets comparable to paved streets in the United States. The capitol building may have been somewhat comparable to the State House in Columbia, South Carolina, but it had been bombed and was left a pile of rubble. The hotels and office buildings also had been severely damaged by the war. Filipino people were living under poverty-stricken conditions. At the same time, there were a few extremely wealthy people living in and about Manila. There was no area of the town comparable to the six-room bungalow subdivision in South Carolina. People either lived in a little mansion or in a building somewhat similar to a barn in South Carolina. Stealing was rampant. Thieves stole an average of 45 jeeps from our Army every month, and the military police boasted of retrieving 30 of them.

I left Manila in late spring of 1946. I was tempted to remain until the fourth of July, because it had been planned that the Philippine Islands would become legally and governmentally self-sufficient and, in effect, an independent new nation would be born on that day. I was tempted to stay just to be a party to the birth of a nation, but a political campaign was just around the corner at home; and I was more concerned with returning to my Princeton Street home in Spartanburg than I was with seeing a new nation come into being.

Although I have never been back, I have watched with much interest the governmental turmoil and problems which have been so prevalent in the Philippine Islands during these last thirty years.

At the end of the war, some ten or eleven million officers and enlisted men and women were returning to civilian life. It was anticipated that an economic depression would quickly ensue. This was expected because the military would not be spending money as before. Actually, the letdown did not come. The economy remained relatively good and the depression we expected has never arrived.

Under the federal law, men and women who went to war were assured of their former employment once they were released. Such assurance was not available to those who held political offices.

There was a sort of camaraderie that developed between those who went to war. After returning to civilian life, they joined the American Legion and the VFW by the millions. These men and women seemed to think that many advantages could be obtained through these organizations. The night I joined the VFW, forty-five others became members also. Over the years, membership in these organizations has continued to diminish to a fraction of their former numbers, and comparatively few continue active membership.

For most persons, returning to civilian life was not difficult. Unfortunately, some were not and have not until this day been able to adjust. It has been my observation that some develop leadership skills by reason of their military assignments and have, in one sense of the word, shown a profit.

It is unfortunate that the burdens of war can never be equalized. Some served by staying, while others served by going. Some served by living; others served by dying. It has been estimated that for every ten persons entering the service only one saw actual combat. Perhaps many who stayed and worked in munition factories contributed more than some who actually donned the uniform. To some, war meant the loss of a husband and father. To others the war meant getting rich by reason of businesses enhanced by war needs. Certainly a lot of people did get rich during the war and as a result of the war. I have sometimes thought that if the government can requisition the limbs and lives of its citizens, it should, by like token, be able to requisition the property of its citizens. Certainly property rights are less important than human rights.

I appreciate, however, the fact that money matters and property rights become somewhat secondary when victory is the goal. I have no happy solution to the problem, but I would hope that in the case of another all-out war, much thought would be given by those in charge of the government in attempting to equalize the burdens of war.

Returning soldiers from throughout the country were anxious to again return to political life. The people were charitable and gave much weight to the fact that a person had been in service. This made getting elected easier.

I was discharged in the early summer of 1946, just in time to enter the House race. It was not difficult for me to decide that I wanted my old job back in the General Assembly in Columbia. I entered the Democratic primary and the voters very charitably elected me at the head of the ticket on the first ballot. The November general election was routine, because there was no political party other than the Democratic party in South Carolina at the time. And so I was on my way back to the Legislature in Columbia, eager and ambitious once again to become a part of state government.

11

THE STATE HOUSE—THE OLD AND THE NEW

If you think things at the State House aren't what they used to be, you are correct.

It seems to be in the scheme of things that all governments get bigger and bigger from year to year. This calls for more employees and more office space. Such has certainly been true every year since I first began going to the Legislature in January of 1937.

When I went to the Legislature in 1937, the capitol building housed the Senate, the House of Representatives, the offices of the Governor, and the offices of the State Treasurer, the Supreme Court, the Comptroller General and the Secretary of State. There was space left over, and it was allotted to the Confederate Relic Room, which was housed upstairs above the Senate.

On the House side of the General Assembly, there were only two committees which had fixed committee rooms—the Ways and Means Committee and the Judiciary Committee. All other committees, of which there were too many, met in these rooms or sometimes in one corner of the House or the Senate. When the Ways and Means Committee or the Judiciary Committee was not in session, which was seldom, other committees might use their rooms. Only the Speaker of the House and the President of the Senate had individual offices.

It was not until the late 1950s that air conditioning came to the State House. It was at that time still considered something of a luxury, and politically-minded members of the Assembly voted against it for fear that the voters back home would consider it unnecessary. At the next election, the air conditioning of the State House was an issue in many counties and a few candidates were defeated because they had voted in favor of a cooling system. The opponents of air conditioning argued that it would only prolong the sessions and cause members to remain in Columbia all summer in order to keep cool.

For many years after I went to the Assembly, there was no carpeting in the State House. The floors were of marble, and the mop was the instrument for cleaning instead of the vacuum cleaner. It is my recollection that a manufacturer of rugs took much pride in contributing a rug with the state seal on it for the lobby.

I remember when two elevators were placed in the state capitol — one on the House side and one on the Senate side. Again, those who challenged the incumbents made this a political issue at the next voting time, claiming that people ought to walk up the stairs to save tax dollars.

One by one the departments of government operating in the capitol building became so large that new quarters had to be found. Now there remains in the State House basically the two assembly rooms, the offices of the governor and the lieutenant governor. The office of the lieutenant governor is one which has grown tremendously. When I was Speaker of the House from 1947 to 1949, George Bell Timmerman Jr. was Lieutenant Governor. He had one part-time secretary. That office has now been expanded to what might be termed a small department of government, although the duties are somewhat negligible.

In between the House of Representatives and the Senate there was for many years what we referred to as the "Engrossing Department." It served the same purpose as the Legislative Council now headed up by Thomas Linton. For many years the Engrossing Department operated under the direction of the attorney general. It was his duty to provide personnel for the drafting of proposed legislation. This he accomplished by calling in some of the fourteen solicitors periodically as needed. It was a very unsatisfactory arrangement, because the better solicitors didn't want to come, and those less apt ended up drawing important legislation. Some of the solicitors enjoyed coming for the recreation. Former Attorney General John M. Daniel took much pride in supervising this activity and spent a great deal of time in the lobby of the State House. Many of the solicitors had little talent for drafting legislation.

In 1949, while I was Speaker, the Legislature created the Legislative Council. It operates throughout the year under the direction of Mr. Linton, doing research for assemblymen and drafting bills for pre-filing. Included within the Legislative Council quarters is a very fine library referred to as the "Legislative Library."

For many years the State House provided virtually no parking space for assemblymen or others desiring to transact business at the State House. Directly in front of the capitol building, facing Main Street, there were twenty or perhaps twenty-five parking spaces. The need for parking space was alleviated to some degree by the fact that many of the members of the House and Senate lived, during the sessions, either at the Wade Hampton Hotel at the corner of Gervais and Main streets or at the Columbia Hotel at the corner of Sumter and Gervais streets. Both of these hotels have been demolished in recent years.

Behind the State House there has now been constructed an underground parking garage sufficient to provide spaces for all members of the House and Senate and for many others who are employed regularly in connection with the Assembly's work. As government grew, the need for committee rooms and office space for House and Senate members became pretty much a necessity. The Edgar Brown Office Building, the Marion L. Gressette Office Building, the Solomon Blatt Office Building and the Rembert Dennis Office Building have been constructed for this purpose. All of these compose what is usually referred to as the "Capitol Complex."

In 1971 the Supreme Court moved out of the Capitol and into the renovated former post office building at the corner of Sumter and Gervais streets. Other offices have been moved from the Capitol, mostly to the Wade Hampton Office Building. These include the offices of the Attorney General, of the State Treasurer, of the Secretary of State and of the Comptroller General.

The State Appropriation Bill now involves the expenditure of more than three billion dollars. It is difficult for my young friends to appreciate the fact that in 1941 the State Appropriations Bill included such items as $132,000 for the Legislative Department, $249,000 for the Judicial Department, $23,000 for the Office of the Attorney General (he had two assistants), $151,000 for the State Penitentiary, and $66,000 for the Industrial Commission. All of these figures have consistently been increased.

Today many committees appointed incident to the work of the General Assembly function throughout a substantial part of the year. The growth of state government in South Carolina is not inconsistent with the growth that has taken place in other states, in cities and in Washington, D.C. It seems to be in the scheme of things that the great mass of people are demanding that the government do more and become involved in more activities. At home, voters fuss about the growth of government. Politicians advocate a smaller budget and lower taxes. In Columbia and in Washington, the lobbyists have been very successful in persuading the politicians that "it ain't necessarily so."

12

BOB-TAILED BILLS

In 1985 the Chamber of Commerce brought an action in the Court of Common Pleas designed to attack as unconstitutional, permanent legislation included in state appropriation bills. The gist of the attack is the contention that more than one subject matter is included in one proposed act and that matter is inserted in the appropriation bill without having had three readings in each house as required by the Constitution. The Constitution of South Carolina, Article III, Section 18, provides:

> No Bill or Joint Resolution shall have the force of law until it shall have been read three times and on three separate days in each house, has had the Great Seal of the State affixed to it, and has been signed by the President of the Senate and the Speaker of the House of Representatives.

Article III, Section 17, provides:

> Every Act or Resolution having the force of law shall relate but to one subject, and that shall be expressed in the title.

When I became Speaker of the House and Lieutenant Governor George Bell Timmerman Jr. became President of and presiding officer of the Senate, we dealt with a kindred matter putting an end to what we conceived to be an unconstitutional handling of legislation.

There had developed in the Assembly a bad habit of bob-tailing bills. It enabled the Assembly to enact legislation without giving a proposal the three readings in the House plus three readings in the Senate on separate days as required by the Constitution. At that time the local delegation pretty well controlled local government back home through what we referred to as local legislation or bills. This system of operating local government resulted in hundreds of bills being introduced each year for such things as setting the fee to be collected for recording a deed. Such is no longer the case since Home Rule, because the Constitution now says that no legislation shall be passed for a particular county.

The bob-tailed bills, which we outlawed, worked like this: Members of a local House delegation would introduce a local bill and give it three readings. The Senate would receive the bill and at the direction of the local Senator give it two readings, never intending to give it the third and final reading so that it might go to the governor for his signature. As the legislative term was nearing an end, the six days needed for passage of an act were not available. The Senator and the House members would want to enact some other bill totally unrelated to the one which had received five readings. The routine was for the Senator to amend the bill by striking out the title and inserting a new title and striking out all after the enacting words and inserting new legislation. After the bill was amended in the Senate it would immediately be sent to the House for concurrence, and accordingly, the whole legislative process was accomplished within an hour. This was unconstitutional, but if the presiding officers certified that the legislation had received the six required readings, the courts would not go behind their signatures.

Upon taking office, Timmerman made a statement to the Senate wherein he said, among other things:

Under these sections, [of the Constitution] it is clear that a bill must receive three readings on three separate days in each house of the General Assembly to become a law.

It is equally clear that a bill becomes a new bill, requiring three such readings, *when amended so that its title relates to a subject not contemplated in its original title.*

Therefore, if a bill is amended so that the title thereof relates to a subject not contemplated in its original title and is up for consideration in the Senate, I shall rule in obedience to the Constitution that it is a new bill and must receive the three readings required by the Constitution for its passage by the Senate.

On or about the same day, as Speaker, I made a statement to the House of Representatives as follows:

The South Carolina Supreme Court has consistently held in all of the cases that it is the duty of the Speaker of the House and of the President of the Senate to determine whether or not a bill received three readings as required by the Constitution, and has refused to look into the Journals of either house to determine whether or not a bill actually had the readings required by constitutional law. This being true, the responsibility of enforcing the provisions of the Constitution in this regard is directly upon the presiding officers of the Assembly and an aggrieved citizenry has no recourse in case a bill is signed unconstitutionally.

It is my opinion that a bob-tailed bill violates both the letter and the spirit of the Constitution in that it prevents the three-day deliberative period in each house, and in that it minimizes the right of the public to hearings on proposed legislation. I therefore deem it my duty to place the House on notice that I shall not falsify the record by signing any bill which contains matter not reasonably contemplated by the original title, commonly called a bob-tailed bill.

It is not always easy to determine when a bill relates to only one subject as contemplated by the Constitution. By supplementing logic with imagination, one can sometimes come up with far-fetched conclusions.

The custom of including much permanent legislation in the State Appropriation Bill had not developed at that time. It is of more recent vintage and involves not exactly the same but a kindred issue to the one the Lieutenant Governor and I dealt with in 1947. We put an end to bob-tailed bills.

13

LEGISLATIVE EXTRA PAY

Compensation provided by law for members of the House of Representatives and the Senate has never been abundant. Certainly the pay has never been extravagant.

When I first came to serve in the House of Representatives in 1937, the compensation was $400 per year. This represented ten dollars per day for the forty-day session contemplated by the Constitution. The amount of compensation was not enumerated in the Constitution, but there were constitutional provisions which circumscribed the appropriation. Those provisions were included in the Legislative Article of the Constitution, Sections Nine, Nineteen and Thirty, which read in part as follows:

Nine
Members of the General Assembly shall not receive any compensation for more than forty days of any one session.

Nineteen
[N]o General Assembly shall have the power to increase the per diem of its own members; and members of the General Assembly when convened in extra session shall receive the same compensation as is fixed by law for the regular session.

Thirty
The General Assembly shall never grant extra compensation fee or allowance to any public officer, agent, servant or contractor after service rendered, or contract made, nor authorize payment or part payment of any claim under any contract not authorized by law; but appropriations may be made for expenditures in repelling invasion, preventing or suppressing insurrection.

Accordingly, it is seen that the Legislature may raise the compensation of its members, but this may be provided for only those members elected next time to serve in subsequent years. Raising compensation for Assemblymen is not a pleasant chore and is certainly not politically rewarding; accordingly, there has been a great reluctance on the part of the legislators to provide additional compensation for the members.

Over the years prior to 1948, there developed a habit at the Legislature of including in the annual appropriation bill, or more often the deficiency appropriation bill, what came to be known as "extra pay." This was accompanied by designating the appropriation "official expenses for each member of the House and Senate." In the Assembly there were many who refused to vote for extra pay on the theory that it was unconstitutional or politically unwise, but normally a majority vote could be rounded up. Nearly all members took the compensation, but a few declined, while others accepted the money and used it to make contributions to churches and/or charitable institutions. Newcomers seeking to unseat members of the Legislature customarily made a big issue of the fact that someone had voted for extra pay or had voted against it and then taken it.

The provisions of the Constitution quoted above had been in the Constitution long before I came to serve in the Assembly and remain parts of that document today. As far back as 1931 the issue of the constitutionality of the extra pay appropriations was paraded before the Supreme Court as then constituted. In the case of *Scroggie v. Scarborough*, the appropriations were tolerated by the Court which refused to upset the practice.

By 1947 regular compensation of members of the Legislature had been raised to $1,000 per year. At the end of the 1947 session an appropriation for official expenses to each member of the Assembly in the amount of $700 was provided. Scroggie, who had brought the 1931 action, brought another action against Jeff Bates, who was at the time State Treasurer, again attacking the appropriation as unconstitutional under the sections enumerated above. On circuit, Judge Marvin M. Mann upheld the validity of the appropriation. Upon appeal to the Supreme Court, all the members of that Court signed certificates of disqualification resulting in the naming of a special court by the Governor under the provisions of Article V, Section 6, of the Constitution. That section read in part as follows:

> In case all or any of the Justices of the Supreme Court shall be thus disqualified, or be otherwise prevented from presiding in any cause or causes, the Court or the Justices thereof shall certify the same to the Governor of the State, and he shall immediately commission, specially, the requisite number of men learned in the law for the trial and determination thereof.

Governor Strom Thurmond appointed C. Granville Wyche as Acting Chief Justice and Henry C. Jennings, Harvey W. Johnson,

Henry Busbee and David W. Robinson as Acting Associate Justices to serve as the Court. The Court as constituted ruled that even though the appropriation was designated official expense, it was in actuality additional compensation prohibited by the Constitution.

Most members of the Legislature had received the $700 and had spent it. Demand was made for the return of $700 from each of the recipients, and nearly all complied promptly. A few members who had not taken the appropriated amount did not have to concern themselves.

One member is said to have advertised the fact that he gave his extra pay to the church. It developed that he applied it to a pledge previously made, and when this fact was discovered, he was somewhat embarrassed.

My friend Charles Plowden of Clarendon County, contemplating the next campaign, gave $100 to each of the seven charitable organizations in his county. Friends teased him when it developed that he had to repay the state with his own money.

At that time E.W. Cantwell was serving in the Senate from Williamsburg County. The Senator was a lawyer who graduated in my law class of 1936 at the University of South Carolina. He was also a Baptist minister. At one time he served as secretary to Governor Olin D. Johnston. Senator Cantwell refused to return the $700, and Attorney General John M. Daniel brought an action for judgment against him in the Court of Common Pleas for Williamsburg County. Cantwell demurred to the Complaint, and when the matter came to be heard before Judge William H. Grimball, the demurrer was overruled.

When I, as a circuit judge, held my first court in Williamsburg County, it developed that Cantwell had failed to answer the Complaint and was in default. The Attorney General moved before me for judgment against him. Cantwell, although in default, happened to be in the courtroom when the matter came to be heard. After the Attorney General made his motion, I asked Senator Cantwell what his position in the matter was. He stated, "Judge, I want you to grant me judgment in the amount of $5,000 on a Counterclaim, because the State owes me additional money for services I rendered over and above the call of duty for an ordinary senator. Not only that, but there is in my family $7,500 worth of Confederate bonds issued by the State of South Carolina which are now due plus interest. I want to offset the debt the state owes me and my family by reason of these bonds."

I appreciated his humor. I did not follow his logic and granted judgment in favor of the state. Soon thereafter Cantwell was defeated for re-election and moved to the New England states and returned to full-time Baptist preaching.

The decision of the special appellate court settled the issue of extra pay and/or expense money. No attempt has been made since 1947, so far as I can recall, to provide additional compensation to members of the Assembly under the guise of expense money.

14

DUAL OFFICE HOLDING

Article VI, Section 3, of the Constitution of South Carolina provides as follows:

> No person shall hold two offices of honor or profit at the same time; *provided*, that this limitation shall not apply to officers in the militia, notaries public, or delegates to a Constitutional Convention.

Notwithstanding this provision of the Constitution, before 1947 it became fashionable for members of the General Assembly to seek, be elected to and serve as members of the boards of trustees of the University of South Carolina, Clemson and other state institutions of higher learning. It was virtually impossible for anyone who was not a member of the General Assembly to defeat a member who sought the office. Over and above the fact that such dual office-holding was unconstitutional, an evil existed in that a member of the Assembly serving on the board had a warped view in favor of his favorite institution.

Member trustees and others attempted to justify their election and service by contending that a member of the board of trustees was not an office within contemplation of the Constitution.

Serving on a board of trustees of an institution of higher learning is prestigious; it entitles one to such fringe benefits as football tickets and influence in getting students admitted.

In 1940, Attorney John Bolt Culbertson of Greenville brought an action in the original jurisdiction of the Supreme Court against several members of the House of Representatives and the Senate, the mayor of Bishopville, and the solicitor of the Fourteenth Circuit, alleging that all were dual office-holders and submitting that each vacated his initial office in accepting a second office as a trustee. The action was brought in his capacity as a taxpayer representing all other persons similarly situated.

The defending trustees argued that Culbertson was without capacity to bring the action in the absence of a personal interest and that he failed to show any right to prosecute the action.

The Supreme Court ducked the issue and dismissed the action holding:

> ... that the constitutionality of legislative action in the form of legislation may not be questioned by one who fails to show in his complaint that he has some personal interest in the situation other than that shared in common by other members of the public.

When Lieutenant Governor George Bell Timmerman became President of the Senate in 1947, he decided to put the members of the Senate on notice that he would perform his duty imposed by Article III, Section 24, by declaring vacant the office of any member of the Senate who accepted a second office and ordering an election to fill the vacancy. His statement was in part as follows:

> But concerning my duties as presiding officer of the Senate, I desire to make my position clear respecting the issuance of Writs of Election to fill vacancies which may hereafter occur in the Senate.

> The State Constitution, Art. III, provides in Section 24, that:

> No person shall be eligible to a seat in the General Assembly while he holds any office or position of profit or trust under this State, the United States of America, or any of them, or under any other power, except officers in the militia and Notaries Public; and if any member shall accept or exercise any of the said disqualifying offices or positions he shall vacate his seat.

> and, in Section 25, that:

> If any election district shall neglect to choose a member or members on the day of election, or if any person chosen a member of either house shall refuse to qualify and take his seat, or shall resign, die, depart the State, accept any disqualifying office or position or become otherwise disqualified to hold his seat, a writ of election shall be issued by the President of the Senate or Speaker of the House of Representatives, as the case may be, for the purpose of filling the vacancy thereby occasioned for the remainder of the term for which the person so refusing to qualify, resigning, dying, departing the State, or becoming disqualified, was elected to serve, or the defaulting election district ought to have chosen a member or members.

> Furthermore, the Supreme Court of South Carolina has held that where a person accepts two offices of honor or profit, the acceptance of the last one vacates the first.

> It is my conviction that the decisions of our Supreme Court should be respected and that the Constitution of our State should be

obeyed, especially by those of us who hold public office, and who take an oath to "preserve, protect and defend" the Constitution.

The Constitution makes it clear that when a member of the General Assembly accepts or exercises another "office or position of profit or trust" a vacancy is created to the same extent as when a member dies or resigns.

I was in agreement with the Lieutenant Governor and, as Speaker of the House, I placed the members on notice that I too would call an election to fill a vacancy created by any members accepting a second office. The last office any House member accepted was membership in the House itself; accordingly, at that point no House seat was in jeopardy. Those members on boards already in violation of the Constitution had actually vacated the other office.

No one seriously challenged our interpretation of the Constitution. It must have been correct, because until this day no member of the Assembly has undertaken to seek a seat on a board of trustees. The Court has, however, tolerated ex officio membership on some of the boards. In addition, members have served on the Board of Trustees at Clemson. The will of Thomas Clemson, which gave to the state Clemson properties, provided that several members of the Board of Trustees should be designated by the Board itself. As of this time, it has not been declared whether these several will-created trusteeships violate the constitutional provision.

An interesting sidelight is the fact that the father of Lieutenant Governor George Bell Timmerman Sr., who was a federal judge at that time, had been serving as a member of the Board of Trustees at the University of South Carolina since 1942. On January 22, 1947, the day after the statement of the Lieutenant Governor, his father resigned. In his letter of resignation, he indicated that he had been serving for five years ". . . in a de facto capacity pending an election of a successor for the General Assembly."

15

OATH OF OFFICE: NO DUEL, PLEASE

I was sworn in as a member of the House of Representatives on six separate occasions: 1937, 1939, 1941, 1943, 1947 and 1949. I was also sworn in as Speaker in 1947 and 1949 and as Circuit Court Judge in 1949 and 1953. At these times the Constitution of South Carolina required me to take an oath of office. Included in the oath of office was the following:

> ... I do further solemnly swear (or affirm) that I have not since the first of January, in the year Eighteen hundred and Eighty-one, engaged in a duel as principal or second or otherwise; and that I will not, during the term of office to which I have been elected (or appointed) engage in a duel as principal or second or otherwise. So help me God.

Over the years, I spent much time explaining to young lawyers and to students why this oath was required. At the end of the nineteenth century in South Carolina, and other places too, disputes were often settled by challenging an adversary to a duel. It was well understood that one could not in good honor refuse to accept the challenge. Refusing to participate proved that the non-participator was a coward. It was not unusual for a person in public office to be challenged to a duel. They had to fight or else be branded as cowards.

When the Constitution of South Carolina of 1895 was written and approved, the founders decided to place into the oath of office a perfect protection and/or defense against being required to duel with pistols, swords or other instruments of mayhem.

Fifty-nine years later, in 1954, an amendment to the Constitution was proposed to strike out the part of the oath of office I have quoted above. The amendment was ratified in 1955, and since that time public officeholders in South Carolina have no longer been required to swear that they have not participated in a duel since January 1, 1881.

Perhaps the inspiration for including this constitutional provision in the oath of office comes from the well-publicized Cash-Shannon duel fought in 1880. The details of this incident are recited in the *Memoirs of Richard Cannon Watts*, who was the son-in-law of Colonel E.B.C. Cash (and who later came to serve as a circuit court judge, an Associate Justice of the state Supreme Court and as Chief Justice thereof).

It appears that two lawyers, Colonel William C. Shannon and Captain W.L. DePass, represented a man named Weinges. Weinges had sued the wife of Colonel Cash, charging her with fraud incident to a judgment confessed in her favor to the detriment of Weinges. The case of *Weinges v. Cash* was tried on circuit, appealed to the Supreme Court and reported in 1881.

Colonel Cash was incensed by the fact that his wife was charged with fraud and challenged Weinges' attorney, W.L. DePass, to a duel. It developed that both DePass and Cash were arrested, thus preventing the duel which had been agreed to in writing.

Thereafter, Weinges' other attorney, Shannon, challenged Cash to a duel. Shannon was killed with the first bullet fired. Cash was arrested and tried for murder before Judge Pressley, resulting in a mistrial. Thereafter, he was tried for murder before Judge Cothran and was acquitted.

The incident created much consternation throughout the state. Preachers denounced duelling and editorials ridiculed Cash.

One year after this duel, a statute outlawing duelling was passed. The statute, still on the books, mandates in South Carolina that one who kills while participating in a duel ". . . shall suffer death, as in the case of willful murder." However, juries were historically inclined to find duellers not guilty, as was the case with Cash.

Apparently, the constitutional provision in the oath of office was inserted to make it acceptable for a public officeholder to decline to duel if someone should challenge.

This interesting comment is found in Chief Justice Watts' memoirs, published in 1938:

> It sounds antiquated now to talk about a duel. When I came to the bar at Laurens there was not a member there at the bar who would not have appealed to the Code Duello as laid down by Gov. Wilson. No good pupose could be served by enumerating the different duels which have been fought by men of South Carolina since I have been a grown man, to say nothing of duels fought before the war. Hon. Eugene B. Gary [served as Chief Justice 1912-1926] and I were intimate friends and, as young men, agreed to live up to the usages and customs of the gentlemen of South Carolina and we agreed that if either ever had to fight a duel, if he were principal that I would be second, and if I were principal that he would be second. The General Assembly passed the anti-dueling statute the next session after the Cash-Shannon duel,

and the Constitutional Convention of 1895 embodied in the Constitution that the officers elected were to take the anti-dueling oath of office that they had not, since the first day of January, 1881 fought a duel as principal or second or otherwise, and that they would not during their terms of office do either. If an attempt had been made to apply this law to all parties who had participated in a duel at any time, the results would have been embarrassing; but they so worded the act as to absolve every one until January 1, 1881.

The part duelling once played in society is further described in a book written by Attorney P.F. Henderson of Aiken entitled *A Short History of Aiken and Aiken County*. He described historic spots in the county:

An equally historic spot, but of a much later period, is the old Sand Bar Ferry Duelling ground, situated also on the Savannah River and about fifteen or twenty miles upstream from Silver Bluff. In the days of long ago all serious disputes must be settled by the letting of blood, especially if it were an "affair of honor." The South presented no exception to this rule. Duelling was banned by the church and being a crime of deliberate violence was, of course, forbidden by law but was still looked upon throughout the world of yore as the privilege of nobility and aristocracy, and there was a lot of the latter in South Carolina and Georgia in those days. As there were even then heavy penalties prescribed for duelling it was found to be quite convenient to keep these affairs as secret as was possible and to arrange matters geographically so as to get out of the jurisdiction as soon thereafter as might be. Therefore it was customary where it could be done to locate the duelling ground close to a state line, fight in one state, and immediately get over the line into another state. Sand Bar Ferry was ideally located for that purpose.

* * * *

But public opinion was finally aroused. There was an especially maladorous affair, the cold-bloodedness of which appalled the state. Murder through duelling was already, of course, illegal, but this legal provision had not been enough. After this affair, however, an Aiken County statesman, backed by an aroused public opinion, got through the Legislature and later wrote into the Constitution of the State, a requirement that every official of South Carolina from Governor down to Notary Public must take a solemn oath that from and after the first day of January, 1881 (the new year date immediately following the enactment of the new law), he had 'not engaged in a duel, as principal or second or otherwise.' Today that oath sounds a bit foolish, and brings on many derisive smiles when it is publicly and solemnly administered, and today the oath is unnecessary, and the requirement should be repealed, but in 1881 it was vital and to the point. It effectively broke up a fearful evil.

It is said that the duelling oath was removed from the Constitution upon the insistence of James F. Byrnes, who served as governor from 1951 to 1955. The story goes that some of Byrnes' friends from Washington came to the inauguration and teased him about having to swear that he would not participate in a duel. He seemed embarrassed about it and as a result advocated and helped to bring about the elimination of this provision from the Constitution.

The part which duelling played in American political life and in American society is illustrated by the famous duel between Alexander Hamilton and Aaron Burr in 1805. In 1800 the election of president was thrown into the House of Representatives in Washington because Thomas Jefferson and Aaron Burr received an equal number of electoral votes. Hamilton exerted his great influence in favor of Jefferson, who had always been his chief political opponent. He opposed Burr, whom he considered to be a man of dangerous ambition. Then, in 1804, Hamilton was instrumental in the defeat of Burr as a candidate for governor of New York state. After his defeat, Burr forced a quarrel on Hamilton and challenged him to a duel. Although he strongly disapproved of duelling, Hamilton felt obliged to accept the challenge. They met in Weehawken, New Jersey on the spot where Hamilton's eldest brother had been killed in a duel three years earlier. Hamilton was mortally wounded and died the next day. Burr's conduct so discredited him that he was never again a political power.

During my tenure of public service, I swore on eleven occasions that I had not fought a duel since thirty-one years before I was born, and I promised not to fight a duel during the term of office I was undertaking. More recently, I have taken the oath of office on eight occasions when I was not required to swear.

Today, people assuming public office may accept a challenge to a duel without violating their oath of office. But it is a fact that duelling remains unlawful by statute, and one who chooses to accept a challenge can only hope the jury is as charitable as those of earlier days—assuming, of course, that he first prevails in the duel.

During my half century at the Bench and Bar, I do not recall a case occurring in South Carolina which involved the law of duelling. I would have thought that duelling was at an end all over the United States, but I was mistaken. In February 1987 a municipal judge in California ordered a Sacramento man to stand trial for violating the state law prohibiting duelling. The case involved an 1854 statute. According to court documents, Kenneth Spanos and Elmer Roy Southern had a shoot-out in front of a lounge. Spanos died in the encounter. The judge ordered Southern to prosecution for duelling rather than manslaughter because the fight resembled more closely the combat described in the duelling law. The news story recites that this law was last used in California twenty years ago. In that case the accused was acquitted.

16

NICHOLLS, WYCHE, BYRNES AND RUSSELL

As we approach the end of the twentieth century, it seems to be in the scheme of things that large law firms dominate the practice. Such has not always been true. When I was a boy, Nicholls, Wyche and Byrnes, with offices in the Cleveland Law Range on Magnolia Street in Spartanburg, was considered a large firm. A substantial portion of Spartanburg attorneys practiced alone. The Nicholls firm was considered large because there were three lawyers and especially because it did a big business. It was understood in the late twenties that people in trouble ought to employ this firm.

Initially, the firm was Nicholls and Wyche (Sam J. Nicholls and C.C. Wyche). In 1924 James F. Byrnes of Aiken, who had served in Congress with Nicholls, came to Spartanburg to join the firm and it became Nicholls, Wyche and Byrnes. In 1930 Byrnes was elected to the United States Senate and discontinued the practice of law. Donald Russell of Union came to Spartanburg about that time, and soon the firm became known as Nicholls, Wyche and Russell.

Lawyers are known for rendering public service and for serving in political office. The public service which the members of this one firm rendered their state and county is of historical note. Two of them served as members of the South Carolina House of Representatives; two served as members of Congress; two served as United States Senators; two served as governors of South Carolina; two served as United States district court judges; one served as a member of the Supreme Court of the United States; one served as a member of the Fourth Circuit Court of Appeals; one served as Secretary of State; and one served as president of the University of South Carolina.

It should be added that one member of the firm, but for a quirk of fate, would have been Vice President of the United States, and one member would, but for a quirk of fate, have served on the Supreme Court of the United States as will be pointed out hereafter.

I will not attempt biographical sketches of these men, but a recitation of their public service is of historical significance.

Sam J. Nicholls

Sam J. Nicholls was a native of Spartanburg County and a son of a probate judge. He was elected to the South Carolina House of Representatives from Spartanburg County and served during the 1907 and 1908 sessions.

Thereafter, in 1914, Nicholls sought to unseat Congressman Joe Johnson of the Fourth Congressional District but was unsuccessful. In 1915 Johnson resigned to accept an appointment as a United States district court judge for the newly created Western District of South Carolina. In a special primary held during the summer of 1915, Nicholls bested several opponents and emerged the winner. He was opposed for re-election in 1916 and 1918 but was victorious. In 1920 he voluntarily retired from politics and devoted his full time to the practice of law, always taking an intense interest in the various political races. His support was always helpful, and candidates traditionally sought his endorsement.

It was during his stay in Congress that Nicholls became a close personal friend of James F. Byrnes, who was simultaneously serving from the Second South Carolina Congressional District. Out of this relationship Byrnes, Nicholls and Wyche came to be partners in the practice of law in Spartanburg in 1924.

Nicholls died as a comparatively young man in 1936.

Charles Cecil Wyche

C.C. Wyche was a nephew of Circuit Court Judge Thomas Sidney Sease. Both of them were born and reared in Newberry County in the Prosperity area. Sease was circuit solicitor in the Spartanburg circuit prior to his election as circuit court judge in 1910. Wyche was elected to the Legislature and served during the sessions of 1913 and 1914. Thereafter he returned to the successful practice of law in Spartanburg.

By 1937 Byrnes had served in the United States Senate for seven years. When Judge Watkins of Anderson died, the President of the United States, on Byrnes' recommendation, appointed Wyche a district court judge for the Western District of South Carolina. In this capacity Wyche served ably and well for approximately thirty years, until the time of his death in 1966. In addition to serving as district court judge, from time to time he sat with the Fourth Circuit Court of Appeals in Richmond.

James F. Byrnes

James F. Byrnes was born in Charleston but moved to Aiken when he was still a young adult. He never attended law school or even college, but he was blessed with a native ability. Byrnes' first public service was as a court reporter, where he learned enough law studying under others to be admitted to practice in 1903. In 1908 he was elected solicitor of the Second Judicial Circuit, but in 1910 he abandoned that assignment to seek a seat in Congress. He was elected and continued to serve as one of the more influential members for a period of fourteen years. He was usually opposed but always victorious.

In 1924 Byrnes, along with former Governor Cole L. Blease and John J. McMahan, sought to unseat Senator Nathaniel B. Dial. The second race was a battle between Blease and Byrnes. Blease won in the runoff, receiving 50.5 percent of the votes.

Byrnes then came to Spartanburg to join the firm of Nicholls and Wyche, and the firm name became Nicholls, Wyche and Byrnes. Although Byrnes was practicing law, he was mostly preparing to run against Blease at the end of his term in 1930. In 1930 Byrnes defeated Blease and began a highly influential tenure of office in the United States Senate in Washington. He was a great help in the nomination and election of Franklin D. Roosevelt in 1932 and again in 1936. He became one of the President's most influential advisors. In 1936 both Roosevelt and Byrnes were re-elected by a landslide.

It had become well known that Byrnes and President Roosevelt had a very close personal relationship. In 1941 the President appointed Byrnes a member of the United States Supreme Court. Rumor had it that Byrnes was never too happy on the Court. With the war coming on, the President needed his assistance in another capacity more important, at the moment, than that of serving on the high court. The United States was at war and winning was paramount. Byrnes resigned in October 1942 to become Director of Economic Stabilization and later Director of War Mobilization.

He was on more than one occasion considered as a vice presidential running mate to President Roosevelt. In 1944 he would have been the nominee, but labor favored Harry Truman. As it developed, President Roosevelt died in 1945 and if Byrnes had been the Vice President he would have become the President of the United States.

At the end of the war Byrnes played an important part in the negotiations for peace and attended many international conferences incident to the ending of the war.

In 1945 President Harry S. Truman, who had succeeded to the office of President upon the death of Roosevelt, appointed Byrnes Secretary of State, in which capacity he served until January 1947, resigning to return to the practice of law. Both Byrnes and Russell were of counsel to a Washington firm.

Byrnes lived in Spartanburg until 1950, when he was elected by an overwhelming vote to the office of Governor of South Carolina. He served with distinction for the four year term. It was during his term as governor that he left the Democratic party long enough to support Dwight D. Eisenhower, the Republican nominee who was elected. In later years Byrnes would continue his support of Republican nominees for high political office.

James F. Byrnes has been one of the great political influences in South Carolina during the twentieth century. He died in 1972 at the age of 92 and is buried in the Trinity Episcopal Cemetery at the corner of Sumter and Gervais streets in Columbia. His wife Maude Busch Byrnes is buried alongside him—and so is his trusted manservant of many years, Willie Byrd.

Across the street, at the corner of Gervais and Sumter on the capitol grounds, a monument to Byrnes has been erected. The inscription on his tomb summarizes his multitude of public services. It reads as follows:

Died April 9, 1972, Age 92, after a Lifetime of Service to State, Nation and the World. Solicitor Second Circuit of South Carolina, US Congress Second District, US Senator 1931-1941, Justice of Supreme Court of the US 1941-1942, Director of Economic Stabilization, Director of War Mobilization, US Secretary of State 1945-1947, Governor of South Carolina 1951-1955; Statesman Jurist Diplomat.

Donald S. Russell

Donald S. Russell was born in Mississippi and moved to Chester when he was a very small child. After graduating with high honors from undergraduate and law school of the University of South Carolina, he came to the practice of law with Gordon Hughes in Union.

The story goes that Russell came to Spartanburg to participate in the trial of a case against Nicholls, Wyche and Byrnes, but they were impressed by the legal skills of this young man from Union and invited him to move to Spartanburg and join them in the practice of law, which he did. Before long Russell was doing a substantial part of the firm's trial work.

In 1930, upon his election to the United States Senate, Byrnes discontinued the practice of law. In 1936 Nicholls died and in 1937 Wyche left the practice for the judgeship, all of which left the firm's business basically to Russell.

When Byrnes moved to the Office of Economic Stabilization, he sent for Russell to join him. In 1942 Russell came to serve as Assistant Director of Economic Stabilization, Assistant Director of War Mobilization, Deputy Director of War Mobilization and Reconversion, and then as Assistant Secretary of State for administration.

When the war had ended and Russell's assignments were over, he was chosen President of the University of South Carolina, serving from 1952 to 1957. He resigned and ran for governor in 1958 but was not successful. In 1962 Russell prevailed and became governor. Upon the death of Olin D. Johnston in 1965, Russell was appointed by Governor Robert E. McNair to the United States Senate and served until the next election.

In 1966, he accepted an appointment from President Lyndon B. Johnson as District Court Judge in South Carolina. In 1972 Russell was appointed by President Richard Nixon to the Fourth Circuit Court of Appeals which sits in Richmond. In that capacity he has served for seventeen years and continues active.

In 1969 President Nixon wanted to fill a vacancy on the United States Supreme Court and wanted a strict constructionist from the South. Senator Strom Thurmond's first choice was Russell, and the time came when it was either Russell or Clement Haynesworth. John Mitchell, the Attorney General, chose Haynesworth; the President appointed him but he was not confirmed. Had Russell been chosen instead of Haynesworth, he would no doubt have been confirmed by the Senate, where he had served. He was thoroughly qualified beyond question.

As the four left the practice of law in Spartanburg, business was turned over to Attorney Erskine Daniel. Sam Means came to be associated with Daniel, and the firm which he and Tom Evins now head up is successor to the original firm discussed above.

Truly, members of the firm from the Cleveland Law Range on Magnolia Street in Spartanburg have served the state and nation well.

Spartanburg must be a good town from which to run for public office—especially the governorship. Between the years 1930 and 1962, Spartanburg supplied the state's governor five times as follows: Ibra C. Blackwood in 1930; Olin D. Johnston in 1934; Olin D. Johnston in 1942; James F. Byrnes in 1950; and Donald S. Russell in 1962.

17

THE DEMISE OF LYNCH LAW

One of the most important functions of government is to provide a forum wherein citizens can settle disputes without resorting to violence. Where money and property are concerned, the forum is found in the civil courts. Where there is a controversy between society on the one hand and an accused person on the other, settlement is accomplished through criminal court proceedings. No organized society can prosper without these forums. No organized society can endure which permits persons without legal authority to perform these important functions.

At the end of the War Between the States, there came into being an organization known as the Ku Klux Klan. It began in Tennessee about 1866 and was formed by a group of former Confederate officers. It was formed as a result of the new relationship between whites and blacks who recently had been freed from slavery. The Ku Klux Klan was a secret organization, and its main purpose was to assure white supremacy and to prevent the newly freed slaves from voting and otherwise participating in governmental affairs. The Klan terrorized blacks and federally appointed public officials with floggings and beatings performed by men attired in white robes and masks. It frightened blacks—and sometimes whites also—by planting burning crosses on hillsides near the homes of those upon whom it looked with disfavor.

The Klan defined and detected crime, apprehended the accused, tried and punished summarily. Its victims were sometimes lynched. The organization was open to native-born, white protestant males who were sixteen or older; Negroes, Catholics and Jews were excluded and were often the targets of Klan animosity. Klan activity continued in varying degrees in some locations throughout the country, particularly in the South, well into the twentieth century.

Klansmen were always greatly interested in governmental affairs, and the influence of the group was felt for many decades. An indication of their political influence is the fact that in 1924 a resolution denouncing the Klan was introduced at the Democratic National Convention and failed to pass after a bitter controversy.

Over the years, candidates for election either quietly sought the support of the Klan or at least refrained from offending it.

The activities of any private individual or individuals undertaking to punish other citizens for wrongdoing has always been illegal. But where mob violence is concerned, it has always been difficult to apprehend members of the group which undertook to administer its own justice.

As race relations improved and the court system became more efficient in dealing with crime, Klan and other mob activity constantly decreased. By the time I came to the Bar in 1936, there was little left of the Klan. There was, however, still some Klan activity, and in actuality a bit continues up to the present time.

During my adult life there have been few lynchings. It is not always easy to determine, after the fact, the difference between lynching on the one hand and murder on the other. This is true because it is not easy to define an organized band or mob. Accordingly, statistics relative to lynching cannot be determined with absolute accuracy.

The South Carolina Code defines a lynching as follows: " . . . any act of violence inflicted by a mob upon the body of another person which results in death of the person . . . constitutes the crime of lynching in the first degree. . . . " A mob is defined as " . . . the assembly of two or more persons without color or authority of law with the premeditated purpose and the premeditated intention of committing an act of violence on the person of another."

I first heard talk of lynching and of the Klan when I was eleven years old. At Pacolet, where I was born and reared, a popular young banker, Ben High, was killed by one of his tenants, a black man. The whole town was up in arms, and it was rumored that the Ku Klux Klan had lynched the accused person and buried him. This was never substantiated but the accused person, whose name was George Hunter, disappeared and has not been heard of from that day to the present, more than sixty years later.

In the early 1930s I was passing through the town of Union en route from Columbia to Spartanburg on a Saturday afternoon when I detected hundreds and hundreds of people milling about the courthouse and along Main Street. It developed that a black man had been accused of raping a white woman and had been lynched.

Other lynchings may have taken place in the area during the next few years, but I do not recall another until 1947, when a mob used force to break into the Pickens County jail and took from the Sheriff's custody one Willie Earl, who was suspected of having stabbed and robbed a man named Thomas W. Brown. Several persons were indicted and tried for the death of Earl, but the jury found them not guilty. Thereafter, the personal representatives of Willie Earl brought an action for damages in the Court of Common Pleas, based on the constitutional and statutory law of South Carolina, seeking recovery against the county. The case was appealed and is reported in the opinions of the Supreme Court of South Carolina.

In my career as a lawyer and a judge, I have never encountered a case wherein a lynching was involved. Perhaps the nearest I came to being concerned with the possibility of a lynching occurred during my first term in court in Aiken, in January 1950. Bert Carter, the solicitor for the Second Judicial Circuit, came to my office and told me that a defendant was being held in the county jail and was accused of murdering a man and his wife who operated a "mom and pop" type grocery store in the rural part of the county. Carter told me that this man had been tried and convicted of murder and sentenced to the electric chair. The conviction had been affirmed in the Supreme Court of South Carolina, but a new trial had been granted by the Supreme Court of the United States, which ruled that the only evidence, a confession, against the accused person was inadmissible.

Carter said that if we proceeded to trial, a directed verdict would have to be granted. He proposed to *nol pros* the case, tell the jailer to free the man at midnight and warn him that he had better be long gone for fear that the Klan, which still had a chapter active in that county, would be looking for him. The solicitor feared a lynching.

The defendant was freed and disappeared. Eight years later another person admitted killing "mom and pop" and pled guilty to the crime. This incident emphasizes the fact that a mistake can be made not only by a mob but also by the court, in spite of all its constitutional and statutory safeguards. The confession was apparently coerced.

Perhaps the first public officeholder in South Carolina to speak out firmly against the Ku Klux Klan was Governor James F. Byrnes, who, in his inaugural address in January 1951, made the following statement:

> In this State there can be but one government, that must be a government of the people under law. There can be but one Governor, elected by the people, whose duty it is to see that the law is enforced. I am going to be that Governor. I do not need the assistance of the Ku Klux Klan nor do I want interference by the National Association for the Advancement of Colored People.

By this time the influence of the Klan had waned, and it has continued to wane ever since. During Byrnes' administration and at his instigation, two statutes were enacted, one of which made it illegal for any person over sixteen years of age to appear upon any lane, walk, alley, street, road, public way or highway, or upon any public property while wearing a mask or other device concealing identity. The statute also declared it unlawful for any person to place or cause to be placed in a public place in the state a burning or flaming cross, or to place such on private property without first obtaining written permission of the owner or occupier of the premises.

The position of the Klan is such today that no candidate for public office would seek or publicly accept the support of the Klan as an organization. Such support would lose more votes than it would gain. Even today, however, the Klan occasionally will seek a permit to participate in a parade. At such times Klansmen are, of course, unmasked but usually robed, and when the authorities grant them a parade permit, security is abundant for fear of a clash between those who support the Klan and those who do not.

In 1987 five cadets at The Citadel entered the room of a black student late at night, robed as if a part of the Klan and carrying some semblance of a burning cross. They were indicted and charged with illegally wearing masks during the hazing of a black student. The grand jury declined to indict them, however, for violating the statute relative to a burning cross. The incident caused much national publicity which The Citadel did not deserve.

In February 1987 a grand jury in Columbia considered a charge against six men of raping and lynching a Columbia woman. It appeared to be the theory of the state that these men constituted a mob as referred to in the lynching law. The grand jury refused to indict.

Even though only a few Klan organizations and only a few Klansmen remain, occasionally they do something newsworthy. At Christmastime in 1987 a Klan organization sought to participate in the Christmas parade to be held in the town of Pelion in Lexington County. The town council voted to deny the request, but when it appeared that the Klan might be permitted to participate, a high school drill team and representatives of a presidential campaign dropped out. State Attorney General Travis Medlock poured oil on troubled waters by issuing an emergency opinion sustaining the right of the city officials to deny the Klan's application. The parade was peacefully attended by many citizens including about twenty members of the Klan who watched peacefully from the sidewalks while robed and hooded but not masked.

18

THE DEMOCRATIC PARTY

When I came to the Bar and entered politics in 1936, the Democratic primary was the equivalent of election. Republican candidates were scarce. There were still a great many people who said, "My granddaddy and his daddy and my daddy always voted Democrat, and I expect to vote Democrat as long as I live."

The Democrats held precinct meetings every two years, usually in late spring, but few people attended. Anyone who appeared would likely be named an officer of the precinct and might be named a delegate to the county convention, which was usually held in May. Sometimes resolutions of different sorts were approved at the precinct meetings. These resolutions were normally of no great consequence. The county convention met approximately one month later; then came the state convention about the last part of June. From 1936 until I went on the Bench in 1949, I usually attended the precinct, county and state meetings.

Actually, the contest for election in South Carolina, with rare exceptions, involved Democrats versus Democrats until about 1970. The state convention was normally attended by public officeholders and members of the Senate and House of Representatives were the dominant influence. This was a good place for a statewide candidate to mingle with important political people from throughout the state.

Traditionally, the Speaker of the House was made a delegate to the national convention. As Speaker of the House in 1948, I was among the twenty-eight delegates, representing twenty votes, designated to go to Philadelphia to attend the 1948 national convention. Harry S. Truman had taken over as President in 1945 after the death of President Franklin D. Roosevelt and had, prior to this convention, taken a strong stand in favor of civil rights—which was at the time an unpopular move in the Southland. The Southern states, including South Carolina, were somewhat the redheaded stepchildren of the convention. Among other things, the South Carolina delegation was relegated to the Lorraine Hotel—a two-bit type establishment with an elevator operated by a wheel. Someone had to turn the wheel one or two rounds to make it percolate.

As we approached the convention, gloom was rampant. It was obvious that Truman had control of the convention with no strong opponents, even though there were several favorite sons nominated. Our delegation supported Senator Dick Russell of Georgia. Sam Rayburn of Texas, who was Speaker of the House of Representatives in Washington, was the permanent chairman. Senator Paul McGrath of Rhode Island was chairman of the Democratic National Committee. Senator Olin D. Johnston was South Carolina's national Democratic committeeman. Mrs. C.L. Wheeler of Dillon was our national committeewoman.

Traveling with me and representing the *Spartanburg Herald-Journal* was my loyal friend Glen Naves, who over the years has been accused of being my press agent. He was not actually my press agent, but I must admit that he was always very charitable to me with his reporting, up until his retirement in the early 1970s. He and his wife Susan helped me with my book *Laugh With the Judge* in 1974.

It was at this convention that Hubert Humphrey of Minnesota first came into national prominence. In an address to the convention, he made himself despised throughout the South at the time by vigorously advocating civil rights and opposing states rights. The South was Humphrey's whipping boy. Over the years his views mellowed somewhat and eventually, when he was a candidate for President in 1968, he received substantial support from throughout the South, including South Carolina. By this time the views of Southerners had changed, too.

It is more or less customary for presidential candidates to be permitted to select their vice presidential running mates. At the Philadelphia convention, no one had the inside track for that office. Alben Barkley had been chosen to make the keynote speech. He was a senator from Kentucky and was considered to be basically a Southerner. Barkley's speech was truly a spellbinder. After he had addressed the convention and received several tremendous ovations, there was no question but that he would be, and he was, designated as candidate Truman's vice presidential running mate. Barkley will be long remembered for the fascinating way in which he told humorous stories.

A Democratic national convention (or any national convention) is a great study in human nature. At the Convention Hall in Philadelphia, there must have been about 10,000 people. Seats had been designated and South Carolina did not fare very well in the seating arrangements. Actually, there was so much confusion that ordinary delegates had difficulty keeping up with the proceedings. In a group of 10,000 people, especially politicians, you always have 400 people on the way to the restrooms and 400 people on the way back. At the same time, 400 are going to get a drink and 400 are coming back after having a drink. The turmoil is tremendous. Seldom is the hall quiet enough to know what is going on at the podium. An exception at this convention was during the Barkley address, when everyone settled down to listen.

It was at this convention that I first came to know television, which was just coming to the South but was already in the big city hotels in the North. A delegate could stay at the hotel and learn far more about what was happening at Convention Hall than if he were actually present.

The convention was pretty well dominated by a small group emanating from the Democratic National Committee, and when the convention adjourned, there was even more gloom than when it began. It was pretty well conceded that Truman simply could not get elected with a divided Democratic party. The South created quite a problem for him. Republican Governor Thomas Dewey from New York was the nominee of his party.

After the Democratic convention, a states' rights group was organized, with Governor Strom Thurmond the nominee for President and Governor Fielding Wright of Mississippi the nominee for Vice President. This party received substantial votes throughout the South and carried four states for a total of thirty-nine electoral votes.

Everyone, including Harry Truman, was amazed when the votes were counted. On the night of the election, the newspapers went to press with big headlines: "Dewey Is President." As more votes were tallied, these early edition papers were taken out of circulation. The late returns favored Truman and resulted in his victory. Truman proudly had his picture taken holding up one of the papers with the "Dewey Is President" headline.

Soon after the election, Truman was asked by a friend if he had been surprised by the results. "No," he replied, "I knew I was going to beat Dewey all the time."

"How did you know you were going to beat him," the friend inquired, "when everyone else in the United States thought you were going to lose?"

The newly elected President smiled as he replied, "People don't trust a man with a mustache."

Dewey did have a small, well trimmed mustache. It has been my observation that cartoonists, in drawing a villain, always make sure the villain has a mustache. Truman may have had a point.

After coming to serve as a circuit judge in 1949, I discontinued active participation in Democratic party activities but continued to take an interest in political happenings, both within and without the parties.

In the summer of 1962, Donald Russell of Spartanburg was elected governor of the state by besting Burnett R. Maybank Jr. of Charleston. Sam N. Burts of the Spartanburg Bar had been one of my most loyal friends and supporters since I came to the Bar in 1936. In 1933 Sam encouraged me and Ray Humphrey, both students at Wofford College, to go to law school. I well remember visiting in Sam's office upstairs on Morgan Square in the spring of 1933.

Sam had been at the Bar about two years and was none too prosperous at the time, but he talked a good game. Prior to 1962 he had been a member of the Spartanburg County Board of Control and Chairman of the Spartanburg County Democratic Party. He was also a loyal supporter and friend of Governor Russell. The Governor appointed Sam a member of the South Carolina Tax Commission, which required him to be in Columbia a good part of the time and placed him in a position of influence within the Democratic Party.

In 1964 Sam was made a delegate to the national convention which was to be held during the summer in Atlantic City, New Jersey. Under party procedures, if it developed that some delegate could not attend, the remaining delegates could select a substitute. When it developed that one of the regular chosen delegates would not be able to be in Atlantic City, Lawyer Burts suggested that I should be designated to fill the vacancy.

Actually, I had reservations about attending, because I was not sure whether a judge should be a delegate to a national political convention, but the group which had selected me was not meeting again, and I hesitated to tell Sam that he should not have nominated me or that I would not go. Not knowing what to do, I attended along with Sam Burts, Simpson Hyatt and E.C. Burnett Jr. of the Spartanburg Bar.

President John F. Kennedy had been assassinated on November 22, 1963 and Vice President Lyndon Johnson had become President and was serving the unexpired term. He was in control of the convention and seeking a full term, and it was obvious that Johnson would be the candidate. The big question was who would be the nominee for vice president. To the disgust of many Southern delegates, Hubert Humphrey was Johnson's designee.

After John F. Kennedy was assassinated, the influence of his brother Robert, who was Attorney General, was substantial. Edward Kennedy also was coming into prominence, and it was apparent that the Kennedys would be a factor in national elections thereafter. Senator Barry Goldwater of Arizona was the Republican nominee that year but fared poorly when the votes were counted in November. Robert Kennedy and Lyndon Johnson worked together within the Democratic party, but it was well conceded that this was a marriage of convenience and each was merely putting up with the other because that was the practical thing to do.

No doubt Robert Kennedy's threatening to run for President in 1968 caused President Johnson to bow out of the race in late winter or early spring of that year. But Robert Kennedy was assassinated while campaigning in California, and the complexion of the contest for president in 1968 was completely changed thereafter.

A national political convention is something like a circus—a big show with much media coverage provided, to the benefit and/or detriment of the candidates. The importance of the convention today has been watered down somewhat, due to the fact that so many states now have primaries which commit their delegates to a candidate well in advance of the convention. A substantial portion of the delegates have no choice but to vote for the candidate who prevailed at the "test voting" back home.

It was not until the early 1950s that blacks came to be actively engaged in the Democratic party. In April of 1944, the Supreme Court of the United States, by an eight to one decision, upset a previous decision of nine years standing and ruled that blacks would have the right to vote in Democratic primary elections in Texas. The Court held that ". . . the great privilege of choosing his rulers may not be denied man by the state because of his color."

There had been on the statute books of South Carolina many sections of the Code which related to primary elections. It was the political thinking of the Democrats, and others, that the Texas ruling would not apply if there were no statutory laws controlling the primaries. At the time of the Court's ruling, the state legislature had adjourned for the year, but on April 12, 1944 Governor Olin D. Johnston issued a proclamation calling the General Assembly into extraordinary session for April 15. The extra session adjourned on April 20, after 147 primary laws had been completely repealed in hopes of avoiding the Texas ruling.

It was the thinking of the assemblymen that primary elections would no longer be a part of state government but would instead operate as a private club called the South Carolina Democratic Party. The party then adopted rules limiting the primaries to whites only.

United States District Court Judge Waites Waring from Charleston struck down the new arrangement as unconstitutional. He pointed out that primaries were an important part of the election process. Gradually blacks began to register and vote in the Democratic party primaries. Later, statutes were again enacted to control primaries. In Charleston, the most Southern of Southern towns, Judge Waring was ostracized. Society there simply would not tolerate him or his views.

About that time an interesting story went the rounds in political circles. Judge Waring had a house at Folly Beach. A summer storm brewed up and lightning struck the adjoining house, ruining the roof. The occupant of the damaged house had a sign painted and placed in his front yard which read: "God, he lives next door."

Judge Waring, as a practicing attorney, had been a lawyer for Burnett R. Maybank, a cotton broker, prior to Maybank's election as governor and prior to his subsequent elevation to United States Senator. In 1948, as Maybank ran for re-election to the Senate, he was lampooned by his opponents with the fact that he was responsible for Judge Waring's appointment. At the time of the Judge's appointment, Cotton Ed Smith was also a member of the Senate from this state and Senator Maybank tended to blame the appointment on Senator Smith.

A newspaper reporter asked Mrs. Waring if it was true that Smith ws responsible for her husband's appointment. She replied, "No, they just blame it on Senator Smith because he's dead."

The popularity of Judge Waring in South Carolina, and especially in Charleston, waned after his ruling on the Democratic primary. Eventually, he retired and moved to New York, where he died many years later. His body was returned to Charleston for burial, but few were in attendance at the funeral services.

In spite of the problems the appointment caused Senator Maybank, he was nominated on the first ballot in the 1948 Democratic primary over four opponents. There being no Republican opponent, Maybank was re-elected and served an additional six-year term prior to his untimely death in September 1954.

The Democratic party continues to be the dominating influence in South Carolina elections—especially local elections. However, we no longer have the day of the "yellow-dog Democrat." There was a time when a multitude of people would say, "I would vote for a yellow dog if he was the nominee of the Democratic party—especially against a Republican." Today, however, there are not many South Carolinians left who have not voted for Republican candidates at some election. This is especially true in the presidential races.

Since 1964, when Senator Strom Thurmond switched from the Democratic to the Republican party, he has been returned to the Senate as a Republican in 1966, 1972, 1978 and 1984.

In 1974 State Senator James B. Edwards of Charleston was elected governor of the state on the Republican ticket, defeating William Jennings Bryan Dorn in an election referred to elsewhere in this book. Gradually, over the last twenty-odd years, more and more Republicans have been elected to the State Senate and House of Representatives. Nomination by the Democratic party is no longer equivalent to election in South Carolina. As of 1989, we have one Democratic Senator and one Republican Senator. We have two Republican members of Congress and four Democratic members of Congress.

Senator Strom Thurmond has always submitted that people ought to vote for the best man, regardless of party affiliation. More and more voters are disregarding party labels and taking Thurmond's advice.

19

THE REPUBLICAN PARTY

Writing a chapter about the Democratic party during my fifty years of watching politics in South Carolina was not difficult. I was present or involved in Democratic political activities from the time I entered the race for the House of Representatives in 1936 until I joined the judiciary in 1949. In any given year there was much news concerning the activities of the Democrats, who had been in control of politics of South Carolina for nearly 100 years.

Writing a chapter about the Republican party during those same fifty years is more difficult, because its activities in South Carolina have been pretty much limited to the last half of the years I write about.

As I began my political career, South Carolina was a part of the "solid South." For many years the Democratic primary determined who would serve in public office, and until the 1960s and 1970s, people generally did not bother to go to the polls at general election time. After a candidate was nominated in the Democratic primary, he considered the campaign over and would often go on vacation.

Activities within the Democratic party organization were for many years rather informal. I cannot recall any precinct meetings on the part of the Republicans prior to the 1960s. Some county conventions convened and the state convention was held mostly to select delegates to attend the national convention. From 1932 to 1952, the Democrats were in control of the White House, and Congress was in large measure controlled by Democrats.

"Republican" was not a four-letter word, but before the 1960s it was a four-syllable word almost as obnoxious in the mind of many South Carolinians. If one had leanings other than Democratic, he did not get around to boasting of it in public.

I date the advent of the two-party system in South Carolina and the rise of the Republican party from 1948, the year South Carolina Democrats conceived that they had been mistreated at the national convention in Philadelphia and came home mad enough to do something about it. Out of that discontent grew the States Rights party ticket and selection of electors to support the candidacy of

Governor Strom Thurmond and Governor Fielding F. Wright of Mississippi.

A majority of the old-line Democrats left the party to vote for electors committed to Thurmond and Wright. The great majority of those who so voted would have found it difficult to vote a Republican ticket but did not hesitate to leave the Democratic party long enough to vote a ticket which in their minds was not tainted by the word "Republican." Having once left the Democratic party, voters found it easier four years later to leave the Democratic party again—not to vote Republican yet, but to continue to show their irritation with the national Democratic party by voting a third-party ticket.

In 1952 the Republicans sought and procured a war hero, Dwight Eisenhower, to carry their banner. He was popular and generally acceptable to both Republicans and Democrats. Actually, being a career Army man, Eisenhower had never become affiliated with any political party. It is my recollection that the Democratic hierarchy hoped he might seek the Democratic nomination, but he chose otherwise. That year the Democrats nominated Governor Adlai Stevenson of Illinois, a very personable candidate but one with leanings certainly more liberal and less acceptable to the South than General Eisenhower.

In South Carolina there came into being a temporary political party called the "South Carolinians for Eisenhower." And electors were named for whom the people, unhappy with both the Democratic and Republican parties, could vote. Along with these electors the old-line Democrats chose their electors and the old-line Republicans selected their electors, so the voters had three choices.

In a general election a plurality prevails. Democratic electors for Stevenson received 173,000 votes; South Carolinians for Eisenhower electors received 158,000 votes and the old-line Republican electors for Eisenhower received 9,000 votes. Although the Democrats won, it should be observed that the margin was only by 6,000 votes out of a total of 340,000 voters. In 1952 Governor James F. Byrnes, who was very popular and influential, supported the independent "South Carolinians for Eisenhower" ticket and was in large measure responsible for the highly complimentary vote which Eisenhower supporters cast that year. And so, for two presidential elections in a row, South Carolina Democrats left the national party—once by majority and the other time nearly so. The "solid South" was beginning to crack.

Two years later, in 1954, United States Senator Burnett R. May-bank died after being nominated in the Democratic primary. The Republicans had not even fielded a candidate. It was September and the Democratic party decided that there was no time for another primary. The Executive Committee named state Senator Edgar A. Brown to run in the November general election. The story of former Governor Strom Thurmond's famous write-in candidacy is told elsewhere in this book; I mention it here to call attention to the fact that Thurmond, in a write-in campaign, defeated the Democratic party's nominee. Once again South Carolinians were becoming accustomed to voting other than Democratic.

In 1956 the Democrats chose as their presidential candidate Adlai Stevenson, with Estes Kefauver as his running mate. Eisenhower and Nixon were again the choice of the Republicans. A third set of electors called "South Carolinians for Independent Electors" were also on the November general election ballot; actually they were for Senator Harry Byrd of Virginia. The Stevenson ticket (Democrat) got 128,000 votes, Eisenhower (Republican) got 75,000 votes, and Byrd (Independent) got 88,000 votes. Certainly "Republican" was no longer an ugly word in South Carolina.

No Republican had served in the General Assembly of South Carolina since 1901. Few had sought a seat in either the House or the Senate. In 1961 Democratic House member Tom Elliot of Richland County resigned. A special election was called to fill the vacancy, and Charles Boineau, a Republican, was elected. Boineau became the first member of his party to serve in the South Carolina House of Representatives in sixty years.

In 1962 Clarence Singletary of Charleston resigned his seat in the House of Representatives to accept the office of Circuit Judge for the Ninth Judicial Circuit. Fred Worsham of Charleston, a Republican, was elected to serve his unexpired term. Worsham was re-elected in 1964.

The growth of the Republican Party in South Carolina is indicated by the number of House members and Senators elected since Boineau and Worsham pointed the way. There are 124 members in the House of Representatives. Republicans were elected in years and numbers as follows: seventeen in 1966, five in 1968, eleven in 1970, twenty-one in 1972, seventeen in 1974, twelve in 1976, sixteen in 1978, seventeen in 1980, twenty in 1982, twenty-seven in 1984, and thirty-two in 1986.

In the Senate, where forty-six members serve, Republicans were elected as follows: six in 1966 plus one independent Democrat. In that year the Senate had attempted to add four additional members, for a total of fifty, to its number; this action was declared unconstitutional and a new election was held in 1968 for a Senate of forty-six members. Republicans were thereafter elected as follows: three in 1968, 1972 and 1976; five in 1980 and ten in 1984. When the General Assembly convened in January 1987, Republican legislators totaled forty-two—ten in the Senate and thirty-two in the House of Representatives.

Republican David Wilkins, an outstanding lawyer and House member from Greenville County, was the first member of the Republican party in modern times to serve as chairman of an important House committee. He was elected Chairman of the Judiciary Committee by a substantial margin over opposition. By the late 1960s the Republican party in South Carolina had grown to the extent that statewide candidates entered races in opposition to the Democrats. These candidates were not successful until 1974, when Charleston's state Senator James B. Edwards defeated William Jennings Bryan Dorn, who came to carry the Democratic banner in the fall of 1974 after Charles "Pug" Ravenel was declared by the Supreme Court ineligible to serve.

In 1956 the Republican mayor of Clemson, L.P. Crawford, challenged Democratic United States Senator Olin D. Johnston but corralled only 49,000 votes.

In 1962 W.D. Workman Jr., a highly respected Republican newspaperman from Columbia, challenged Senator Johnston and received 133,000 votes representing forty-two percent of the total.

In 1964 Strom Thurmond was serving his tenth year in the Senate. After prevailing in the write-in campaign of 1954 against Edgar Brown, he had resigned in 1956, in keeping with his pledge, so that the people of the state could have a free choice, Thurmond had been elected not only in 1954 as a write-in candidate, but also in 1956 and 1960 as a Democrat. The time came (in 1964) when Thurmond was uncomfortable with his liberal Democratic colleagues from the North, and he announced that he was switching to the Republican party. He has since that time been re-elected as a Republican in 1966, 1972, 1978 and 1984. Thurmond's switch to the Republican party gave South Carolina Republicans a shot in the arm, as they now had a popular, sagacious leader.

In the 1950s Roger Milliken moved the Milliken Research Center to Spartanburg. He brought with him many influential people who were employed by his company in high-income brackets. These people were interested in and influential in political matters, and they became active and have been active ever since in Republican party political matters. Roger Milliken's influence has been substantial in many national as well as statewide and local campaigns during the last quarter of this century.

In 1970 Republican Albert Watson relinquished his seat in Congress to run for governor against Democratic nominee John West. Watson was not successful, but he received 221,000 votes against 251,000 for West. Floyd Spence, who had served in the General Assembly as a Republican, was elected to fill Watson's vacancy on the congressional delegation and continues as of 1989 to hold that office.

In 1966 Marshall Parker, who had served in the General Assembly as a Republican, challenged Senator Fritz Hollings but was defeated by a narrow margin of 11,000 votes—Hollings received 223,000 votes and Parker 212,000 votes. Republican Joe Rogers ran for governor against Democrat Robert McNair. Rogers got 184,000 to McNair's 255,000.

In 1974 my fellow townsman of Pacolet, General William Childs Westmoreland, had retired from the Army after a distinguished career as Commander in Chief during the Vietnam War. He had never concerned himself with politics and admitted that he had never voted. He announced his candidacy for governor on the Republican ticket. State Senator James B. Edwards of Charleston also entered the race. This was the first year the Republicans held a statewide primary. Before this time nominations for state offices had been agreed upon at the state conventions.

Thirty-five thousand South Carolinians went to the polls and voted in 1974. Edwards prevailed by a vote of 20,000 (plus) against Westmoreland's 14,000 (plus). It is worthy of note that Charleston gave 8,152 votes to Edwards and only 658 to Westmoreland. This county's one-sided vote was largely responsible for Edwards' victory.

While Edwards was winning the Republican primary, Charles D. "Pug" Ravenel was defeating the field of Democratic candidates for governor. They were L. Maurice Bessinger, John Bolt Culbertson, Bryan Dorn, Milton J. Dukes, Earl E. Morris and Eugene N. Zeigler. In a second race for the nomination, Ravenel received 186,000 votes to Dorn's 154,000 votes. Ravenel's eligibility to serve under the Constitution was challenged in court. The Supreme Court of South Carolina held that he had not resided in South Carolina during the last five years, as required by the Constitution for one who wishes to serve as governor. The Democratic Executive Committee named

Dorn to run in the general election against Edwards. Edwards was declared the winner and became the first Republican governor to serve in South Carolina since Reconstruction days.

Statewide candidates have not fared too well on the Republican ticket. Congressional candidates have experienced more success. In recent years Thomas Hartnett, Floyd Spence, Carroll Campbell, Ed Young and John Napier have served. Since 1964 South Carolina has had one Republican and one Democratic United States Senator.

Democrat Richard W. Riley of Greenville was elected Governor in 1978 and re-elected in 1982. The office went back to the Republicans when Carroll Campbell defeated Lieutenant Governor Mike Daniel in 1986.

I think it a fair summary to say that South Carolina is now truly a two-party state. No longer can it be said that the Democrats have everything in the bag. A majority of the members of the General Assembly are still Democrats. Of the 170 members of the General Assembly, almost one-third is Republican. Republicans have provided a serious challenge for many seats now held by Democrats. In addition, a few Republicans are winning in local, county and municipal races, but the vast majority of officeholders at the municipal and county level are still Democrats. The growth of the Republican party in this state has been gradual but constant. It has been interesting to watch.

20

LAUGH WITH THE JUDGE

Preachers, teachers, lawyers and doctors—and anyone else whose work requires them to be in touch with the public—experience a great many humorous happenings. All of them, especially lawyers and doctors, could write a book. It is interesting to hear people in all walks of life say they have considered writing a book. Few get around to it.

After I had been on the bench for twenty-five years, I decided to write about the humorous incidents which occurred during my legal, political and judicial career.

Here is how it came about. My first assignment to hold jury court was in Aiken in January 1950; I was scheduled to make a banquet address about a month later. Several amusing incidents occurred during the first weeks of my presiding, and I made a note of each incident to remind me so I could use this material in my speech at the banquet. The audience received my anecdotes rather charitably, and I formed the habit of recording such amusing incidents in a little black book to keep me from forgetting.

Over the years there came to be about 180 such anecdotes. Most of them involved my personal experiences, but some involved true happenings in the lives of friends. None of them was a repeat of an old war story which I heard at a lawyers' or judges' meeting. Insofar as I know, all the incidents recited in my book, *Laugh With the Judge* (published in 1974 by Sandlapper Press, Inc.), are originals.

After being elected as an Associate Justice of the Supreme Court, I drove 100 miles from Spartanburg to Columbia and back each time a term of court was held. This gave me idle time which I utilized to dictate my anecdotes into a cassette recorder. My secretary then took the cassettes and transcribed them into a rough draft. When the work was completed, I offered the manuscript to the University of South Carolina Press in hopes that it would undertake to publish it. Instead, the director (I believe his name was King) reported that I simply did not have the makings of a book and returned the manuscript to me.

Thereafter, publisher Robert P. Wilkins of Sandlapper was in touch with me and eagerly bought all rights, undertaking to publish my book without any investment on my part and to pay royalties. Sandlapper sold 3,000 copies in the first thirty days, but I never learned whether Mr. King had seen a copy. Over the years the book continues to sell, though typically the sales diminish with time. All in all, however, *Laugh With the Judge* has experienced excellent sales in South Carolina as well as substantial sales throughout the country.

In writing the book, I endeavored to emphasize the fact that the courtroom is no place for levity. Certainly a humorous situation should never be provoked. It is, however, inescapable that in and about the court there will occur from time to time incidents which are good for a smile, a grin or even occasionally a belly laugh. When this occurs, there is no reason why the incident should not be shared with others. This I have attempted to do.

21

STATE CONSTABULARY AND
THE SOUTH CAROLINA
LAW ENFORCEMENT DIVISION

The Constitution of South Carolina provides for the separation of powers. There is allocated to the General Assembly the authority to make laws. There is allocated to the judiciary the chore of interpreting and declaring the law. It is the duty of the governor or the executive branch of the government to see that the laws are enforced.

The military department of the state, headed up by the adjutant general, is at the command of the governor for the purpose of seeing that laws are executed. It may be remembered that Governor Johnston called out a unit of the national guard in 1935 to take over the South Carolina Highway Department. It was declared by him to be in a state of insurrection.

Over and above the military department of the state, there was, during the first eleven years of my political career, an organization within the governor's office referred to as the "State Constabulary." Members of the constabulary were appointed at the discretion, or oftentimes the whim, of the governor. Until 1947 these appointments were pretty much political. It was well known that candidates running for governor obligated themselves to appoint constables in exchange for political support.

The duties of these constables were not well defined. In a general way, it can be said they went where the governor told them to go and enforced such laws as the governor wanted enforced. Many of them devoted a great deal of time to raiding illegal liquor stills. Some of them were helpful to the office of the local sheriff, and some were a thorn in the flesh of local law enforcement officers. As late as 1947 the constabulary was not large. The total appropriation for the entire law enforcement division of the governor's office amounted to less than a quarter of a million dollars.

When Strom Thurmond was elected governor in the fall of 1946, he inaugurated a new plan for the work of the state constabulary. By executive order in 1947 he created the South Carolina Law

Enforcement Division (SLED) to take the place of the state constabulary. Thus began a truly professional organization the duty of which would be to assist local law enforcement officers in solving problems they were not prepared to deal with.

Most sheriffs, particularly in the smaller counties, are not prepared to make ballistic examinations, provide lie detector tests, examine blood samples, analyze illegal drugs or compare fingerprints. Both Governor Thurmond and Governor James F. Byrnes, who succeeded him, were generally of the view that the basic authority and responsibility for enforcing the criminal laws was with the county sheriffs and with the chiefs of police of the various towns. It is my recollection that Governor Byrnes would not send SLED people into a county unless assistance was requested by local law enforcement people.

My friend Oren Brady, who had spent many years in law enforcement in Spartanburg County, was one of the first chiefs of SLED. In 1956 Governor George Bell Timmerman Jr. appointed J.P. "Pete" Strom to be the director of the organization. Strom was truly a professional and his administration of the law enforcement division has been likened to the administration of the FBI by J. Edgar Hoover.

Over the years the organization grew and Strom made of it a truly professional organization. When local enforcement people had problems they could not solve, Strom's men were always available. He continued as chief for a period of thirty-two years and died in 1987 of a heart attack.

Of all the people I have known in public life over the years, none has come to my attention who was more highly respected than was Chief Strom. He never knew anything except law enforcement. His father was sheriff of McCormick County, and as was customary at the time, the family of the sheriff lived in the jail. That custom has long since been abandoned, and no sheriff today lives in a jail in South Carolina.

Pete Strom had been in law enforcement many years prior to his appointment as chief. During the era of integration of the schools, law enforcement people had many problems. I particularly recall Strom's part in admitting Harvey Gantt to Clemson College. Gantt was the first black student enrolled. Then I recall the tremendous problems which Governor Robert E. McNair and Chief Strom had in the middle 1960s in Orangeburg. Strom did outstanding service for the state in both instances.

The editor of *The State* newspaper had high praise for the chief:

The folksy cop, who died Monday at age 69, had to combine deft police skills with masterful politicking to survive more than 30 years as chief of the State Law Enforcement Division.

"Pete" Strom became chief only nine years after SLED had replaced the old State Constabulary, known as much as a political football as a law enforcement agency. He carried SLED to a new level of professionalism.

On the way, Chief Strom himself learned the lessons of politics. He was not above endorsing a political favorite for governor and, when the potential election of a hostile chief executive threatened his job, his legislative supporters rallied round and loosened the governor's control over the job.

The chief of SLED is appointed by the governor of the state. Among those who reappointed Strom were governors Hollings, Russell, McNair, West, Edwards, Riley and Campbell.

It was not until 1974 that the Legislature gave statutory status to SLED. Prior to that time it existed and operated purely under the executive order issued by Governor Thurmond in 1947. Rumor had it in and about the Legislature that Governor Edwards might not reappoint Chief Strom. His support in the Legislature was so strong that the act giving his department legislative status included a provision that the chief would have to be confirmed by the Senate after being appointed by the governor. If Governor Edwards had not reappointed Strom, many believed that the Senate would simply have refused to confirm a successor, thereby leaving Strom in office. Governor Edwards reappointed him.

Pete Strom will long be remembered in law enforcement circles and admired by people who believe in firm enforcement of the criminal laws of the state. He leaves a son, Pete Jr., who practices law in Columbia.

Gone are the days when the only prerequisite for serving as a law enforcement officer was the possession of a badge and gun. Substantially all persons working in law enforcement today are required to be trained at the South Carolina Criminal Justice Academy. Chief Strom was an ex officio member of the board in charge of the academy. His contributions in improving personnel who serve as law enforcement officers has been great.

Upon Chief Strom's death, many people expected Governor Carroll Campbell to appoint Sheriff James R. Metts of Lexington County, a highly respected and capable Republican sheriff. The

governor surprised many by appointing Chief Strom's first assistant, Robert Stewart, who had succeeded Leon Gasque (de-
ceased) as first assistant to the chief. Chief Stewart bears an
excellent reputation. It is expected that the office, under his direction, will continue to render the fine service to which the people of
South Carolina have become accustomed.

22

FOR THE SAKE OF A CALF

I began the practice of law in 1936 in Spartanburg. My office was upstairs over Ralph Broome's Liquor Store. In order to get to it, I walked upstairs between the liquor store and Babe Thomason's Pool Room. We did not have the modern conveniences which lawyers enjoy today. There was no air conditioning, and in the summertime, I raised the window and hoped that a breeze would not blow all the papers off of my desk. Business was usually none too good and I spent some time gazing out the window onto Morgan Square. At that time there were some city police cars, but downtown police officers walked the beat.

I used to gaze out the window and admire Policeman Joe Frank Logue. A native of Edgefield County, Logue came to Spartanburg to be a part of city law enforcement. He was handsome, tall and erect, always well groomed and weighed about 190 pounds. He was truly a perfect specimen of what a police officer ought to look like. I enjoyed chatting with him, and he was a good supporter of mine politically.

Back in Edgefield County, Joe Frank Logue had an uncle named George Logue and an uncle named Wallace Logue whose wife was named Sue. Edgefield County is one of the smallest counties in the state. A great portion of the people who live there know a great portion of other people who live there. In such a county, politics are important and oftentimes jealousies, loves and hatreds are quite prevalent. In that county lived also a man named Davis Timmerman who operated a country grocery store type of enterprise.

Timmerman and Wallace Logue developed a difficulty arising from the killing of a calf. I cannot remember whether Wallace Logue killed Timmerman's calf or Timmerman killed Wallace Logue's calf, but out of the killing of the calf there arose a dispute in 1940 and Davis Timmerman killed Wallace Logue. Timmerman was charged with murder, but the jury wrote a verdict of "not guilty" and he went free and returned to the operation of the country grocery store. Almost immediately Sue Logue, whose husband had been killed, and George Logue, whose brother had been killed, began plotting to avenge the death of their kinsman. They seized

88

upon the idea of procuring the help of their policeman nephew, Joe Frank Logue of Spartanburg. After many conferences, the police officer agreed to be a party to the crime and hired Clarence Bagwell, a Spartanburg house painter, for the sum of $500 to go to Edgefield and kill Davis Timmerman.

In a later trial it would be testified that Bagwell told the policeman that he would kill everybody in Spartanburg County for $500. On September 17, 1941, with Bagwell driving a car borrowed by Joe Frank Logue, the two drove to Edgefield County. While Bagwell went in Timmerman's store, Joe Frank concealed himself under a raincoat in the back seat. After Bagwell shot and killed Timmerman, the two immediately returned to Spartanburg in the automobile which Joe Frank had borrowed from a friend.

As the result of a tip, Bagwell was questioned and confessed his part in the murder of Timmerman. The state then charged Bagwell, George, Sue and Joe Frank with the murder—some of them for murder and some for being an accessory before the fact.

Arrest warrants were taken and the sheriff of Edgefield County, W.D. Allen, along with his only deputy, a man named Clark, undertook on Sunday morning to go to the residence of George and Sue Logue to arrest them. They refused to be arrested. George shot and killed the sheriff and a farm tenant named Fred Dorn shot Deputy Clark, who in turn shot and killed Dorn.

Clark lived about two days and was able to tell the authorities what had taken place. When the news got around, Circuit Court Judge Strom Thurmond, also of Edgefield, went unarmed to the home of George and Sue Logue, arrested them and persuaded them to go to jail. So far as I know, this is the only instance in the history of South Carolina where a circuit court judge has undertaken to arrest persons charged with a violation of the law. Circuit Court Judge Thurmond has been well known for doing unusual things over the years and so far as I have been able to learn, he is the only one who has this distinction.

It was determined that George and Sue Logue and Clarence Bagwell could not get a fair trial in Edgefield County, where the people who would be members of the jury knew too much about what had taken place. The court moved their trial to Lexington County. Joe Frank Logue did not want a change of venue and his case was tried later. The trial in Lexington resulted in a conviction of all three without a recommendation of mercy, which carried with it a mandatory death sentence by electrocution. The case was appealed to the Supreme Court of South Carolina and affirmed.

At that time there was no such thing as getting a state-tried case heard in the federal courts, and so the execution of the three took place rather promptly. Sue Logue may have been the first and the only woman electrocuted in this state, but I am not at all sure of that.

Joe Frank Logue came to trial in July 1943 in Edgefield County. He had turned state's evidence in the Lexington trial against his three cohorts and had hoped that the fact that he had helped the state would bring about a verdict of "guilty with a recommendation to mercy," which would spare his life. Instead the Edgefield County jury found him guilty of murder without a recommendation of mercy, and he was sentenced to be executed. His conviction (and sentence) was upheld on appeal to the Supreme Court. At a later date, Governor Olin D. Johnston commuted Logue's sentence to life in prison. He was assigned to the South Carolina Law Enforcement Division as a trusty and placed in charge of the bloodhounds. He made quite a record for himself as keeper and runner of the hounds and was eventually paroled. It is my recollection that he came to be a used car salesman in the Laurens area.

Since George and Sue Logue and Clarence Bagwell were sentenced to death for the killing of Timmerman, they did not come to trial for the death of Sheriff Allen or his deputy Clark.

After Bagwell's electrocution, his body was brought back to Spartanburg and lay in state in the Green Gables Pool Room, located about halfway between Spartanburg and Inman. It is my understanding that the funeral was preached there. The Green Gables was operated by Bagwell's good friend, or maybe she was his wife, who was known as "Ma Smith." These killings gained much notoriety throughout the United States, and several detective magazines wrote up the story.

There is an old saying which goes: "Big oaks from little acorns grow." It can also be said that many troubles may grow out of the death of a calf. In this case the troubles included the deaths of eight persons: Wallace Logue, Davis Timmerman, Sheriff Allen, Deputy Clark, George Logue, Sue Logue, Clarence Bagwell and Fred Dorn.

23

THE FIFTY-MAN SENATE

The opinion of the Supreme Court of the United States in *Reynolds v. Sims* in the early 1960s required that the apportionment of members of legislatures be made on a substantially equal population basis. This decision caused pandemonium in many legislatures, including South Carolina's. Under South Carolina's Constitution of 1895, the Senate was composed of one member from each of the state's forty-six counties. One county was inhabited by approximately 8,000 people, while other counties had a population of well over 200,000 each. Each county had at least one House member, with large counties having members depending on population.

The General Assembly of South Carolina began wrestling with the problem of reapportionment. The question brought about prolonged debates, particularly in the Senate. It was obvious that small counties like McCormick, with a population of 8,000, could not have one senator; likewise, it was apparent that counties like Charleston, Richland, Greenville and Spartanburg would have more than one. Reapportionment became a difficult problem and a somewhat emotional issue because, in order to comply with the mandate of the United States Supreme Court, seats which had been held by the same individuals for years became endangered. Every senator understandably began to wonder how any proposed plan would affect the possibilities of his re-election.

During the debate, someone came up with the novel idea of adding senators to accommodate a maximum of the incumbents. The problem could be solved to the satisfaction of enough senators to assure passage of a bill if the total number of senators was fifty instead of forty-six. A statute was enacted accordingly; and in the fall of 1966, fifty senators were elected from the senatorial districts created by the legislative act.

It is difficult to define those things which should be dealt with in a constitution as contrasted with statutes. However, it seems pretty well universally agreed that the composition of the legislative, judicial and executive departments is a matter for constitutional determination.

As expected, the question of the constitutionality of the statute arose in the original jurisdiction of the Supreme Court soon after the fifty-man Senate began its legislative duties in January of 1967. In the case of *State ex rel. McLeod v. West*, our Supreme Court made the only logical determination. The Court held that Article III, Section 6, of our Constitution limited the number of senators to forty-six.

The opinion was filed in March of 1967 while the Legislature was in session. The question then arose: "Is the Senate dissolved?" Strong argument could be made for the proposition that there was no legal Senate—which, of course, would have caused unlimited turmoil. The Court went on to hold that since the fifty-member Senate was adopted in good faith, the actions of the Senate as then composed would be treated as valid ". . . but only until the next general election."

Had the Court permitted the Assembly to statutorily determine its own composition, the number of House members and the number of Senate members would have been negotiable every ten years when the results of the United States census were declared.

For many years, the United States Supreme Court avoided the issue of apportionment of legislative bodies. The abuses throughout the United States became so obnoxious and unfair that the court finally decided to enter what has been referred to as a "political thicket."

Routinely, prior to 1970, every ten years the General Assembly reapportioned the House of Representatives by statute according to a formula. Normally there was no debate, it being understood that South Carolina's constitution mandated reapportionment of the House. The Constitution of 1895 anchored down the Senate at one senator per county; accordingly, the Senate was never reapportioned prior to the middle sixties, regardless of the fluctuating population.

The ruling of our Court in 1967 forced the Assembly to again consider reapportionment. It came up with a plan whereby one senator or several senators would represent the people in a given area. The area might be one or more counties, or one senator might represent several counties.

Later came single-member districts for both Senators and House members. Republicans and blacks have generally favored the single-member district, as it enhances the possibility of their being elected. I have never served in a single-member district legislature, but those who have served under this system tell me that it is the worst thing that ever happened to the state of South Carolina. It appears that every delegate to the General Assembly, whether senator or House member, is more interested in his district than in the general welfare of the county and the state—and this is bad.

Routinely, Republicans and Democrats have determined single-member district lines in a way that enhances the possibility of the controlling party winning a maximum of elections. This is called gerrymandering. In the summer of 1986, the Supreme Court of the United States, with reluctance, decided to become involved. It will determine the question: Is it unconstitutional, as a violation of the Fourteenth Amendment, for a legislative body to create political districts for egregiously partisan purposes? The decision has potentially explosive implications. The Court has decided to enter one more political thicket.

24

HOME RULE

Under the Constitution of 1895 (effective prior to 1973) there was nothing to prevent the Legislature from enacting local laws such as the County Appropriation Act, referred to as the County Supply Bill. It could, and oftentimes did, enact laws for a particular county which determined such insignificant things as the salary of an employee or the cost of recording a deed in the Office of the Clerk of Court or of the Register of Mesne Conveyance. For all practical purposes, the local courthouse and the county government were controlled by acts of the General Assembly passed at the instigation of the local county delegation.

This did not mean that all members of the General Assembly concerned themselves with local legislation. It was common knowledge that only the legislative delegations from the counties affected read local bills. Over the years, this system of operating county government became tremendously undesirable, and several county governing boards were created before Article VIII was ratified in 1973. This article brought into being what we commonly refer to as "Home Rule."

The Home Rule Amendment to the Constitution was designed to bring about local governing boards in each county, much like local governing boards for the cities. Most legislators were delighted to be relieved of operating the county government and were content to be state legislators. On the other hand, there were a few members of the House and Senate who desired to keep on running the counties as had been the case since 1895.

The new 1973 Article VIII (Local Government) Amendment mandated that the General Assembly provide by general law for county home rule; it required the Legislature to provide options "not to exceed five" forms of government. A most important part of the new provision required "... no laws for a specific county shall be enacted and no county shall be exempt from the general laws or laws applicable to the selected alternative form of government."

The Assembly enacted a statute providing options as follows: Form 1 (Council); Form 2 (Council-Supervisor); Form 3 (Council-Administrator); Form 4 (Council-Manager); and Form 5 (Board of

Commissioners). Any one of the first four forms brought about home rule. Form 5 permitted the Legislature to continue to govern the respective counties. The constitutionality of the act came into contest in the original jurisdiction of the Supreme Court, and the opinion fell to me for writing. Forms 1, 2, 3 and 4 were not under attack. The Attorney General submitted that Form 5 was repugnant to the new amendment and especially to Section 7 thereof. By the narrow margin of a vote of 3 to 2, the Court held Form 5 to be unconstitutional. We wrote:

> We think that Form 5 is constitutionally repugnant to Section 7 of Article VIII, because it permits a county to carry on business as before, after the people, speaking through the constitution, have mandated a change.

The effect of the Court's ruling was to approve the first four forms of government enumerated above, and all counties came to operate under one of these. Our ruling was completely consistent with the mandate of people speaking through the new amendment that local county government be taken out of the State House and returned to the county courthouse, where it should have been all of the time. The transition was not without its problems, but the problems were largely political.

It was not easy for legislators to give up their authority to control county matters which were now delegated to local governing boards. Some legislative delegations continued to introduce and have passed in the House and Senate bills which related to a single county. Governor James B. Edwards, who was inaugurated in January 1975, recognized the unconstitutionality of these local acts and proceeded to veto the first of them. His veto was promptly overridden and, rather than take issue with the Assembly regularly as other local bills were passed, he simply let them become law without his signature. This pattern of operation continued throughout his four-year administration as governor. All counties have adjusted to the new Home Rule government, and if any legislator would revert to the old system, it has not come to my attention.

As time goes on, fewer and fewer of these local bills have been introduced, and legislators have been more content to allow local governing authorities to attend to local matters. There continue, however, as of 1989 a few local bills which are purely unconstitutional, but, with rare exception, no one raises the issue.

The change brought about by Article VIII is one of the more important changes during my fifty years at the Bench and Bar. Home Rule is working well in South Carolina.

25

A NEW DAY IN LEGISLATIVE POLITICS

Rex Carter was elected Speaker of the House in 1973 and served with distinction as such until 1980. He has been a friend of mine over the years and was highly helpful in my election as Associate Justice to the Supreme Court in 1967.

It was about 1979 that he commented to me: "Bruce, when you were Speaker of the House in 1947, 1948 and 1949, the work of the Speaker was greatly different. You served with all male, white Democrats. Today in the House of Representatives we have Democrats and Republicans, whites and blacks, men and women. There is a Republican caucus, a black caucus, a women's caucus and a Democratic caucus. In making every move, the Speaker of the House must take into consideration these several groups. On a matter as simple as appointing a committee to escort a visiting Speaker to the podium, I must keep in mind all of these groups for fear of offending some."

The fact that I did not, as Speaker, have to contend with these various factions made my work more pleasant. I reflect upon the way the changes have come about and the effect which the changes have had on the operations of both the House of Representatives and the Senate. Today the work of a senator and/or House member has become almost a full-time job. The pay is very different, and the support personnel available to members of the General Assembly is far more abundant.

Ladyfolks were pretty much unknown to the General Assembly until the 1960s. My brief research indicates that Mrs. Mary G. Ellis, a Democrat from Jasper County, was the first woman elected to the Senate in a regular general election for a full term. She served from 1929 to 1932.

Mrs. Thomasine Grayson Mason, a Democrat from Clarendon and Sumter counties, served in 1967 and 1968. Elizabeth Johnston Patterson (daughter of Olin D. Johnston), a Democrat from Spartanburg, and Norma Caldwell Russell, a Republican from the Aiken-Bamberg-Barnwell-Edgefield-Lexington senatorial district, came to the Senate in 1981. Senator Patterson served until she was elected to Congress in 1986. Nell Whitley Smith, a Democrat of the Abbeville-Anderson-Oconee-Pickens senatorial district, came to the Senate in 1983. She was elected to fill a vacancy created by the death of her husband, Senator Harris Smith.

In the House of Representatives it would appear that Mrs. Harriet F. Johnson, a Democrat from York County, was elected and served during the 1945 and 1946 sessions. Mrs. Emma Jane McDermott, a Democrat of York County, was elected and served during the 1953 and 1954 sessions. Mrs. Martha T. Fitzgerald, a Democrat of Richland County, served from 1951 to 1962. Mrs. Ruby C. Wesson, a Democrat from Spartanburg County, served in 1959 and 1960. Miss Virginia Gourdin, a Democrat from Charleston, served from 1959 to 1962. Miss Ruth Williams (now Mrs. Ruth Cupp), a Democrat from Charleston, served during the 1963 and 1964 sessions. Mrs. Carolyn E. Frederick, a Republican (the first female Republican member of the House) of Greenville, served from 1967 to 1974. Other women who served more recently in the House of Representatives are named in the Appendix.

After Reconstruction, many Republicans served in the General Assembly of South Carolina, but from 1901 to 1961 only Democrats were elected. It was in 1961, when Tom Elliott resigned his seat in the Assembly to accept appointment as Treasurer of Richland County, that a Republican, Charles E. Boineau Jr., came to serve again in the House. His tenure was for only one year, but in 1962 Republican Fred Worsham of Charleston was elected; and he was for several years the only Republican member.

It was in the November election of 1966 that the service of Republicans became meaningful in the General Assembly. Seventeen of them beat seventeen Democrats in the general election to the House. They were as follows: Wayne P. Farmer, Zack G. Fulmer, S. Eugene Hamlet, Delmus I. Weeks, George D. Grice, Julian Sidi Limehouse III, John K. Earle, Mrs. Carolyn E. Frederick, George N. Gault, Mac V. Patterson, Jack E. Shaw, W.H. Stroud, Robert L. Watkins, Jarvis R. Klapman, Lucius O. Porth, Ryan C. Shealy, Fred Connor Jr. and Jerry M. Hughes Jr. Grice resigned and Limehouse filled his unexpired term. Other Republicans serving since that time are indicated in the Appendix.

In that same year of 1966, six Republicans defeated six Democrats for seats in the state Senate. They were as follows: Marion H. Smoak, Nathaniel W. Cabell, G. Fred Worsham, John E. Bourne Jr., Eugene C. Griffith and Floyd D. Spence. Other Republican senators serving since that time are enumerated in the Appendix.

It should be noted that since 1960 Republicans have elected fewer members some years and more members other years. As of 1987 there are 33 Republicans serving in the House of Representatives and 12 Republicans serving in the Senate. All of this emphasizes once more the fact that South Carolina is no longer a one-party state.

It was in 1970 that black persons came to serve in the General Assembly for the first time since Reconstruction. In that year three, all Democrats, were elected: Herbert U. Fielding of Charleston and James L. Felder and I.S. Leevy Johnson of Richland County. In 1972 the number increased to four, Fielding by re-election along with Ernest A. Finney Jr. of Sumter and Benjamin J. Gordon Jr. of Williamsburg and Robert R. Woods of Charleston. Finney came to serve later as the first black Circuit Court Judge in South Carolina and still later as the first black Associate Justice of the Supreme Court of South Carolina.

In 1974 the number of black House members was increased to thirteen, all of whom, together with others serving more recently, are enumerated in the Appendix.

No woman, black or Republican has, during this century, served as Speaker of the House. Republican David Wilkins of Greenville was the first Republican to serve as chairman of an important House committee. Juanita White is the first woman to serve as chairman of an important House committee. She is a black Democrat from the Jasper-Beaufort district.

Nancy Stevenson, a Democrat from Charleston, is the only woman who has served as presiding officer of the Senate and as Lieutenant Governor. She was elected in 1978 and served for four years. Many thought she would seek the office of governor, but she decided not to run. Dick Riley was elected in 1982 for his second consecutive term. At a later date Mrs. Stevenson moved to Columbia and ran for Congress. She was defeated in the Democratic primary by a black candidate who in turn was defeated by the incumbent Republican Floyd Spence.

The coming of women, Republicans and blacks to the General Assembly has made legislative activities considerably different. The impact of these changes is almost as great as the coming of one-member districts.

Today the election laws in South Carolina, and in several other states, cannot be changed without the approval of the Justice Department in Washington. This results from legislation enacted by the Congress more than a decade ago. It is patent that the Justice

Department leans toward single-member districts for all governmental entities, and election areas are being turned more and more into single-member representation because the Justice Department can veto any proposed redistricting by local authorities.

It would appear that only the United States Senate was not concerned with reapportionment. New York State has two United States senators and Rhode Island has two United States senators. The day may come when the United States Supreme Court will delve into this matter. It has delved into almost everything else.

One of the chores undertaken by the Legislature by reason of the constitution or statutory law is the election of many officeholders, including eighty-eight members of the judiciary. Many other offices are also filled by the members at a joint meeting of the House and Senate. For example, they elect members of the boards of trustees of many state supported colleges and universities. Minority groups within the Assembly are inclined to block voting. This gives each group a tremendous weapon to influence the selection of important officeholders. A comparatively small block vote is oftentimes the balance of power. Of course, this is also true in all elections throughout the country. The majority group will normally split almost fifty-fifty. When this is true, a small block of voters can dominate an election. They become the balance of power.

The coming of single-member districts for members of the House of Representatives has changed the complexion of the election process considerably. Formerly candidates seeking seats in the House would do what we refer to as "run with the pack." Persons seeking a House seat (except in those counties where there was only one representative) would never run against any other candidate. For example, in Spartanburg we had eight House members. We would normally have fifteen to thirty candidates seeking those eight offices. A candidate would never run against anybody. This was true because if a candidate lambasted some other candidate, it would not assure votes for the lambaster and would only make friends of the lambasted mad. Now that there are single-member districts, one seeking a seat in the House must challenge the incumbent. If there are no incumbents seeking re-election, the candidate must contest "head on" with others seeking the same office. Fewer people are willing to make the challenge, and accordingly it is now possible for a substantial portion of incumbents to run unopposed.

In the Senate, prior to 1967, this was not true, because each senator was the only senator representing a particular county.

From 1967 to 1984, in some areas more than one senator represented the area, but during this short period, prior to single senatorial district seats, the seats were numbered so that incumbent senators did not run against each other.

The Constitution of 1868 (reported by historians to have been controlled by carpetbaggers, scalawags, freed slaves and Republicans) forbade slavery in any form and assured freed slaves the right to vote. The Democrats moved in under the leadership of General Wade Hampton in 1876, and the influence of Republicans and freed slaves waned in South Carolina until the turn of the century, when it pretty much vanished.

It is difficult for my young friends to believe that there was a time, prior to about 1948, when persons voting in the Democratic primary were required to swear that they would support the nominees of that party in the general election. Even if the Democratic nominee committed grand larceny between the primary and the general election, Democrats were sworn to support him. The requirement was patently unconstitutional but went unchallenged. In 1947 United States District Court Judge Waites Waring of Charleston opened the Democratic primary to black voters.

By the Nineteenth Amendment of the Constitution of the United States, ratified in 1920, the right of women to vote becamed fixed. Prior to that time a state might or might not permit female persons to cast a ballot. In South Carolina it was not until 1967 that women were permitted to serve on juries. During the first half of the twentieth century, comparatively few women participated in elections and practically none sought public office. In 1984 Walter Mondale, the Democratic nominee for President of the United States, chose Geraldine Ferarro, a Congresswoman from New York state as his running mate, rationalizing that this would fortify his chance of election. It became apparent that the people were not ready for a woman to be one heartbeat from the presidency. Actually she was not a good choice for the office, and beyond debate Ronald Reagan, the Republican, was a shoo-in and Mondale, even with a strong female candidate, would have lost.

An Associated Press story printed in November 1987 indicates that in the United States blacks hold less than one and one-half percent of all elective offices in the country, even though they comprise about eleven percent of the total population. In South Carolina ten and one-half percent of the elective offices are held by blacks.

Isaiah DeQuincy Newman was the first black man in modern times to be elected to the South Carolina Senate. He filled an unexpired term (in 1983) brought about by the resignation of Alexander Sanders, who was elected Chief Judge of the newly created South Carolina Court of Appeals. Other blacks who have served in the Senate more recently are Herbert U. Fielding, John W. Matthews, Theo Mitchell, Frank Gilbert and Kay Patterson.

In 1989 Sherry Lynn Shealy Martschink joined her father Ryan Shealy as a member of the Senate. This brought about the first father/daughter arrangement to serve in that body.

Some of the other blacks, women and Republicans serving in recent years but not mentioned in this chapter are enumerated in the Appendix at the end of this book.

Now that blacks and whites, men and women, Democrats and Republicans, actively pursue office in single-member districts, a new day in South Caroina legislative politics has arrived.

26

JOHN BOLT CULBERTSON, BETTER KNOWN AS "COTTON CULBERTSON"

The story of the political activites of Attorney John Bolt Culbertson of Greenville during the half century from 1933 to 1983 would fill a book. It is not easy to discuss him and his influence in South Carolina in a chapter, but this book would not be complete without reference to his life and political career.

"Cotton" Culbertson was one of thirteen children born to humble but honest parents in Laurens County. He came to the University of South Carolina without resources and enjoyed telling about spending his first night in Columbia in a free bed provided by employees at the Columbia Fire Department. Moving on to the campus, he completed his undergraduate education and then his law school training with virtually no outside financial support. He took odd jobs of all sorts and during his last year in law school contributed substantially to his sister, who was a student at Columbia College.

It was in the fall of 1933, when I entered law school, that I first came to know him. He was about to graduate from law school and I was entering the freshman class. Cotton was well known to the entire student body, and if the campus had a political boss at the time, he was it. There was much activity on election day, and the endorsement of Culbertson often formed the balance of power and was sometimes the equivalent of election.

For years Culbertson had been known as "Cotton." He was about as blonde as one could be, and the nickname "Cotton" followed him throughout his career and until his death in 1983. Somehow I was attracted to him, and we spent considerable time together talking about both campus politics and state politics. He was already involved in state politics and was closely affiliated with Congressman John J. McSwain as his assistant secretary. McSwain represented the Fourth Congressional District, which was composed, at that time, of Greenville, Spartanburg, Union and Laurens counties. Culbertson's close relationship with McSwain continued through the congressman's retirement in 1936 and until his death soon thereafter.

As a freshman in law school, I always appreciated the fact that Cotton (a senior) had time to pause and discuss a problem with me. At that time I recognized the basic characteristics that followed him throughout his life, including absolute independence, courage, fairness and honesty. Many questioned his philosophy, but none questioned his integrity. He was one of the few people who had the courage to tell a friend the truth when the truth was not what his friend wanted to hear. By nature I found him to be fair and magnanimous in 1933. I visited him at age 74, a month before his death, and he continued to exhibit these same basic qualities.

After graduating from law school, Culbertson spent two years with the Federal Bureau of Investigation before opening his law office in Greenville, where he continued an active practice until his death in 1983.

Cotton Culbertson had an ambition to serve in public office, but it was not easy for him to get elected. The only public office he held was that of House member from Greenville County in 1949 and 1950. At the same time he was always helpful to friends, including me, who were seeking election. His endorsement was always good for a substantial block of votes because he consistently had a following, particularly among the underprivileged.

If there ever was a true Democrat in South Carolina, I think it was Culbertson. He referred to himself as a "double dipped Democrat." At the same time he was on occasion a loyal supporter of Republican U.S. Senator Strom Thurmond. His admiration for Strom was inspired by Strom's sense of right and wrong and honesty. The two had this basic characteristic in common.

Cotton Culbertson might have been elected several times except for his outspoken support of black people. He was the first politician in South Carolina to speak out loud and long in favor of permitting black people to vote. He advocated much earlier than other politicians extending the right of suffrage to all people, black and white. When he first began espousing this view, it was a very unpopular view in South Carolina—but it was the view which all politicians came to have some twenty years later.

Culbertson ran several times for the House, once for Governor and at least once for the United States Senate. On one occasion he ran for Congress in the Second Congressional District, where he did not reside. His right to run in a district where he was not a resident was at first contested, but later it came to be conceded that one did not have to live in a congressional district in order to represent the people in that area.

Cotton Culbertson never represented corporations or people of great wealth. His clientele was among the downtrodden. There was a time when he had perhaps as many worker's compensation cases as any single law firm in South Carolina. He oftentimes represented people who were unable to pay, but he never attempted to force collection. At the same time, the volume of his business brought him substantial income, which enabled him to accumulate a substantial estate.

At campaign meetings where he was scheduled to speak, people often came just to hear him and left when his speech was concluded.

There are many who have convictions but no courage. A few have convictions and courage, and such a person was Cotton Culbertson. Instead of waiting until change became popular, he had the courage to speak out when he knew that not only his enemies, but sometimes his friends as well, would criticize him. When he was nearing death, he was quoted as saying: "All the politicians are now repeating the things I was ridiculed for saying some thirty years ago."

Stories incident to Cotton Culbertson's political career will be recited and repeated for years to come. He was one of my most loyal supporters in all my political endeavors, and I was always grateful for his friendship.

He was also known for his devotion and loyalty to his family. He was married to Mary Symmes Thomason Culbertson and they had five children: Nancy L., John Dennis, Patrick O., Symmes W. and Manning Y. Culbertson. The latter two also pursued careers at the law.

I was complimented to be invited to speak at his funeral. Also on the program was his friend the Reverend Bryan Crenshaw, who eulogized Culbertson as follows:

> Those who knew him as friend knew that he was one for whom friendship was no pretense. His friendship spanned the spectrum of people—from the mightiest in power who enjoyed wealth, fame and prestige, to those without power who knew only poverty, anonymity and hopelessness. He had the quality of speaking the word that was needed—be it a word of affirmation, gratitude, gentle rebuke or appreciation. There are many of us present whose lives have been enriched by his gift of a quiet word of wisdom, or a needed word of affirmation or by some surprising word of wit and humor.

* * * *

He was accused of being a LIBERAL, and he was—especially in the deeper meaning of that word: to liberate, to set free. He was accused of being a RADICAL, and he was, in the same sense that a surgeon performs radical surgery in cutting deep to remove a life-threatening malignant mass. He often ran for public office, not for the primary purpose of winning, but seeking instead a public forum where he could give voice to the voiceless and demand that his opponents address the basic issues. Had he been willing to compromise his positions, he could possibly have held high office and certainly gained a greater measure of this world's goods, but the word "compromise" was neither part of his vocabulary or his life....

In conversation with several people recently, as we spoke of John, the word has come more than once: "Through the years, John Bolt mellowed." I feel sure that this statement was true and may God grant to all of us that type of "mellowness" that comes as experience enriches and time adds wisdom. In that sense I hope that every one of us will know a certain type of mellowing....

But I think that closer to the truth is not that John mellowed, but the rest of us *matured*. His vision outran our vision, and many of the things that he espoused have, thank God, come to fruition and general acceptance.

The *Greenville News*, reporting his death, said:

The "lonely liberal" of South Carolina politics is dead at 74.

John Bolt Culbertson was called everything from "flamboyant veteran of the political wars" to a "circus" in the 46 years he practiced law and politics in Greenville County.... Known for his streaming white hair, his booming voice and his courtroom theatrics, Culbertson was a champion of the underdog, a civil rights advocate and a man who stood willingly against the mainstream of public opinion if he believed the cause was right.

Friends and foes alike remember him as a man of integrity, courage and strength.

My friend will be long remembered by those who have followed his political career. He was beloved by many and despised by a few, but he was respected by all.

27

MAGISTRATES AND POLITICS SINCE 1936

During the years of my political observations, magistrates have played an important part in elections. In South Carolina there are more than 300 judges who hold the offices. The exact number varies from year to year, depending on resignations, vacancies, etc.

In the past every community wanted its own judge, referred to in some states as "justices of the peace" but called "magistrates" in South Carolina. It seemed to be the thinking of the people that such a judge in the community was a keeper of the peace. Many times neighbors with problems would go to the magistrate and bare their souls. He (in theory at least) would pour oil on troubled waters and settle the dispute. Magistrates gave advice freely.

Before automobiles came into common use, it was important that magistrates be conveniently available for the procurement of warrants and for the bringing of small claims. This made it unnecessary to travel many miles to the county seat for the purpose of seeking the services of a judge.

Today few people in the entire state are by car more than twenty or thirty minutes from their county seat. Accordingly, the need for magistrates in rural areas has been rapidly diminishing. People have known for the last fifty years that the state could get along with fewer magistrates and fare just as well, but each magistrate had a political base and it has not been easy to abolish the office of magistrate because of political fears.

The state's Constitution of 1895 provided that "[a] sufficient number of magistrates shall be appointed and commissioned by the Governor, by and with the advice of the Senate, for each County...." In actuality, this gave to the forty-six senators, the authority to designate these local judges. The appointment is initiated by the governor, but it has been well understood over the years that he should not appoint anyone until clearing the matter first with the local senator. Senators, and House members too, have been reluctant to abolish any office of magistrate, not because of need but because of political expediency.

With the writing of new Article V, Constitutional Amendment ratified in 1973, the magistrate system was for most intents and

106

purposes continued. This Constitutional Amendment provided that "[t]he Governor, by and with the advice and consent of the Senate, shall appoint a number of magistrates for each county as provided by law." It further provided that the jurisdiction, both civil and criminal, would be, by statute, determined by the General Assembly. Magistrates now have jurisdiction to try a case involving not more than $2,500 on the civil side and not more than a $200 fine or prison for thirty days on the criminal side. The Constitution of 1895 limited the jurisdiction of magistrates to $100 civilly and a fine of $100 or thirty days imprisonment criminally.

Many senators, especially lawyer senators, have been over the years anxious to retain the authority to designate local judge magistrates. In turn the lawyer senators have not usually hesitated to practice law before the appointees they brought about. In such cases it can be logically argued that the judge should recuse himself, but I know of no South Carolina case where this issue has been raised or determined.

At the same time, the appointment of magistrates has brought to many senators many headaches. It has not been unusual for several citizens to seek a single appointment, and the senator oftentimes could satisfy one and irritate several. In order to avoid this political problem, many senators had local legislation enacted requiring a prospective magistrate to seek election at the polls. In turn the governor would appoint the winner and the senator would "advise and consent." The Constitution never contemplated such a procedure, but it was not until several years after new Article V was adopted that the matter came in contest. The Supreme Court of South Carolina held that the Constitution imposed upon the governor the duty of selecting the appointee and the duty of the Senate to approve or disapprove. It held that the Senate and the governor could not avoid constitutional duties by wishing the chore off on the voters. Since that time, magistrates have not appeared on the ballots, and the governor and the Senate proceed without the advice of the people.

In years gone by it has not been unusual for magistrates with more political than judicial qualifications to be appointed. When magistrates came into the Uniform Court System, the Chief Justice learned that some magistrates kept a trust bank account as was proper; others deposited fines and fees in their personal accounts and periodically sent their own personal checks to the county treasurer; others kept cash in their desk drawers or their billfolds until a trip was made to the county treasurer's office. The Chief

Justice has inaugurated a bookkeeping system, and now all magistrates have trust bank accounts which may be audited from time to time.

The work of the magistrates, like the work of all courts, has become increasingly more difficult, demanding and technical. The success or failure of a prosecution of a capital offense, or other serious crimes, often hinges on whether the magistrate followed constitutional law in the issuance of a search warrant. There is considerable thinking to the effect that magistrates should be members of the Bar or at least should have undergone substantial training in preparation for their work. Both the United States Supreme Court and the Supreme Court of South Carolina have declined to hold that magistrates are required to be lawyers. It can be logically argued that even as one accused of crime should be represented by counsel, one accused of crime should be tried before a judge also learned in the law.

In Spartanburg, for many years, the senators responsible for the appointment of the magistrates at the courthouse have approved only members of the Bar, and this has been a great blessing to the county and to the practicing Bar. I have been informed that last year the three magistrates at the Spartanburg courthouse collected almost two million dollars in fees and fines.

Contrast this to the work of one magistrate in the Low Country who was cited to appear before the Supreme Court of South Carolina to answer for some irregular conduct. As the hearing progressed, then Associate Justice J.B. Ness asked the judge, who was pleading his own case, how many cases he handled during the previous year. The judge gazed up toward the ceiling as though to seek inspiration from above, and replied, "About six."

"Do you mean to tell me that during the entire year you handled only six cases?" Justice Ness inquired.

Looking again toward the ceiling for supplemental inspiration, the judge replied, "Could have been about eight."

This is an example of a political ward healer who obviously stood in great favor with the senator or senators from that county.

The work of the magistrates in South Carolina continues to grow. In 1987 the magistrates disposed of 701,000 cases, broken down as follows: traffic, 449,000 or 64%; non-traffic, 123,000 or 17%; civil, 128,000 or 18%. It should be observed that these courts touch the lives of almost 25 percent of the entire population of the state every year.

While the magistrates were disposing of some 700,000 cases, there were filed in the Family Courts 71,000 cases, in the Court of General Sessions 50,000 cases, and in the Court of Common Pleas 54,000 cases. All courts disposed of approximately as many cases as were filed during that year.

It was in the late 1970s that the Supreme Court of South Carolina held that Magistrates' Courts came within the orbit of the Unified Judicial System and were answerable to the Chief Justice administratively and otherwise. The Court in effect ruled that the Magistrates' Courts, as then operated, were not in keeping with the new Constitution. The Legislature was, however, given a reasonable time in which to bring about uniformity. As of 1988 the problem had not been solved. In that year the General Assembly undertook to enact legislation which would make the system uniform. The system of appointment will, of course, be continued, but hopefully the number of magistrates will be reduced, the requisite training will be enhanced, the salaries will be made uniform and the administration of justice in the Magistrates' Courts improved.

Magistrates will continue to play an important part in the elections hereafter, but the day of a magistrate being the political boss in his bailiwick is mostly a thing of the past.

The Judicial Code of Ethics promulgated by the Supreme Court in 1976 includes canons for all judges, including the magistrates, and forbids them to participate in political elections. This limitation on the magistrate's activities lessens his political base and should enhance the possibility of abolishing many unneeded offices.

28

INFLATION AND MONEY

Throughout this book I have mentioned the tremendous changes which have taken place in the political, social, economic and educational worlds since I began running for public office in 1936. There is no change more dramatic than the value of the dollar.

I once commented to a friend that the dollar doesn't do for me what it used to do. In reply he said, "And Judge, you don't do what you used to do to earn a dollar."

My friend was correct. Money is merely a medium of exchange. It isn't easy for someone born in 1913, as I was, to become accustomed to new money, new dollars and new values.

During my first year in the Legislature, in 1937, the total of the State Appropriation Bill was $10,326,323.26. It is difficult for my young friends to envision that dollars in those days would procure so much. A legislator's salary was $400 per year with no expense allowance. The governor drew $7,500 per year, and members of the Supreme Court drew $5,000. Most constitutional officers had a salary of $3,600 per year, but the attorney general drew $5,000.

That year the Legislature appropriated $93,000 to the penitentiary, $54,000 to the Industrial Commission, $265,000 to the University of South Carolina, $115,000 to Clemson and $140,000 to the Medical College.

My young lawyer friends were never acquainted with what I refer to as "old money." It is difficult for them to appreciate old money, and it is difficult for me to understand new money. A person my age has a tendency to keep thinking about the time when hot dogs were a nickel, hamburgers were a dime and lunch could be bought for a quarter. An Arrow shirt was priced at $2, and a suit of clothes could be bought for $25. Before 1938 employees worked pretty much at the mercy of their employers. Not long before that a farmer could hire a hoe hand for a dollar a day plus dinner.

President Franklin D. Roosevelt undertook to improve working conditions throughout the country by firmly establishing the right of labor to organize. Along with this he advocated, and it was enacted into law, a statute entitled "The Federal Fair Labor Standards Act" which provided that employers engaged in commerce or in the production of goods for commerce should pay wages of at least 25 cents per hour beginning in October 1938. There was much weeping, wailing and gnashing of teeth in industrial employer circles. Employers abhorred the idea of the government moving in to control contracts between employers and employees. It was argued vigorously that such a requirement would bankrupt the industrial plants. It did not.

Nowhere is the change in money values more clearly demonstrated than by the increases in minimum wages which have been brought about by Congress during the last half century. The act has been amended from time to time to increase the scale and to exclude, or more often to include, additional employers and employees. The minimum wage figures that follow were supplied me by my friend Edgar McGowan of the South Carolina Department of Labor:

Year	Per Hour
1938	$ .25
1939	.30
1945	.40
1949	.75
1956	1.00
1963	1.25
1967	1.40
1968	1.60
1976	2.30
1978	2.65
1979	2.90
1980	3.10
1981	3.35

A few mathematical calculations will show that a worker receiving today's minimum wage of $3.35 for 40 hours work for 52 weeks a year receives more dollars than did the governor when I went to the Legislature. Such minimum wage earners are handling about ten times as many dollar bills as in 1938, but their income purchases only a little more. As wages have risen, the cost of living has risen also.

We complain perpetually of inflation and talk about the days when just about everything could have been bought with fewer dollar bills, but there is comfort in the fact that the great mass of people in the United States today are enjoying more of the abundant life than was the case prior to inflation. Wages received and prices paid for commodities form a spiral. Wages are increased to make it possible for people to buy more goods. Then the price of those goods is raised, requiring more wages to buy them. Where the spiral will end, nobody knows.

At the time of this writing, Congress was debating the advisability of increasing the minimum wage to $4.35 an hour or some kindred figure. Wages paid in the United States are substantially higher than compensation received in Japan and other foreign countries which export many products, including automobiles, to the United States. Our workers enjoy a higher standard of living, but it becomes more difficult for our manufacturers to compete.

In the old days we used to refer to the one-cent piece as "a penny," "a brownie" or "a copper." It is still a penny, but only a few oldtimers continue to call it a brownie or a copper. Actually, inflation has almost made the one-cent piece a nuisance. The day may come when the penny will be phased out and replaced by a nickel. (And the nickel has already lost its usefulness in favor of the dime and the quarter.)

As I came to politics in 1936, people were fussing about the fact that the Post Office Department in Washington had increased the cost of mailing a first class letter from two cents to three cents. At that time the penny was still useful, because a postal card could be procured for a brownie. For one cent, a person could mail a message all the way from South Carolina to California.

Of the things which have changed dramatically between 1936 and 1988, money is among them.

29

THE MEDIA CHANGED POLITICS

The Constitution of the United States and the Constitution of South Carolina provide for a separation of powers. We refer to the departments of government as the Executive, the Legislative and the Judicial. Some people add a fourth department of government, which they refer to as "the Press" or, more comprehensively, "the Media." We certainly could not function without all three departments of government, and many people are of the opinion that our government could not function without the media. I am inclined to agree. The media is important to democratic government and to the election of people to run that government, because the average citizen must depend almost entirely on newspapers, radio and television for information essential to choosing the right candidates at the ballot box.

Campaigning for public office was changed greatly when radio came into being. And then when television came into being, campaigning was changed even more. There was a day, some fifty or sixty years ago, when the way to campaign for statewide public office in South Carolina was to visit all the county seats. Traditionally, each county had a campaign meeting at the courthouse and several hundred—or sometimes thousands—of people would come to hear the candidates make long, loud speeches extolling their own virtues. The oldtimers will remember that big outdoor campaign meetings were traditionally held in the summer at Silverstreet in Newberry County and at Filbert in York County. And then it was traditional to have a big opening meeting at Gallivant's Ferry in Horry County.

At the county level, the Democratic primary was in years past equivalent to election. The county Democratic party organization traditionally arranged a candidate's itinerary for campaign speeches in all the small towns throughout the county. Over and above those scheduled meetings, in Spartanburg County, we usually had quite a few campaign speakings, which we referred to as "wildcat meetings." These were hatched up by the citizens of various communities or crossroads all over the county. One year there were forty-one wildcat meetings in Spartanburg County, and

113

it was not unusual to have twenty-five or thirty. Candidates knew that few local people would attend, but they were afraid not to appear because the few local citizens who did show up would hold it against them. It was traditional to have a big meeting at the Spartanburg County Courthouse on Saturday before the first primary on Tuesday. Over the years citizens, and candidates also, became less enchanted with this type of county campaigning. By 1986 the local campaign meetings had become pretty much a thing of the past.

It does not seem many years ago that candidates for President of the United States would get on a train and conduct what was referred to as a "whistle-stop campaign." It would be arranged for a passenger train with many cars for the accommodation of the press to go across the entire country. The train would stop in town after town long enough for the candidate to make a speech off of the rear end car of the train. In South Carolina some of us remember that in 1938 President Franklin D. Roosevelt did a "whistle-stop" tour. He was not running for re-election that year but was campaigning for and against various candidates for the Senate and the House of Representatives. Roosevelt stopped in Greenville long enough to make a talk to a huge crowd from the observation car of the train, and it was there that he attempted to purge Senator "Cotton Ed" Smith. South Carolinians would have no part of it, however, and elected "Cotton Ed" Smith over Governor Olin D. Johnston. It was not until 1944, six years later, that Johnston defeated Smith. Smith died a few months later.

In the 1920s it was in the scheme of things that candidates were orators. There were few microphones then, radio was little used and TV was years away. Roosevelt taught public speakers the fireside chat approach to convincing people. He used a conversational tone and had the ability to make people think that he was talking to each of them alone. With the advent of radio and television, the political orator came to be a thing of the past.

When one campaigns personally (as we used to do), it isn't possible to reach a great many people. Most people just aren't sufficiently interested to take the time and effort to attend a campaign meeting. Now people want the campaign message brought to them while they enjoy the conveniences of home. A candidate can get on the radio or on television and speak to tens of thousands of people in a few minutes, whereas in the old style of campaigning personally, it would be difficult, if not impossible, to reach several thousand throughout the entire campaign season.

It was about 1958 that one of my friends said to me, "If people aren't careful and if they don't stop and think, television will cause them to start electing a batch of actors instead of the best man."

We know that public speaking is acting. In a public speaking course, the teacher will tell the student to stomp, to pause, to whisper, to point with pride, to raise or lower the voice—all that is acting. Former President Ronald Reagan is such a good public speaker because he has been an actor for decades; when Reagan gets on television he is a real actor-charmer, and that is why he came to be known as the "great communicator."

Television has brought about the day when advertising agencies undertake to sell a candidate to the people just as they might go about selling corn flakes. It is unfortunate but true that television tends to sell a personality instead of selling the best man. When one campaigns by way of the newspaper or other written word, a candidate comes to be liked or disliked because of the ideas he or she conveys. On the other hand, when a candidate talks to the public by way of television, he or she is in effect selling a personality. The ideas are minimized and the personality is maximized. This may be good or bad. I am not at all sure but what television has, in effect most helped those who can act a part.

When Richard Nixon was running for President in 1960, he did not have a good television personality. Many people are of the opinion that he lost the election to Jack Kennedy because he was unable to act the part in the famous campaign debates when Kennedy bested Nixon. The story is told that when Nixon began to run for President again in 1968, he undertook to take TV appearance training. While I never looked upon Nixon as a good TV personality, he was certainly greatly improved in 1968 compared with his TV appearance in 1960.

In 1968 Nixon beat Hubert Humphrey, the Democratic candidate. Humphrey has been quoted as saying later: "The biggest mistake in my political life was not to learn how to use television." Certainly Hubert Humphrey and Lyndon Johnson were never heavyweights as TV personalities. Johnson was somewhat bunglesome and Humphrey's fast talk irritated the public.

The mass media have also lessened the importance of the political party. When voters could not learn a great deal about the candidates, they would vote a party ticket. Now that every citizen has a radio—and most likely a television set—the tendency has been for each voter to say, in effect, "The heck with the party. I will make up my own mind based on such information as the media has seen fit to feed me."

It goes without saying that the way to reach voters now is by way of the mass media. The media does a good job of pulling a man right up on the television screen where people can look at him and appraise not only what he is saying but his manner and attitude. One of the things a candidate needs to do is to make the voters like him. This has always been true, of course, but it brings to mind what Jack Benny once said. Someone asked Benny what was the most important thing for a comedian to remember. The most important thing for a comedian to remember, he said, was to make the audience like him. "If the audience doesn't like you," he continued, "they aren't going to laugh at your jokes no matter how funny they are. On the other hand, if the audience likes you, they will laugh whether the joke is funny or not."

Mo Udall, in a book entitled *Too Funny to be President*, made a similar comment. Udall said that if the people like you they will vote for you, but if the people don't like you they won't vote for you no matter what your platform. TV does a good job of letting candidates get through to the average voters so those voters can determine whether they like a candidate or not. Popularity is part of every election—and I am not talking only of political elections, I am talking about elections for members of the board of deacons at the Baptist church or for president of the Lions or Rotary Club. People vote for candidates they like.

A young friend of mine who was running for office about twenty-five years ago asked me if he should buy some television time. My response was, "By all means get on TV if you can raise the money and if you can put on a show. But if you cannot put on a show, it will lose you votes instead of getting them, so make sure that everything is just right if you get around to appearing on television."

It is well known that many TV commercials are done again and again and again, throughout a half day or a full day, until they get just exactly the right poses and the right inflection. If you are going to tape a program for television, you can always do it again and again until it is right—but if your program is live, it is sort of like parachute jumping; you've got to do it right the first time.

Jack Kennedy started something about 1960 which I have always felt was bad for the country. He began press conferences where he would stand before the audience and virtually bare his soul and permit sharp-shooting reporters to ask him anything they wanted to. If I could, with a wave of the wand, abolish that practice, I would.

I have never heard a President say, "I simply don't know." Oftentimes that would be the correct answer. The President always feels a compulsion to respond to a question, whether it is relevant and whether it should be answered off the cuff or not. Many questions call for cogitation, and I would prefer that my President, whoever he might be, not stand before an audience and attempt to give answers to all kinds of fool questions coming from the press. These press conferences should be discontinued.

The press is an important part of political life in the United States. It is no credit to people in government that many of the scandals which have been detected in the last few years were brought to the attention of the public not by reason of any check and balance system within the government, but by some newspaper or television reporter who snooped around and discovered something unlawful. Certainly all of us in public life have attempted to conduct ourselves a little more properly by reason of the fact that the media does exist. The media itself is a check and balance—a protection to citizens who have no other way of getting information relative to wrong-doing in government. In another chapter I talk about the Pug Ravenel fiasco of 1974. I will not repeat what is said in that chapter, but Pug Ravenel was among those candidates who used television to the maximum and made it pay, at least temporarily, until the Supreme Court of South Carolina declared that he was not eligible to serve as governor of the state.

Most of us can remember at least one candidate who was virtually run out of the race by the media and some who probably were elected by the media. There are still a lot of people in the world who will say, "I know it's true because I saw it in the newspaper." To the credit of the media, television, radio and newspaper reporting usually is accurate. Accuracy is essential to credibility in the media.

An example of someone being run out of a race for all practical purposes is the candidacy of Gary Hart of Colorado for president. In the summer of 1988 *The Miami Herald* broke a story about Hart (a married man) having a girlfriend on the side. The story went all over the United States by way of newspapers, radio and television and before long Hart withdrew from the race. It is true that later on he became a candidate again but for all practical purposes his candidacy was dead.

Another example is that of Joe Biden, a senator from Delaware who was getting along very well with his Democratic candidacy for president of the United States in 1988. It developed that in his speeches Biden was using quotations from other speakers, some good and some bad, without giving credit to the real authors of the statements. The people of the United States simply did not like that. Upon being exposed, Biden bowed out of the race.

I don't think quoting someone, even without giving them credit, is too great a sin. After all, none of us knew anything when we were born, and anything we know and anything that we say we learned from others. To plagiarize another speaker or another writer is not so bad when you realize that all high public officials have speech writers; when they make speeches they are merely saying something that a speech writer hatched up for the orator of the day.

Over the years the media have been very charitable to me, and I have no quarrel with them. A friend of mine taught me many years ago never to pick a quarrel with people who buy ink by the barrel. I have found that to be good advice. My mind goes back to a class in English when I was a freshman at Wofford College. Professor John W. Harris was perhaps the best teacher I ever had in my life. One day he said, and I have remembered this over the years, that reporters can write up a story in three ways and tell the truth three times and leave a different impression each time. He explained that the press could say: "Wofford holds Furman to a scoreless tie," or "Furman holds Wofford to a scoreless tie," or "Wofford and Furman play to a scoreless tie." In each instance the writer told the truth, but in each instance a different inference was created. And so I have always thought it was beneficial to someone in public office to have reporters thinking nice things when they start to putting a story about that person into production.

More and more people in public office are coming to live in a fishbowl. There was a time when the media did not publicize anything about a public official unless it affected his official duties. That day is gone. Now the media publishes everything about people in public office, whether it affects their official duties or not. It has a tendency to chase a lot of good people out of government and to cause a lot of good people who would like to be a part of government to refrain from public activities. There is some comfort in the fact that people in public office conduct themselves more properly because they realize that their product may be publicized. And so maybe there is good and bad in what the media now does to expose the activity of individuals in government. I agree with my friend who said that democratic government as we know it today could not exist without an active press.

A 1936-type campaign will not produce the desired result today.

The author (center) at a banquet honoring him when he assumed the office of Circuit Court Judge in 1949. With Associate Justice Dewey Oxner (left) and J. D. Kerr (right).

Five Speakers of the House of Representatives (left to right): Bruce Littlejohn, 1947-1949; Rex Carter, 1973-1980; Robert Sheheen, 1986-present; Ramon Schwartz, 1980-1986; Thomas H. Pope Jr., 1949-1950.

30

EARLY CAMPAIGNING

Campaigning before radio and television became popular was truly an interesting experience. In the 1930s and 1940s, people were not so busy as today, and this was especially true during the great Depression, when so many people were unemployed and had time to attend campaign meetings.

In order to reach the voters, we travelled the county, stopped at all the grocery stores and oftentimes stood at the textile mill gates to shake hands with the employees as they either went to work or left the job. It was not unusual for several candidates to stand at the same mill gate simultaneously, introducing themselves and giving cards to potential voters. Sometimes the cards were kept, but oftentimes they were taken and thrown on the ground within a few yards of the place where they were accepted.

Those of us who were serious about getting elected would often spend an entire day working crowds wherever we could find them assembled, or shaking hands with individuals when groups were not available. We especially liked to attend events like funerals, fish fries, barbecues and baseball games. At these we were assured of getting acquainted with a maximum number of people with a minimum of time and effort.

Meeting people under those circumstances was educational. It gave us an opportunity to learn what the voters were interested in and what they were thinking about. Normally, they appreciated our devoting time and attention to them.

Those of us who were young lawyers often developed friendships while campaigning and in turn came to represent those friends in legal matters. One of my older lawyer friends once said, "The best thing a young lawyer can do is run for the Legislature and get beat." He rationalized that this gave a young attorney an opportunity to "advertise" and get acquainted with a lot of people, to make an impression on them and, by so doing, to develop contacts and clients. Most of us who campaigned can attribute at least a few of our clients to the fact that we became acquainted with them at a campaign meeting.

Normally there were so many candidates running that the speaking time for each had to be limited; candidates for the House of Representatives were only allotted three minutes. Three minutes is not long enough to discuss vital issues, but it is long enough to make an impression, good or bad, on voters.

At least a few people at each of the speakings had attended other campaign meetings, and there were some referred to as "campaign followers" who went to practically all the meetings. Normally these people knew for whom they wished to vote, but it was always well to cater to them because they liked to talk politics.

During the campaigns of the 1930s, some of these "followers" solicited what they referred to as "gas money." It was their contention that they wanted to work for a candidate on election day and didn't want any pay except some money for the gas they used in hauling friends and neighbors to the polls. Most often, this was merely a slick way of picking up a few dollars. In the 1940s, when T. Wright Cox of Woodruff was campaigning at Chesnee, a fellow named Pace bounced him for five dollars to buy gasoline. Cox told him, "I know you don't even have a car, but you have harassed me from meeting to meeting for gasoline money, so I'll make you a deal. I'll give you three dollars if you'll quit bothering me during the rest of the race." Pace accepted the proposition.

There were some thirty or forty textile plants in Spartanburg County when I first began campaigning. At that time there was a feeling of political distrust between the cotton mill management and the employees. Of course, those of us who sought office wanted the support of both, but we meticulously stayed away from the mill office because employees would often vote against those supported by management. I made it a point to never be seen at any of the mill offices, preferring to contact management at home or by telephone.

At almost every precinct there were persons whom we referred to as "ward healers." We came to know that a few people, particularly at the textile plants, were influential in helping to carry a particular voting box. Oftentimes these would be employees who we referred to as "second hands." A "second hand" is about half way between the average employee and management. He was an assistant to an overseer. In addition, we attempted to cultivate the operators of country stores. The operator of such an establishment would always be coming in contact with a lot of people and, if so minded, could be very helpful at the local level.

It was not unusual for some organization at a particular precinct to invite all of the candidates to a "wild cat" speaking. The purpose was not so much to learn for whom to vote but to sell ice cream or something else for the purpose of raising money for groups such as the Women's Missionary Society. Only a few people would usually show up, but we were afraid not to go and, accordingly, over and above the meetings scheduled by the Democratic party, many other campaign meetings were held.

In the race for the House of Representatives, candidates did not attack one another. Each voter would vote for eight candidates, and criticizing another candidate in this area would not enhance one's likelihood of election. On the other hand, in races such as sheriff, clerk of court, auditor and treasurer, there was some "mud slinging." Only one person could be elected to each of these offices, and one candidate did not hesitate to talk about his opponent, because weakening the support would more often strengthen the one who was critical. The term "mud slinging" has pretty well trickled out of common usage. It was not until well into the 1970s and 1980s that people began to talk about "negative campaigning." These two terms may be used interchangeably, and there is no accounting for the fact that the new term "negative campaigning" has pretty well completely replaced "mud slinging" of yesteryear.

Occasionally a person would run for the Legislature for want of something better to do. Such a person was Raymond Brown from Pacolet. Brown had little formal education, but he had much native ability and was quite an entertainer. He entered the race in 1932 or 1934 when I first began attending Democratic primary campaign meetings. One could enter the primary for twenty-five dollars, and on at least one occasion, and I think two, Brown's friends at Pacolet raised the money at the barber shop to get him into the race.

The campaign had not been long started when the newspapers began quoting Brown. People came to the campaign meetings to enjoy the entertainment he provided. He had a habit of ridiculing everybody who had anything to do with the government, together with a knack for extolling his own virtues.

On one occasion Brown meant to refer to "ignoramus people" but got his words confused and said from the stump, "The trouble down in Columbia is that they have too many amoramouses."

On another occasion he yelled, "What we need down in Columbia is more people with less education and more horse sense."

"What," interrupted a member of the audience, "is horse sense?"

Quick as a flash, Brown retorted, "It's the kind a jackass like you ain't got."

The audience applauded at length. It was not unusual for half the audience to go home after Brown had spoken, without waiting to hear the other speakers.

At this time Hoover had just gone out of office a very unpopular president, and Roosevelt was attempting to improve the economy throughout the country. Brown told one audience, "Hoover tried to make me sleep in a hollow log, but I foxed him. I picked muscadines, made wine and sold it, and no rat has ever flopped its tail in the bottom of my flour barrel yet." This earned him the nickname "Rat Tail Brown."

Oldtimers will remember that there were many large families during that era. People bought flour in fifty and one hundred pound sacks and dumped it into barrels from which the flour was taken from day to day as biscuits were cooked. Brown's point was that he was ahead of the game, since there was always flour in his barrel while others had empty barrels where mice could flop their tails on the bottom.

The day is long gone when anyone can get in a political race for the entertainment of it. The cost of campaigning has become prohibitive. In addition, campaign meetings of the type I have described are a thing of the past. Few public speakings are held, and candidates now reach the public mainly through television, radio and newspapers.

Fifty years ago, election night was quite different from election nights today. In the 1930s, we would normally not know who was elected in local campaigns until late at night or early the next day. In Spartanburg County paper ballots were used in approximately 100 precincts. Each ballot had to be unfolded and the names (often as many as thirty or forty) called off so that those who tallied the vote could record and total the results. Where several hundred ballots were cast in a precinct, this was a slow, laborious process. The small precincts (up to 100 or 150 votes) could be counted in a relatively short period of time, but in some of the larger boxes, several hours would be required. There were no television stations, and radio stations had not at that time developed much sophistication for tabulating votes and announcing the results over the air.

In Spartanburg, *The Herald* newspaper did a very good job of receiving the reports from the precinct managers by way of the telephone. The newspaper then undertook, through a projector, to send the results across Morgan Square onto a king-sized bed sheet hung on the outside wall of the Cleveland Hotel. Several hundred people would traditionally gather on the street to await the results and talk politics.

Today many of the larger counties, including Spartanburg, have voting machines. Tabulating the vote is somewhat like pushing the total button on an adding machine. Local results are normally declared in an hour or two after the polls close and statewide results (or at least trends) long before midnight. With the use of computers, the television networks now undertake to predict and declare the results for the whole United States, often before precincts in the Western states close and before the voting is completed.

Somewhere along the line in the 1940s the radio people, and later television people, established election central. They do a great job of announcing the election results promptly.

Part II
THE POLITICAL CAMPAIGNS

31

CAMPAIGN OF 1936

In 1934, after my freshman year in law school, I toyed with the idea of running for the House of Representatives from Spartanburg County. I had barely turned twenty-one years of age and in the last analysis decided that I ought not to undertake it. There were a few students at the law school who were serving as members of the House, and on campus they were looked upon as modern-day heroes. Elected that summer were students Wylie Brown of Bishopville, Lonnie Causey of Conway, Drufus Griffin of Pickens, Ira Koger of Charleston, James P. Mozingo of Darlington, Rufus Newton of Anderson and Frost Walker Jr. of Union. That was the year Olin D. Johnston ran for governor the second time and was elected. I was a supporter of Olin, my support growing largely out of the fact that my brother, Boyd Littlejohn, had attended Wofford College with Olin. They also had worked together reading proof at the *Spartanburg Herald* at night in order to pay their tuition. I had much admiration for my brother, and he sold me on the idea that Olin would make a good chief executive for the state.

Having postponed my candidacy in 1934, I was, after my graduation from law school and admission to the Bar in June of 1936, definitely in the running. There is an old saying about anyone who is very anxious to get elected and willing to work hard at it: "He's Hell bent for election." I suppose that expression would have been applicable to me. I was graduated from the law school on June 3. I had been admitted to the Bar on the previous day, as permitted under the diploma privilege rule. No bar examination was required. I opened my office seven days later, on June 10, in Spartanburg and made my announcement to run on July 19, 1936, which was three days before my twenty-third birthday.

Elections then were greatly different from today. There were no single-member districts, and eight members were to be elected countywide. The Democratic primary held in August was equivalent to election, since there simply were no Republicans or other adversaries for the November general election.

I had spent all of my life, except for my college and university years, at Pacolet, where I still lived with my parents. Although I

127

had attended Wofford College for three years before entering law school in Columbia, I knew very few people in Spartanburg County. I therefore had the chore of making myself known to the voters.

My father was a rural letter carrier who farmed on the side and had never concerned himself with political matters. He loaned me $400 to open my office and pay my entrance fee for the campaign. Of this $400, I spent $225 buying a second-hand 1932 model Ford.

The money soon ran out, and I went to the store of my cousin Broadus Littlejohn, on Trade Street, to ask him to lend me $100 — which he did for a period of thirty days. At the end of thirty days, I had to go back and tell him that I did not have the $100. He suggested that I keep it for thirty more days, which I did, but at the end of the next thirty days, I still did not have $100 and was embarrassed to ask Broadus for an extension. Instead, I went to Mr. Frank Vincent at the C & S Bank. By then I had been elected, and he granted me a $150 loan. I immediately reestablished my credit with Broadus by paying my debt. He never knew that I had to "borrow from Peter to pay Paul."

While I had a minimum amount of money to spend on the campaign, I had the advantage of youth and vigor. I drove my second-hand Ford 3,500 miles and personally met a maximum number of people in 100 precincts. In 1936 that was the way to campaign. It was in the scheme of things that candidates went from community to community to stump speakings. A few of the meetings were officially arranged by the Democratic party, but different groups, such as clubs and churches, scheduled unofficial meetings, which we felt compelled to attend. Usually very few people attended, but we were afraid not to appear.

During one campaign (it was either 1936 or 1938), there were a total of forty-one campaign meetings, seven of which were held on Saturday preceding the voting on the third Tuesday in August. On that Saturday, we were at Wood's Store at nine in the morning, Fairmont at ten, Victor at eleven, Appalachia at two, Beaumont at six, Drayton at seven and Spartan Mills at eight. Candidates would make their speeches at one location and move on to the next meeting. During that year we had a total of thirty-three candidates seeking the eight seats in the House. Twenty-six other candidates sought other local offices.

When I began the campaign in 1936, I did not know Governor Johnston except for having been introduced to him in a crowd. I had, at age twenty-one, cast my first vote in any election for him in 1934. It surprised me to learn early in the campaign that ardent

Johnston supporters were not going to be elected to the House of Representatives from Spartanburg County. There was much resentment there, as elsewhere, over the fact that Johnston had called out the national guard and taken over a department of government without any real justification as was held by the Supreme Court. Spartanburg's business people, textile executives and substantial farm operators had organized a campaign to make sure that dyed-in-the-wool Johnstonites did not go to the Legislature.

Several of Olin's friends advertised from the stump: "I am one-hundred percent for Governor Johnston." None of them was elected. On the other hand, Attorney H.K. Osborne, who had argued the case for Ben Sawyer in the Supreme Court, won by a substantial vote as a well advertised opponent of Governor Johnston. Charles M. Pace, whose uncle Ibra C. Blackwood defeated Johnston for governor in 1930, was also elected by a substantial margin. It was beyond question—Johnston's home county was not to send candidates committed to his support to the Legislature. Only anti-Johnston people and middle-of-the-roaders, like me, were elected in Spartanburg that year. Olin was definitely the issue.

If a candidate received a majority of the votes in the first-race voting, he was declared nominated. In the second race, there would be twice as many candidates for the House as there were vacancies remaining. Charles C. Moore and T. Wright Cox made it on the first ballot; I was tenth among the twelve permitted to seek the remaining six seats. After several political difficulties and much vigorous campaigning for an additional two weeks, I was nominated by the "skin of my teeth," along with Paul M. Allen, Charles M. Pace, Jerome McAbee, H.K. Osborne and T.J. Hendrix.

Campaigning for the Legislature in the old days was an education in itself. I will always be indebted to my distant cousin, Broadus Littlejohn, and to my friend of many years, L.A. Odom, for their substantial contributions to the chore of convincing others that I ought to be in the Legislature.

This was the same year Franklin D. Roosevelt was re-elected President of the United States by carrying all but two states. It was also the year that Senator James F. Byrnes was re-elected to the United States Senate from South Carolina by a landslide. The Great Depression was still with us, but the many actions of the federal government were helping to make it more possible for people to have food and other essentials.

My dream was coming true. I was on my way back to Columbia, where I had spent three delightful years at the University.

No sooner was the election over than the phone started jumping up and down. Claude Taylor had vacated the office of Speaker to run for Congress. A hot race was brewing between Speaker Pro Tempore Sol Blatt Sr. and Caston Wannamaker. Blatt was considered the anti-Governor Johnston candidate; Wannamaker was supported by Johnston. The race went "down to the wire" with Blatt winning 62 to 57. The House could not have been more divided if one had been a Democrat and the other a Republican.

The Constitution provided for a forty-day session of the Legislature for which members were paid ten dollars per day. Accordingly, the salary of a legislator was $400 per year.

Charles C. Moore, Jerome McAbee and I reserved a big room for three at the Jefferson Hotel during the 1937 session of the Assembly. We each paid $1.75 per day for these lodgings. For three dollars we could get three satisfactory meals at the cafeteria.

On January 14, 1937 those of us who had been elected to represent the various counties throughout the state appeared at high noon in the House chamber. The first order of business was to elect a Speaker of the House and a Speaker Pro Tempore.

The Spartanburg delegation was all new except for T.J. Hendrix, who had served in previous years. The rest of us were unacquainted with the work we had been elected to perform in the Legislature. In the previous session, 1935, there had been much bitterness because of the feud between Governor Olin D. Johnston and the South Carolina Highway Department. Many members who were perceived to be on the wrong side of the issue refrained from seeking re-election or were defeated, and accordingly there was a substantial turnover in the membership of the House and some in the Senate.

In preparation for my service in the House, I had taken the advice of Jennings Thompson, a well known Spartanburg lawyer, who had advised me during the campaign. He told me that if I would master the rules of the House prior to its meeting, I would be head and shoulders above those members who had not become acquainted with them. Between the election in November and the meeting in January, I made an intense study of the rules governing the activities of the House as well as the rules which governed both Houses. I have on many occasions since admonished new members of the Assembly to master the rules of procedure, but few get around to it.

In the House I found many friends from my Wofford College and University of South Carolina days. Some of my colleagues at the law school had been elected, and I also came to develop new friendships rapidly. In the House of Representatives, as well as in the Senate, I found a cross-section of South Carolina people. They came from all walks of life and were engaged in just about all occupations and professions. They were old and young, rich and poor, fat and lean, learned and wanting. Over the years I have concluded that this mixture is good for the state. It brings to the law-making body the thinking of people who represent varied interests and ways of life.

It did not take me long to learn that a great portion of the work of the House of Representatives takes place in committees. It simply is not feasible to debate with any degree of satisfaction the great mass of legislation which must be acted upon.

I came to realize early in the game that the chairmen of the important committees and the Speaker of the House were dominant influences. Deep down, I dreamed of the day when I might be Speaker of the House, but at that time I did not think it would ever come to pass. It is difficult to unseat an incumbent in Congress, and it is virtually impossible to unseat a sitting Speaker of the South Carolina House. Speaker Blatt was only forty years old and loved legislative service. I could not envision that he might after ten years step aside and that I might be fortunate enough to succeed him.

There are many unpleasant aspects of service in the General Assembly, and most of us would from time to time swear we would never run again. At the same time, there are many pleasant experiences associated with legislative work. There is also something fascinating about it which induces one to change his mind just before the next election and decide that he will serve "just one more time."

All members of the Spartanburg County Delegation had voted for Speaker Blatt in a hotly contested race. This put us in an enviable position so far as committee appointments were concerned. Representatives T.J. Hendrix, T. Wright Cox and I were appointed to the powerful Ways and Means Committee. Henry K. Osborne, Charles C. Moore and Charles M. Pace were assigned to the Judiciary Committee, which is also prestigious. All the members of our Spartanburg delegation were given other assignments to several committees, most of which were relatively unimportant.

If politics were not already in my blood, it was on the way.

32

THE SPEAKER'S RACE—JANUARY 1937

The feud between Governor Olin D. Johnston and Chief Highway Commissioner Ben M. Sawyer had a tremendous impact on the race for Speaker in January 1937 when I first came to serve in the General Assembly. Supporters of the highway department had for several years opposed the governor. In 1930 they had aided Ibra Blackwood in defeating Johnston and in 1934 they had unsuccessfully supported Johnston's opponent.

In January 1935 Claude A. Taylor of Spartanburg was elected Speaker of the House and Solomon Blatt of Barnwell was elected Speaker Pro Tempore. Both were supporters of the highway department in the Johnston-Sawyer feud. After the Legislature adjourned in the spring of 1936, Taylor announced that he would be a candidate for Congress, and so the Speaker's office was up for grabs when the House convened in January 1937.

The office of Speaker has sometimes been described as second in power only to the Governor. This cannot be proved or disproved, but suffice it to say the Speaker is a highly potent cog in the legislative wheel. Much legislation hinges on the influence exerted by the presiding officer of the House of Representatives.

Governor Johnston's ability to accomplish his purposes during the last two years of his first gubernatorial administration was dependent on the election of a friendly Speaker. Many candidates throughout the state had campaigned for a seat in the House as avowed supporters of Governor Johnston. Many had also campaigned as avowed opponents of Governor Johnston. And then there were many middle-of-the-road candidates who never declared an allegiance. Few were outspoken against the Governor, but many said, in effect: "I am for the Governor when I think he is right."

When the Democratic primary was over in the summer of 1936, the election, for all intents and purposes, was over too. While the official election was not until the first Tuesday in November, no one at that time would dare challenge a Democratic nominee after the primary. And so the race for Speaker of the House became hot quickly. Johnston supporters selected as their candidate Caston

Wannamaker, a highly respected lawyer from Chesterfield County. Wannamaker had served in the Assembly in 1921 and 1922 but had not been a member in more recent years.

The highway department faction supported Speaker Pro Tempore Solomon Blatt of Barnwell. Blatt had come to the Legislature in January 1933 and was made Speaker Pro Tempore two years later.

This became one of the most vigorously contested campaigns in my experience. Much was at stake. The Governor used all the influence at his command to persuade members of the House to vote for his candidate. The highway department, together with most business and professional people, was adamant for Blatt.

Solomon Blatt, who died in 1986 at the age of ninety-one after having served in the General Assembly for more than a half century (thirty-two years as Speaker) was one of the most persuasive individuals I have ever known. Among his supporters were eight members of the Spartanburg County Delegation. This was perhaps the support which "broke the camel's back." It was persuasive in getting votes from other counties that no member of the House from Johnston's home county was voting for his candidate. In the final analysis, Blatt received sixty-two votes, and Wannamaker got fifty-seven.

And so my first experience in the General Assembly was with a membership split almost down the middle. For the time being we had a two-party system, but Speaker Blatt immediately began to cultivate his opposition. Every member, for reasons understandable, would like to curry the favor of the Speaker. Under the rules, the speaker appoints all the standing committees, which is a very important function.

At that time the House rules called for the appointment of twenty-nine standing committees. Many of these—such as the committees on Accounts, Engrossed Bills, Police Regulations and Railroads—were insignificant and never met. A few committees were relatively important, but the prize which every member wanted was to be on the Ways and Means Committee or the Judiciary Committee. It was well known before the election that both candidates were either promising committee assignments for votes or at least leading supporters to believe that they would receive appointments to the committees of their choice. Rule 17 of the House said: "The Speaker of the House shall not appoint more than twenty-one (21) members on any standing committee of the House."

After the Speaker had been elected, the rule quoted above was adopted along with all other rules of the previous session. Many of us had wondered how Speaker Blatt was going to appease everybody he was supposed to take care of by way of committee appointments.

A day or two after the election, committee assignments were announced from the podium. Blatt solved the problem by naming twenty-eight members to the Ways and Means Committee and twenty-six members to the Judiciary Committee. A Wannamaker supporter promptly raised a point of order, but Blatt solved the problem by simply leaving it up to the House. A majority of the members had received satisfactory appointments and refused to upset the Speaker's actions.

Speaker Blatt was elected again in 1939, 1941, 1943 and 1945, serving a total of ten years before January 1947. In another chapter I will tell of his political career in later years.

33

CAMPAIGN OF 1938

Having served for two legislative sessions, my term expired in 1938, and I was again, "Hell bent for election." The entrance fee was twenty-five dollars and twenty-eight of us, including all the incumbents except Charles M. Pace, were running for re-election. Pace ran successfully for probate judge. Again we campaigned the entire county with approximately the same number of campaign meetings. By this time I had learned some of the tricks of the trade, had become acquainted with a lot of people in Spartanburg County and had established a political base. Campaigning this time was much easier. I was generally acceptable to capital and labor. The teachers were for me, and the courthouse ring was in my corner.

Of the twenty-eight candidates, I was the high vote-getter and was elected on the first ballot. Representatives Cox and Moore, who had bested me two years before, ran second and third and were also nominated on the first ballot. Also elected, in the second race, were T.J. Hendrix, Jerome McAbee, Dr. N.T. Clark, Tracy Gaines and Virgil Evans, who barely defeated incumbent H.K. Osborne. This was the year for the election of governor, and there was less emphasis on the local races. Contesting for governor were D.T. Blackmon, Cole L. Blease, John Hughes Cooper, F.M. Easterlin, Wyndham Manning and Burnett R. Maybank. Maybank and Manning ran the second race with Maybank winning.

Running for re-election was quite different from campaigning the first time. When one runs the first time, he has no record to defend; he has no accomplishments to point to with pride. At any subsequent election, one always has to answer questions such as: "How come you didn't _____?" There were advantages and disadvantages. People were charitable to me again, and I was headed back to Columbia for the opening of the General Assembly and for the inauguration of the newly-elected governor, the former mayor of Charleston Burnett R. Maybank.

Voting practices were rather loose and subject to many irregularities, if not actual fraud. The Democratic Party was for all intents and purposes an entity little controlled by law. It was customary to have an enrollment book in each of the approximately

100 precincts at some public place such as a grocery store. The book might be moved from one grocery store to another within the same precinct. Any person who thought he or she might want to vote could merely sign his or her name on the book. People signed for each other. The enrollment books were picked up a few days prior to the election and delivered to the box managers along with paper ballots.

If one did not get around to signing the book, all was not lost. He could, upon petition, get a court order from either a county court judge or a circuit court judge directing that the petitioner be allowed to vote in the Democratic primary. It was not until about ten years later that there came to be meaningful statutory law controlling primary elections.

The Governor's Race

The local races in Spartanbury County created a minimum of interest in 1938. There was no Spartanburg County State Senate campaign, and all members of the House delegation who ran were re-elected except one. Two years previously, Olin Johnston had been a substantial issue in the legislative races, but in 1938 this was no longer true.

The center of attention in 1938 was on the governor's race and the race for the United States Senate. Burnett F. Maybank had served several years as mayor of Charleston and had become rather well known throughout the state because he was chairman of the Santee Cooper Authority, which was, at the time, developing the power generating project near Charleston financed largely by the federal government. Jobs were scarce throughout the state, but many were available in the construction of the dam and power unit. It was well known that one must see Maybank in order to get a job.

In addition, Maybank had as mayor sponsored the annual Azalea Festival and had entertained political people from throughout the state rather lavishly. Along with several others mentioned above, he announced his candidacy for the governorship in the Democratic primary. Maybank was one of the more astute politicians known to the state, and he ended up in the second race together with Wyndham Manning. The voting was comparatively close, with Maybank winning 163,000 to 149,000. Maybank became the first elected Charleston governor since the Civil War—except for Wilson G. Harvey who, as lieutenant governor, succeeded to the office in 1922 upon the resignation of Governor Robert A. Cooper. At the same primary, J. Emile Harley was chosen lieutenant governor again.

Governor-elect Maybank began a colorful political career which was to last sixteen years, until his untimely death in 1954.

United States Senate Race

In 1938 Senator Ellison D. Smith, better known as "Cotton Ed," was completing thirty years as a member of the United States Senate from South Carolina. He had been a vigorous campaigner, emphasizing over the years two basic propositions: (1) "Cotton is King" and (2) "White is Supreme." He had defeated Edgar A. Brown in a hotly contested race in 1926 and was challenged in 1932 unsuccessfully by Ashton Williams, Leon W. Harris and Cole L. Blease, who had lost his Senate seat to James F. Byrnes two years previously. The second race was between Blease and Smith, with Smith receiving 150,000 votes to Blease's 114,000.

These were the years of the Great Depression. President Franklin D. Roosevelt had taken office after his tremendous victory in November 1932 and was doing a very good job of restoring the country to at least a moderate degree of prosperity. James F. Byrnes had been in the United States Senate for two years when Roosevelt took office, and Byrnes was truly one of the President's right-hand men and supporters. In 1936 Byrnes was up for re-election and opposed by Thomas P. Stoney, a former mayor of Charleston, and William C. Harlee, a retired Army officer from Florence, both of whom were ardent critics of Roosevelt and his New Deal. Byrnes was re-elected as a Roosevelt supporter by a landslide, receiving 200,000 votes to Stoney's 25,000 and Harlee's 12,000.

Unlike Byrnes, Senator "Cotton Ed" Smith was opposed to a substantial portion of President Roosevelt's New Deal. As his term of office was coming to an end in 1938, it appeared that he was "ripe for picking." Roosevelt had been re-elected in 1936 by a landslide, and Byrnes ran correspondingly strong in South Carolina the same year. State Senator Edgar A. Brown had run a respectable race against "Cotton Ed" in 1926 but had not repeated the challenge in 1932. At the same time, Brown had not given up his ambition to end his political career in the Senate of the United States. He envisioned 1938 as the year to make his dream come true. He was a close personal friend of Senator Byrnes, an admirer of President Roosevelt and a supporter of The New Deal.

Governor Olin D. Johnston was in the last year of his gubernatorial term. He too envisioned this as being a good year to unseat the incumbent and transfer his public service from the governor's office in Columbia to the Senate chamber in Washington. Johnston was just as ardent a supporter of Roosevelt, if not more so, than was Brown.

Originally Ashton Williams of Florence County and Theo Vaughn of Anderson County announced that they would be candidates for the Senate to challenge incumbent Smith, but both withdrew early in the game.

One of the most vigorous campaigns coming to my attention during my fifty years observation of the political world ensued with Brown and Johnston as advocates of The New Deal challenging Smith, and accusing him of being an anti-new dealer.

Smith was an old cowhand at vote getting. He was an accomplished orator and took much credit for protecting the interests of the farmers, who at that time were a substantial portion of the voting population of the state. Smith's opponents ridiculed him for opposing many of the Roosevelt programs, and he in turn referred to both of them as "coat-tail swingers." Smith's campaign was an uphill battle in a state which vigorously supported Roosevelt and new dealer Byrnes.

Whereas Johnston had come into the office of governor with great popularity, he did not leave the office with similar admiration on the part of the voting public. His gubernatorial programs had not fared well, and a multitude of people could not get over the fact that he had, in an era of peace, called out the militia to take over the State Highway Department. His stock and his support about that time was at perhaps its lowest ebb during the era from 1934 until his death in 1965. Johnston emphasized throughout the campaign his support for the President. To advertise his connection with Roosevelt, he had announced his candidacy from the steps of the White House in Washington.

Johnston and Brown had never been closely allied. About the only thing they had in common at the time was that both were supporters of Roosevelt and both wanted to go to the United States Senate. In 1936 Brown was up for re-election to the State Senate in Barnwell County. Johnston was in the middle of his first gubernatorial term. Johnston went to Barnwell during the campaign and attempted to purge Brown. They were truly political adversaries and each thought that he was the one to replace "Cotton Ed." Brown had received the support of labor in 1926 when he ran against Smith, but this support was not available to Brown as against Johnston.

As the race was coming to a close, it became apparent to Brown that he could not win. He feared that Johnston might beat Smith in a second race. On Saturday night before the primary vote on Tuesday, Brown announced his withdrawal from the race but did not indicate a preference as to the two remaining candidates.

Johnston fired off a stinging rebuke in the form of a telegram to Brown, challenging him to tell the voters to vote for him and against Smith. The stinging rebuke inspired a reply from Brown to Johnston advertising to the public that Brown favored Smith. The exchange embittered Brown's friends and was appreciably helpful to Smith.

The outcome of the voting was 186,000 votes for Smith to 150,000 for Johnston.

Accordingly, Smith was headed back to Washington to continue his opposition to portions of The New Deal. Johnston would soon be leaving office to return to the practice of law in Spartanburg. Many people were of the view that this was the end of Olin D. Johnston's political career. Johnston loved politics and immediately began mending his political fences, working to the end that he would again return to statewide politics when the opportunity presented itself. Such an opportunity was forthcoming in 1941 when James F. Byrnes resigned as United States Senator to take a seat on the Supreme Court of the United States. Governor Maybank, Johnston and Congressman Joe Bryson sought the vacated office. Maybank was victorious. The next year (1942) Johnston was to fare better when he was elected to an additional term to the office of governor.

Once again it had been proven that it is difficult, or nearly impossible, to unseat an incumbent United States Senator or a member of the House of Representatives.

34

CAMPAIGN OF 1940

All persons who seek and serve in public office at times become thoroughly disgusted with the office and say they will never run again. I was among those who made such a statement during the 1937, 1938, 1939 and 1940 sessions of the Legislature. Most of these officeholders, including me, get something "under the skin" and "in the blood" that makes one change his mind when time for announcing for a new term arrives.

And so in 1940 I decided that I would run one more time for the House of Representatives. In 1936 there were thirty-three candidates for eight seats in the House; in 1938 there were twenty-eight candidates, and in 1940 there were only twenty-one. The Delegation's services were approved by the people, except for those of Senator W.D. Burnett.

Senator Burnett was perpetually disgusted with the Senate, in which he had served for eight years, and would go to Columbia and to the Assembly only when something was taking place in which he was intensely interested. At that time each county had one senator. The courthouse was operated by the Delegation through the County Budget Bill. The Senator was intensely interested in this facet of his work and was normally able to prevail insofar as legislation that pertained to Spartanburg County was concerned. The people came to know of his attitude and generally disapproved.

Charles C. Moore, who had served in the House with me for four years, moved over into the contest for Senator for Spartanburg County and ran against Burnett. Except for the feuding between Burnett and Moore, this campaign was comparatively uneventful. Moore made no secret of the fact that Burnett had been absent much more often than he had been present when there was voting in the Senate. Moore was successful in his campaign, but his term was short-lived because of World War II. He held a reserve officer's commission and was called into service before the end of his term. He was succeeded by Howard McCravy, who served until 1948.

The 1940 campaign was a good year for incumbents. T.J. Hendrix, Tracy Gaines, T. Wright Cox and I were re-elected. Newcomers were Leroy Sellars, J. Hertz Brown, Paul Allen and Claude Taylor, who had served in the House previously. Leroy Sellars resigned in 1941 to accept an appointment as the Register of Mesne Conveyances for Spartanburg County, and W.B. Champion was chosen to serve his unexpired term. Taylor had served as Speaker in 1935 and 1936. He was made Speaker Pro Tempore in 1941, succeeding J.W.D. Zerbst, who left the Legislature to serve as auditor of Charleston County.

While there was a minimum of interest in local races, the presidential race made big news. Traditionally, the President of the United States had served for not more than two terms, or a total of eight years. Inasmuch as there was no constitutional, or even statutory, prohibition against a third term, Franklin Roosevelt announced for re-election. It will be recalled that he had carried all but two states four years previously in 1936. By this time the country was well on the way to recovery from the deep Depression. People remembered the tremendous job he had performed in restoring prosperity and voted for him to be President again, defeating Republican Wendell Wilkie by a substantial margin. The Republicans attempted to make much of the fact that Roosevelt was breaking tradition, but to no avail.

Four years later Roosevelt sought and was elected to a fourth term but died before its completion. This was the inspiration for the Twenty-Second Amendment to the Constitution of the United States. It was proposed by Congress in 1947 and ratified in 1951. Under the terms of this Amendment, no President may serve more than two terms.

35

CAMPAIGN OF 1942

The Japanese bombed Pearl Harbor in December of 1941. Congress immediately declared war, and activities in all facets of life changed tremendously.

I was married to Inell Smith of Inman in February of 1942.

Members of the Legislature had a 4B classification in the draft. This meant, for all practical purposes, that they would not be called for military service. Anyone who was physically or mentally disabled was rated 4F, so one might say that Legislators would be called just prior to mentally incompetent persons. There was a great temptation on my part to leave the Legislature and volunteer for military service. I had completed three years of R.O.T.C. at Wofford College but had not returned to Wofford the fourth year and, accordingly, did not have a commission.

There was considerable thinking to the effect that the war would soon end. Proceeding partially on that basis, I announced for re-election in the summer of 1942 without fully knowing just how the voters would feel about re-electing someone my age. I was twenty-eight at the time.

The people must have been pretty well satisfied with the job the Delegation was performing, because all of us were re-elected on the first ballot. Since gasoline was scarce, and many necessities were being rationed, the campaign meetings were minimized. A newcomer had a hard job getting to the people, as there simply was little forum within which to work. Except for radio and newspaper advertisements, the only way to get to the people was to go to see them personally. Re-elected along with me were Paul M. Allen, J. Hertz Brown, T.J. Hendrix, T. Wright Cox, Tracy Gaines, W.B. Champion and Claude Taylor Sr.

This was the year to elect a governor. Olin D. Johnston, after having gone out of office fairly unpopular in January 1939, had mended his political fences and was successful in his quest for a second term as governor of the state.

In the race for lieutenant governor there was a red-hot contest between Senator George Laney of Chesterfield and businessman Ransom Williams of Marion. Prohibition and liquor were the principal issues. Legalized whiskey had returned to South Carolina in 1934, but the Women's Christian Temperance Union was active, and efforts were made almost yearly to vote the state dry again. Laney was the dry candidate. Williams was the wet candidate. With 200 of the state's 1,500 precincts unreported, there was a difference of five votes. It was nip and tuck down to the last precinct, with Williams edging out Laney in the final count. The precinct results from many Low-Country counties, which were traditionally wet, were late coming in, and many people firmly believed that the wets stole the election from the drys.

Johnston, upon his election, immediately began building his fences for the United States Senate race two years ahead against Cotton Ed Smith. Williams began helping to promote Johnston for the office. Governor Johnston was personally and politically dry. Williams needed to help get him promoted so that he could take over the Governor's office. That is exactly what took place in the election of 1944.

This was another good election year for me. The people were generous in permitting me to lead the ticket one more time. Claude Taylor, who bested me in 1940 and relegated me to second place, ran second to me in 1942. In Spartanburg County there had been a great tendency over the years to oust members of the House Delegation. It was almost unprecedented for an entire delegation to be re-elected—especially on the first ballot.

As the 1943 legislative session came to an end, it became apparent that the short war of which we dreamed was not to be. In the summer of 1943 I resigned, waiving my 4B classification, and volunteered for military service. Edwin W. Johnson of the Spartanburg Bar was elected to fill my unexpired term. In the early fall of 1943, I reported for induction at Camp Croft and was soon thereafter sent to the reception center at Fort Jackson for assignment. My first assignment was to Camp Lee at Petersburg, Virginia, for basic training. I was among a multitude of young lawyers who left the practice to enter a military world, wondering what fate had in store.

36

CAMPAIGN OF 1944

During all the campaigns from 1934 to 1988, I have been on the scene and a first-hand observer except during the campaign of 1944. I was at that time serving in the United States Army and stationed at Camp Lee, Virginia. Although I was not in the South Carolina area, I kept a subscription to a South Carolina paper and followed with intense interest the campaigns of that year.

By 1944 "Cotton" Ed Smith had served thirty-six years in the United States Senate. He had defeated Olin D. Johnston six years previously in a hotly contested race, but in 1944 Smith's health was failing. Johnston was in the middle of his second gubernatorial term. I have been told Smith was really not equal to the campaign. Be that as it may, Johnston defeated him in the Democratic primary, and the general election was only a formality. The Democrats were still winning without contest in our state.

As it developed, Smith died a few days after the general election, and Johnston, still serving as governor, appointed his friend Wilton Hall, publisher of the *Anderson Independent* newspaper, to serve in the Senate until his own full term would commence in 1945.

Johnston's moving to the Senate caused Lieutenant Governor Ramson Williams to be elevated to the office of governor. Williams served the unexpired term but was defeated two years later when he sought a full term in his own right.

One significant change in the legislators elected in 1944 was the age of the members chosen to serve. A substantial portion of the young lawyers (and others as well) were away in the service. Normally many of them would have been seeking to be a part of the General Assembly, but the average age serving from 1944 to 1946 was substantially older than during previous years and during the years to come.

At the national level, President Franklin Delano Roosevelt was seeking his fourth term. A third term for him in 1940 had been unprecedented. Certainly a fourth term was also unprecedented.

People were generally satisfied with the way Roosevelt, as Commander-in-Chief of the Armed Forces, was conducting the war. Normally a President probably could not have been elected to a

144

fourth term but for the plea: "Let's not change horses in the middle of the stream." Roosevelt was successful in his fourth campaign and chose for his running mate Harry S. Truman, a Senator from Missouri. Henry Wallace had been the President's vice presidential choice in 1940, but Americans in general and Roosevelt in particular had become dissatisfied with Wallace. He was dumped.

John Nance Garner of Texas had been Vice President from 1932 to 1940 but chose not to pursue the office again. Accordingly, Roosevelt had had the chore of selecting a new running mate in 1940. The general consensus was that Wallace had been a mistake.

37

CAMPAIGN OF 1946

Many of us who had left our businesses and professions to join the armed forces dreamed of returning when the opportunity first presented itself. As soon as I was released from service, I announced that I would again be a candidate for the House of Representatives and reopened my law office. Although I was not entitled to return to my former employment as a matter of right, the fact that employees in industry were entitled as a matter of law to be reinstated was of appreciable help to me in convincing the people that I should be elected again to serve in the General Assembly of South Carolina.

Nineteen forty-six was an interesting political year. Candidates came out of the cracks in the wall, and there were plenty of them running for all offices. Seven members of the delegation from Spartanburg County who had been elected in 1944 sought re-election. It was not a good year for incumbents, however, and a majority of those elected to serve Spartanburg County were newcomers. The people were most charitable to me and sent me back to the Assembly on the first ballot with about 3,000 votes to spare. This was truly the year for young candidates and especially for those who recently returned from the service. It was my easiest race.

Elected along with me in either the first or second races were incumbents Tracy Gaines, Matthew Poliakoff and T.J. Hendrix, and newcomers Thomas B. Butler, Walter B. Miller, Paul McChesney Jr. and Arnold Merchant. The office of county senator was not opened until 1948, and Senator Howard McCravy continued to serve.

Even as many sought seats in the House of Representatives, there were plenty of candidates for the office of governor. They were: A.J. Beattie, Carl B. Eppes, John D. Long, James McLeod, Del O'Neal, Roger W. Scott, Marcus A. Stone, John C. Taylor, Strom Thurmond, Ransom J. Williams and A.L. Wood. Williams was the incumbent, of course, having succeeded Olin Johnston when Johnston was elected to the United States Senate in 1944. Always a political issue and somewhat of a political accident, Williams was not a strong contender in the race.

Strom Thurmond and Dr. James McLeod were the two front-runners; accordingly, they ran the second race of the Democratic primary. Thurmond won.

Contending for lieutenant governor were E. Coke Bridges, R.E. Hannah, George Bell Timmerman Jr., John C. Williams (former partner of Olin D. Johnston) and J.W.D. Zerbt. In the second race, Timmerman was the victor over Williams; he continued to serve in that office for a total of eight years before being elected governor of the state in 1954.

There was particular interest in the election of the Spartanburg legislative delegation, because it was obvious that Judge Thomas S. Sease, who had served for almost forty years as circuit judge, would soon be retiring. There was much interest at the Bar in the Seventh Judicial Circuit (composed of Spartanburg, Union and Cherokee counties) in naming a successor. It was well known then that lawyers in the Legislature have a big advantage over others who seek election as circuit judge at a joint session of the House of Representatives and the Senate.

Arnold Merchant had served as Spartanburg County Court Judge for a period of twelve years. This was a court of limited jurisdiction, and the pay was comparatively low. He had an ambition to serve as circuit judge, and in order to be strategically situated when the votes were cast in 1949, he ran for the House of Representatives and was among those elected. Merchant had friends at the local Bar, but he also had enemies who were particularly anxious to have him retire as county court judge and to see to it that he was not promoted to the office of circuit court judge.

Also entering the race in order to be strategically located when the votes were cast was Spartanburg lawyer Thomas B. Butler, whose father had served as lieutenant governor some twenty or thirty years previously. Butler was an excellent lawyer, engaged basically in defending insurance companies and other corporations. He, too, had many friends and opponents at the local Bar.

Although I had it in the back of my head that I might run when the time came, I did not advertise this fact. It seemed to me that part of the wisdom was to "keep my powder dry" and await developments. The vacancy would not occur until 1949.

In this same year, Congressman Joseph R. Bryson of Greenville was seeking re-election. The Fourth District at that time was composed of Spartanburg, Greenville, Union and Laurens counties. Charles C. Moore of Spartanburg had served in the House of Representatives from 1937 to 1941 and in the Senate from 1941 to 1942 but had resigned to enter the armed forces and serve in World War II. When he returned in the summer of 1946, that office was not up for grabs; he ran for Congress and attempted to unseat a Congressman who had been in the office for eight years. Although Senator Moore ran a highly respectable race, he found, as we all know, that it is almost impossible to unseat a member of Congress. Two years later Senator Moore regained his old seat in the Senate by defeating incumbent Howard McCravy and challenger Tracy Gaines.

Strom Thurmond went into office as a popular forty-four-year-old bachelor with lots of good ideas relative to state government operations. He married Jean Couch his first year in the governor's office.

It was not until about three weeks after the election that I decided to run for Speaker of the House.

38

MY CAMPAIGN FOR SPEAKER—1946

World War II had come to an end in the summer of 1945. During the previous two years comparatively few young men, especially young lawyers, had served in the General Assembly. They were in service. By primary time 1946, just about all of the young lawyers had returned to civilian life. They were as a general proposition eager to seek public office.

Among those lawyers who had returned from military service by 1946 was Strom Thurmond. A circuit judge before the war, Thurmond had been granted a leave of absence so that upon return he would be circuit judge again. He resigned his judgeship in the late spring of 1946 and announced his candidacy for governor. In his candidacy he was opposed to the "Barnwell Ring," said to be composed of Speaker Solomon Blatt and Senator Edgar A. Brown.

Blatt had, at that time, already served ten years as Speaker of the House of Representatives. In Barnwell County, where Blatt was up for re-election, Calhoun Lemons mounted a vigorous campaign which gave to Blatt perhaps the most serious challenge for public office of his career. Blatt prevailed.

Normally the Speaker of the House would get enough commitments from House members during the previous session to ensure his re-election the next year, and it has been unusual for a sitting Speaker to have opposition for the office. Rationalizing that there would be no opposition to his candidacy, Blatt did not get the commitments sufficient to assure his re-election. While a Speaker never knows who will meet him in the House at the next session, it is traditional that a substantial portion of the membership will be re-elected, and canvassing incumbents will normally assure re-election.

About the time of the Primary voting in Barnwell County, Thomas H. Pope Jr. of Newberry, who had been assured of re-election to the House and who had just returned from the war, announced that he would be a candidate for Speaker. Charles N. Plowden of Clarendon County was also toying with the idea. I was ambitious to serve in that office also, and after Speaker Blatt announced that he would stand aside and not seek the office again, I announced my candidacy. Even as I had been in Thurmond's corner, the newly elected Governor was in mine. His support was appreciable, because even as House members like to be in favor with the Speaker, they also want to be in favor with the Governor.

During the fall of 1946, I spent a substantial portion of my time on the road, visiting with House members and soliciting their support. Many friends with whom I had served prior to the war were still House members, and many friends I had known at Wofford and the University were coming to the Assembly for the first time. It was the day of the young veterans, and there was to be a new way of thinking in the General Assembly. Most of the Senators had been too old to participate in the war, and no great change was evident there.

It developed that Plowden withdrew from the race, and the race took place between Tom Pope and me. Tom and I were born within a week of each other. We had attended the Law School together and had served in the General Assembly together prior to entering military service. He was a capable and likable lawyer and House member. There was simply nothing unkind I could say about Tom Pope, and so far as I know, he never spoke unkindly about me. The only problem between the two of us was that we both wanted the same office and only one could have it. The contest did not diminish our friendship or the respect we had for each other; that continues until this day.

The Legislature convened on Tuesday, January 14, 1947 and the first order of business was the election of a Speaker. Representative Perrin Anderson of Greenwood placed my name in nomination. Aubrey Harley of Newberry nominated Tom. I received 67 votes; Tom received 50.

As Speaker, it became my duty to appoint the standing committees. I offered my opponent the committee of his choice, and he chose the Judiciary, where he served with distinction. Blatt, who voted for me, chose the Ways and Means Committee, to which I appointed him.

A contested race for Speaker of the House brings about, at least for the time being, the equivalent of a two-party system. While all members as of that time were male, white Democrats, they were also supporters of either Littlejohn or Pope. My supporters expected me to deal charitably with them when the committee assignments were made. There were twenty-nine standing committees, many of them of no real importance. The main committees, in order of desirability, were Ways and Means; Judiciary; Education; Agriculture; Roads, Bridges and Ferries; and Fish, Game and Forestry. The real gems were Ways and Means and Judiciary. We amended the rules to provide for the appointment of thirty-one members to this committee. It goes without saying that Littlejohn supporters fared well.

As it developed, both Representative Morrison Tuten of Hampton, who had served as Chairman of the Ways and Means Committee for four years, and Representative Calhoun Thomas of Beaufort, who had served as Chairman of the Judiciary Committee for fourteen years, opposed my candidacy and voted for my opponent. Upon my election, each became a convert and sought my blessing in hopes of continuing to serve in the same capacity. They began buttonholing members they thought would be appointed to the respective committees. In the meantime, some of my supporters were buttonholing the same people. Rather than permit the contest to get out of hand and divide my group, I simplified the matter by merely leaving both Tuten and Thomas off their respective committees and giving to them other assignments. This was a drastic move, but it was the only logical way to handle the matter. Charles N. Plowden of Clarendon was elected Chairman of the Ways and Means Committee, and Perrin Anderson of Greenwood was elected Chairman of the Judiciary Committee, both without opposition. Tuten continued to serve in the House but later moved to the Senate. Thomas was unhappy without his chairmanship and did not seek re-election.

Upon being elected, I became very popular at the University of South Carolina. The Speaker had nineteen page appointments. These were desirable assignments and comparatively lucrative. Students who needed financial assistance, and some who did not but were interested in politics, sought these jobs. There must have been sixty to seventy applications for the nineteen positions. The appointments available to the Speaker for page jobs have increased constantly; it is my understanding that today each House member has at least one appointment. My popularity at the University waned greatly after I turned down about fifty who desired to work in the General Assembly.

It had been apparent to me since I came to the Assembly in 1936 that the committee structure in the House was terribly inefficient. With much hesitation I appointed all twenty-nine committees and immediately began thinking about remedying the situation, which I did two years later.

While I was assuming office as presiding officer of the House of Representatives, my friend of many years, George Bell Timmerman Jr., was assuming the position of presiding officer of the Senate because he had been elected Lieutenant Governor.

Accordingly, three of us who had recently returned from World War II had come to hold the offices of Speaker, president of the Senate and Governor of the state. Obviously, those who had left public service in order to participate in the war were given preferential treatment at the ballot box.

It has often been said that Speaker of the House is the most powerful office in the state short of the governorship. This cannot be proved or disproved, but I soon learned that the office of Speaker carried with it substantial prestige and influence. I am not at all sure but that the Speaker has more influence than any person not answerable directly to the voting population should have.

Having been made Speaker, my election to a judgeship to succeed Judge T.S. Sease was practically assured. It came on February 9, 1949 at a joint assembly of the Senate and House.

39

CAMPAIGN OF 1948

During my first two years as Speaker of the House, Governor Thurmond and I developed a close working relationship. It is my recollection that Spartanburg County had only had the office of Speaker on two previous occasions. In the early 1920s, Attorney J.B. Atkinson was elected Speaker and served two years. In 1935 Attorney Claude A. Taylor Sr. was elected Speaker and served two years. Serving as Speaker would normally give one a tremendous advantage in seeking re-election to the House, and it was of substantial advantage to me. This race, however, came to have substantial problems which I had not anticipated.

At that time the appropriation for the State Welfare Department was comparatively low. F.M. Easterlin, a retired railroad worker and an ardent union man, had undertaken some four or five years earlier to organize the Southern Old Age Pension Association. He pretended to be a lobbyist for the old people and urged them to send him dues. In connection with his activities, he published a newspaper periodically.

In the spring of 1948, it became my duty as Speaker of the House to appoint a free conference committee on the State Appropriation Bill. Easterlin, who was from Spartanburg, came to me and said that he thought he was entitled to name one member of the free conference committee of three because of his representation of recipients who were seeking a higher appropriation. I would, of course, have no part of this and told him so.

That summer Easterlin became a candidate for the House of Representatives from Spartanburg County and in his next newspaper publication told the people to vote against me and Tom Butler. He stated that we had not voted for the highest appropriation for the Welfare Department that had been proposed. In actuality, we had voted for an increase in the appropriation, but in an endeavor to curry favor with the senior citizens, someone had proposed a ridiculous amount which would have completely thrown the budget out of kilter. Easterlin continued his tirade by lambasting Butler and me from the stump. In our three-minute speeches at precincts throughout the county, we simply did not have time to "unscramble the egg" which Easterlin was scrambling.

I came to realize that far more people than the recipients of welfare were greatly concerned with the appropriation. For example, many children of senior citizens realized that if welfare were not forthcoming, contributions would have to be made. I overcame the problems through newspaper advertisements and radio speeches. Mr. Butler was unable to overcome the problem and was narrowly defeated. I was elected on the first ballot with approximately 2,000 votes to spare, but the campaign was not an easy one. Elected along with me that year were F.M. Easterlin, Raymond Eubanks, Arnold Merchant, John C. Williams, Tom Woodruff, Matthew Poliakoff and Paul McChesney Jr.

Also in that race were my good friends at the Bar, Sam N. Burts and Edwin W. Johnson. They were active practitioners, intensely interested in my candidacy for the judgeship, which by this time was deep into the rumor stage. Unfortunately for them and for me, both were defeated in the second race. Both however, played important parts in my election as judge, even though they were not members of the House of Representatives at the time the vote was taken.

It was in this campaign that Charles C. Moore was returned to the State Senate, in which he served for several terms before his retirement in the 1960s.

A race which also created substantial interest was that in which John C. Mooneyham sought to unseat Sam R. Watt as Solicitor of the Seventh Judicial Circuit. Watt was an excellent lawyer and a good solicitor who had enemies at the Bar and among the populace. He was always opposed. In 1936 and in 1940, John C. Williams challenged him; in 1944 Allen Lambright opposed him; in 1948 Mooneyham ran against him.

Solicitor Watt had originally been appointed to the office of Solicitor when his partner, Ibra C. Blackwood, left the Solicitor's Office to become Governor in January 1931. Watt served ably and well for some twenty-two years before he retired. I roomed with his brother T.S. Watt at the law school. He, too, was a good lawyer.

In that same year, incumbent United States Senator Burnett R. Maybank soundly defeated four opponents in the first primary. They were Neville Bennett, W.J. Bryan Dorn, Allen Johnstone and Marcus A. Stone.

Senator Strom Thurmond congratulates the author at a South Carolina Bar Convention banquet honoring the newly-elected Chief Justice.

The author and classmate Marshall Williams (right) in 1986 at a fiftieth anniversary celebration of their graduation from law school.

Having retained my seat in the House of Representatives, I immediately began running simultaneously for Speaker of the House and circuit court judge. Running for one office is difficult enough; running for two at the same time is like walking a tightrope. But fate was kind to me in both races.

40

CAMPAIGN OF 1950

From 1936 through 1948 (with the exception of 1944, when I was in the Army) I had been actively engaged six times in political campaigns incident to my own seeking of office. In 1949 I had been elected circuit judge and had assumed office the same year. So the campaigns were different for me as the summer of 1950 approached. Where I had previously been a participant, I was now to be a spectator. While there was no official judicial code of ethics at that time, it was understood by unwritten law that judges were not supposed to be actively engaged in political matters.

In 1950 there was plenty for a spectator to observe. Over and above the local races, there was a red-hot race for the United States Senate and a race for governor of great interest.

The campaign for the Senate brought out two powerful political figures who were well known to virtually every voter in South Carolina. They were incumbent United States Senator Olin D. Johnston and outgoing Governor Strom Thurmond. Both had been very successful at the chore of making South Carolina voters want to favor them at the ballot box.

Johnston had served in the House of Representatives from both Anderson and Spartanburg counties. He had run unsuccessfully for governor in 1930 but had been defeated by a very narrow margin. He had been elected governor in 1934 and again in 1942. In 1944 he had moved to the Senate by defeating incumbent Senator "Cotton Ed" Smith, an old war horse with thirty-six years seniority in Washington. Smith had defeated Johnston in 1938, and Burnett Maybank had defeated him for the unexpired term of Senator James F. Byrnes, who resigned in 1941. By 1950 Johnston had served in the Senate for six years and was well entrenched politically.

Strom Thurmond had been elected Superintendent of Education in Edgefield County and then to the State Senate from the same county prior to his election as circuit judge in 1938. After a distinguished career in the United States Army during World War II, he returned to the judgeship, then ran for governor and was elected over several opponents in the summer Democratic primary of 1946.

During his tenture of office as governor from 1947 to 1950, Thurmond made a splendid record for himself, and he too was deeply entrenched politically.

Both were vigorous in health; Thurmond was forty-eight and Johnston only six years older. Radio was in fairly common use for campaign purposes, but at that time campaigning from the stump was still the way to reach the voters. Campaign speakings were held in every county seat, and additionally at many other places.

A major issue in the race was the relationship between the state Democratic party and the national organization. Johnston was critical of the national administration and of President Truman but preferred to settle differences from within the framework of the party. Thurmond had broken with the Democratic party in 1948 and had been the leader of a group opposing the national party and the candidacy of President Truman.

No other campaign within my memory has been fought so vigorously. It brought back memories of the days when Ben Tillman and Cole Blease campaigned—when voters would fight you because of your views on various candidates.

When the votes were counted, Johnston had received 186,000, representing fifty-four percent of the total, with a lead in twenty-five counties. Thurmond received 158,000 votes, representing forty-six percent and leading in twenty-one counties. This race, like several others, was in large measure a matter of Low Country versus Up Country, with Johnston carrying the Up Country fairly solidly. With few exceptions, Thurmond carried the Low Country counties. Johnston returned to Washington, and Thurmond, upon leaving the governor's office in January 1951, went to Aiken to resume the practice of law with his friends Dorcey Lybrand and Charles E. Simons Jr.

The big political show was with the Senate candidates, but the race for governor was of substantial interest also. After a distinguished career in many facets of public office and public life, James F. Byrnes had returned to South Carolina to a state of retirement upon resigning as Secretary of State under President Harry Truman. After some two or three years in South Carolina, Byrnes decided that he would like to bring down the curtain on his political career by serving as governor of his native state. He had many years previously served as a court reporter, as solicitor, as a member of Congress, as United States Senator, as a Justice on the Supreme Court of the United States and in several administrative capacities under President Franklin D. Roosevelt. He was war mobilizer and war stabilizer during World War II and was appointed by President Truman as Secretary of State—a relationship which ended less than pleasantly. Byrnes' name had truly become a legend in South Carolina.

Lester Bates, a native of Berkeley County, had come to Columbia and organized a substantial insurance company called "Capitol Life Insurance Company." He had as of that time served several years as a member of city council in Columbia. Bates was a good organizer and a good promoter and had an ambition to serve as governor of the state.

Thomas H. Pope Jr. of Newberry was a grandson of former Governor Eugene B. Gary, a nephew of former United States Senator Frank B. Gary and a cousin of former Governor John Gary Evans. Pope had served as a member of the House of Representatives prior to the war and had a distinguished record as an officer in World War II. After the war he had returned to the Legislature and served as Speaker of the House during the 1950 term. Pope was also a candidate for governor. In addition, Marcus Stone of Florence announced his candidacy.

Byrnes campaigned somewhat like a Southern gentleman, not feeling the necessity of carrying on a person-to-person candidacy as others might. In the last analysis, the people welcomed Byrnes home by taking him out of retirement and electing him on the first ballot with seventy-two percent of the vote—a total of 248,000 votes. Bates received 63,000 votes; Pope 29,000; and Stone 5,000.

It was during Byrnes' administration that the United States Supreme Court went about abolishing segregated schools. To cope with the situation financially, the Legislature, under Byrnes' leadership, brought into being a general sales tax to finance school expenditures.

Lieutenant Governor George Bell Timmerman Jr. was re-elected in the summer of 1950, besting Dr. Frank C. Owens, the mayor of Columbia, by a vote of 195,000 to 146,000.

South Carolinians were becoming gradually more uncomfortable with the national Democratic party, but the Democratic primaries of 1950 were still the equivalent of election in South Carolina.

41

CAMPAIGN OF 1952

In 1952 I was again a spectator to the elections, but I was still intensely interested in political campaigns, not only at local levels, but also as relates to the national elections.

In this year there was no United States Senate race and no governor's race in South Carolina. There were some interesting local Spartanburg County races, but everyone was primarily concerned with who would serve as President of the United States during the next four years.

In the Seventh Judicial Circuit, composed of Spartanburg, Cherokee and Union counties, Sam R. Watt was retiring after twenty-two years as Solicitor. J. Allen Lambright, who had served as County Solicitor, and John C. Mooneyham were contesting for the vacancy. Lambright was victorious and served eight years, until his untimely death in 1960.

Senator Charles C. Moore was returned to the Senate, defeating F.M. Easterlin and Paul S. McChesney, both of whom had legislative experience in the House. Horace C. Smith, a newcomer to politics, was elected to the House of Representatives for the first time. With this election Smith began a long, distinguished career in the General Assembly of South Carolina as both a House member and a Senator.

The voters of Spartanburg County re-elected Sheriff B.B. Brockman over challenger George P. Pruette.

There was nominal interest in local campaigns, but there was intense interest in the race for President of the United States. The state was being watched by voters throughout the nation because of events in the presidential campaign of 1948. In that year South Carolinians had for the first time broken with the old line national Democratic party and voted for electors committed to Governor Strom Thurmond of South Carolina and Governor Fielding Wright of Mississippi, for President and Vice President respectively. Prior to 1948 it had been virtually accepted that South Carolina was in the bag for the candidate nominated by the Democratic National Convention. Now that Thurmond had carried South Carolina as well as three other states on a State's Rights ticket, people were anxiously awaiting the events of 1952. Would South Carolina return to the Democratic fold and vote for Adlai Stevenson of Chicago? Inasmuch as Truman had declined to run again, the local voters were not quite as mad at the Democratic party as they would have been if he had sought another term.

It had been rumored that General Dwight D. Eisenhower, the commander of the European Theatre of Operations during World War II, would be the nominee of the Democratic party. It is my recollection that Senator Olin D. Johnston of South Carolina urged him to run as a Democrat. Eisenhower, who had never been concerned with political matters, decided otherwise and agreed to be the candidate of the Republican party. In selecting a distinguished hero of a popular war, the Republicans virtually assured his election.

Eisenhower's running mate was Senator Richard M. Nixon of California, who made big news when during the middle of the campaign it was revealed that he was being subsidized by private interests in California. You may recall that Eisenhower seriously considered removing him from the ticket, but Nixon went on TV and with a tear-jerking speech about his dog and his wife's cloth coat sold himself to the public, and the Republicans kept him as the vice presidential candidate.

While James F. Byrnes had not been outspoken in support of the State's Right ticket in 1948, it was well understood that he was unhappy with the National Democratic party, with President Truman and with Adlai Stevenson. Many were convinced that if Byrnes had joined in Thurmond's campaign enthusiastically in 1948, the election might have been thrown into the House of Representatives. This can never be proved or disproved.

In 1952 Byrnes was in the middle of his gubernatorial term. He was always one of the state's most highly respected citizens, with much influence and a tremendous following.

The Governor gave his support to a ticket of electors called "South Carolinians for Eisenhower." Simultaneously, there were two other sets of electors—the regular Democrats in support of Stevenson and the regular Republicans in support of Eisenhower. In a general election, a plurality prevails and the winner takes all.

The old line Democratic electors for Stevenson received 173,000 South Carolina votes; the old line Republican party supporters received 9,000 votes, while the "South Carolinians for Eisenhower" received 158,000 votes. Accordingly, the Democratic electors for Stevenson prevailed but only by a small margin.

Once more it had been indicated that the yellow-dog Democrats were rapidly vanishing in South Carolina. The voters again had evidenced the fact that they were willing to break away from the Democratic party. This was comforting to the Republicans, because more and more people were willing not only to leave the Democratic party but to join another. This was the second meaningful step in the rise of the Republican party in South Carolina.

Nationally, Eisenhower received approximately five million more votes than Stevenson. The election was a landslide, with Eisenhower breaking into the "solid South" by carrying Florida, Virginia, Tennessee and Texas, together with some border states.

Governor Byrnes was elated. He was quoted as saying: "South Carolina is out of the bag of any political party and we do not intend to get back into the bag. . . . I hope that henceforth that we will let all political parties know that we are going to vote for the best qualified candidate and not blindly follow a label." Byrnes further stated that election day for South Carolina was independence day, since more than half of the states comprising the Southern Governor's Conference voted for Eisenhower.

Growing out of this election, there came to be a political split between Governor Byrnes and his friend of many years, state Senator Edgar A. Brown. Byrnes had hoped that Brown would join in the move to elect Eisenhowever, but Brown chose to remain with the Democratic party. Brown had been a leader within the Democratic party for nearly forty years and had run in the Democratic primary for the United States Senate unsuccessfully in both 1926 and 1938. He was at the time the senior state senator in South Carolina.

The breach between Brown and Byrnes was never healed and was to have a significant impact in the election of a United States Senator to succeed Burnett R. Maybank.

There were many factors which contributed to Eisenhower's victory and Stevenson's defeat. Among those factors was the fact that Stevenson was a divorced man. In South Carolina divorces had been prohibited by constitutional law from 1895 to 1948, and there was still a tendency here, as well as throughout the United States, to look with disdain upon divorced persons. Certainly being divorced was anything but an asset for a political candidate. Compared to modern statistics, there were relatively few divorces. We will never know how many persons voted against Stevenson because of his divorce. The time came, comparatively soon thereafter, that divorce would touch the lives of nearly all the families in the country in one way or another.

Whereas a divorce was a political liability at that time, it is significant to note that this is no longer true. Ronald Reagan was divorced many years ago and remarried. In 1980 and 1984, I do not recall any mention of the fact that he had divorced his first wife and married Nancy. Divorce would appear to be no longer an issue and no longer an impediment to election.

It has often been said that a Democrat cannot be elected President without the help of the "solid South." Keeping this in mind, Stevenson had chosen as his running mate Senator John Jackson Sparkman of Alabama. In chosing a Southerner, he followed the pattern of others. In 1932 and 1936, President Roosevelt chose as his running mate John Nance Garner of Texas. In 1944 he chose Harry Truman of Missouri. Truman in 1948 chose Alben Barkley of Kentucky. In 1960 John Kennedy chose Lyndon Johnson of Texas. When Lyndon Johnson and Jimmy Carter (of Georgia) ran for President, they both, being Southerners, selected running mates from other parts of the country. When Walter Mondale ran for President in 1984, he tried a new angle by choosing a woman, Geraldine Ferraro of New York.

We can never prove with certainty the effect of choosing a running mate. If Stevenson's choice of Sparkman was any help in getting votes throughout the South, it was negligible.

42

CAMPAIGN OF 1954

In 1954, South Carolina's two United States Senators and six members of Congress were still products of the Democratic party. Those nominated in the June Democratic primary were assured of election in November, and normally candidates went on vacation after the primary vote was tabulated.

Senator Olin D. Johnston was not up for re-election, and Senator Burnett R. Maybank was unchallenged. At the congressional level in my home district, Robert Ashmore was being challenged by State Senator Charles C. Moore of Spartanburg. Ashmore had defeated Moore the year before for an unexpired term brought about by the death of Congressman Joseph R. Bryson. Ashmore won again.

The principle interest during the primary was in the race for governor and lieutenant governor. George Bell Timmerman Jr. had served as lieutenant governor for eight years and announced his candidacy for governor. Lester L. Bates, an insurance executive in Columbia, had been runner-up four years previously when the contest was between him, James F. Byrnes and Thomas H. Pope Jr.

Most lieutenant governors perform two functions: they preside over the Senate and they run for governor during their entire terms of office as lieutenant governor. Timmerman did very little of the latter and actually never went through the motions that most candidates go through to get elected. As Lieutenant Governor he would usually come to the Senate just before the opening of the session, preside and return to his home in Lexington County upon adjournment each day. Despite the fact that he was not greatly politically inclined, the voters had confidence in him and elected him each of the three times he offered for statewide office. Timmerman had the benefit of the fact that his father was a highly respected judge who bore the same name as he did. In addition, Governor Byrnes was still a very popular and influential person in South Carolina, and Byrnes did not want to see Bates elected. Timmerman defeated Bates for governor in nearly all counties. His administration from 1955 to 1959 was peaceful; he fully respected the separation of powers.

By winning the election, Governor Timmerman established a precedent. It seemed to be in the scheme of things before that a lieutenant governor simply could not win the governorship. Since the beginning of the primary system, seven had attempted the promotion, but each had failed. Eight years is the longest any lieutenent governor has served.

Once more, in the defeat of Bates, the state had refused to elect a Columbia citizen governor. Columbia has never in modern times produced a governor of South Carolina, though several have attempted to win the election. By a similar token, it is interesting to note that within my memory no Columbia attorney had served as a member of the Supreme Court until Jean Toal was elected in 1988.

While Timmerman was being elected governor, there came on the statewide scene a candidate for lieutenant governor who was to play an important part in state and national politics in years to come. He was Ernest F. Hollings, better known as "Fritz" Hollings. He had come to the House of Representatives from Charleston in January 1949 and was a supporter of mine in both my candidacy for re-election as Speaker of the House and for Circuit Court Judge. After two years Hollings was made Speaker Pro Tempore, and in the spring of 1954 declared his candidacy to succeed Lieutenant Governor Timmerman. In that race there was also a popular member of the House of Representatives from Kershaw County, Clator Arrants. Hollings' victory was substantial, and he began "eye-balling" the governor's office, looking forward to the election in 1958.

The office of lieutenant governor, like most other offices and departments of government, has shown a marked change from the day Lieutenant Governor Timmerman occupied the office. In the State Appropriations Bill of 1948, the Lieutenant Governor was listed as drawing a salary of $1,000. His secretary was paid $300 for part-time work, and he was allowed $300 for office expenses. The total cost of operating his office was $1,600. As years have passed, the office has grown so that in 1986 the lieutenant governor drew a $35,500 salary and the total appropriation for the office was $199,000.

The campaign of 1954 was comparatively quiet. The quietness vanished on September 1, when the Democratic party was called upon to supply a new nominee for the general election to replace United States Senator Burnett R. Maybank who had been nominated in the June primary and died shortly thereafter.

By 1954 blacks were coming to participate in the Democratic primaries but not in large numbers. It will be recalled that Federal Judge Waites Waring had opened the primary to them seven or eight years earlier. For several years after the order of Judge Waring, candidates for public office were anxious to have the support of blacks but did not want their support to be widely advertised. Candidates felt that if it were known that black voters were supporting them, a percentage of white voters would be opposed.

This feeling continued for about a decade but having black persons participate in the Democratic primary gradually became more acceptable to all people. Every two years the black vote came to be a larger percentage of the total vote. By the mid 1960s, candidates openly welcomed and actually sought the support of black voters, who are now often the balance of power.

43

THE 1954 WRITE-IN CAMPAIGN

On September 1, 1954, United States Senator Burnett R. Maybank who was only fifty-four years of age, was dealt an unkindly blow by fate; he died unexpectedly of a heart attack at his summer home at Flat Rock, North Carolina. This brought to an end a colorful and successful political career. Maybank had served as mayor of Charleston and at the age of thirty-nine was elected Governor in 1938.

In 1941 Senator James F. Byrnes, who had served in the Senate since 1930, had resigned to accept an appointment as a Justice on the United States Supreme Court. This threw the office of Senator open. It became the duty of Governor Maybank to appoint an interim senator, and he appointed Judge Alva Lumpkin, an excellent lawyer and federal judge who resided in Columbia. Lumpkin went to the Senate and died unexpectedly ten days later. Maybank then appointed Roger Peace, publisher of *The Greenville News,* who served until an election could be held.

After calling an election, Maybank announced that he himself would be a candidate for the unexpired term. Joining him for the fray was former Governor Olin D. Johnston of Spartanburg and Congressman Joseph Bryson of Greenville. Maybank showed his political strength by besting them on the first ballot but was forced into a second race with Johnston. In the second race Maybank received 92,000 votes to 70,000 for Johnston.

The full six-year term would come open one year later in 1942, and Maybank had to run again. There was usually substantial opposition to Maybank, but never enough to defeat him. In 1942 friends of former Chief Justice Eugene S. Blease of Newberry had persuaded him to get in the Democratic primary race. Maybank defeated Blease by a vote of 120,000 to 114,000.

By 1948 Maybank was well entrenched. He had mended all his political fences but was challenged again for the primary nomination in the summer of 1948. In that race were Neville Bennett of Marlboro County, Allen Johnston of Newberry, Marcus Stone of Florence and W.J. Bryan Dorn of Greenwood. Maybank surprised the state by beating them all on the first ballot.

This brings us down to 1954, when everyone remembered how strong Maybank had run in 1948. No one wanted to challenge him, so he had the luxury of running in the June primary unopposed. On September 1, 1954, Maybank died unexpectedly. The general election was coming up the first Tuesday in November, and general elections cannot be postponed.

The Maybank funeral was held in Charleston in the early afternoon on September 3. It is not unusual in South Carolina for politicians to go to funerals of other politicians. It is not unusual in South Carolina for politicians at the funeral of other politicians to plan a successor. Many friends attended the church service but skipped the graveside service and rushed back to Columbia to a called meeting of the Democratic Executive Committee late that afternoon. With the election only two months away, there was nothing good the Democratic group could do. There was time for a primary, but that created problems—including the considerable expense connected with it and planning that was necessary. The Executive Committee could not resist the temptation to name one of its own as the Democratic candidate—which under the law it had the right to do. State Senator Edgar Brown of Barnwell was chosen as the nominee of the party.

Brown had run for the United States Senate in 1926. He had served as Speaker of the House of Representatives in the mid-1920s. He had come to the Senate about 1930, had been there more than twenty-four years and by 1954 had great influence, seniority and power. Brown had been active in the Democratic Party all of his life, although I think he strayed in 1948 when South Carolina rebelled at the nomination of Harry Truman for President.

The fact that the voters were to be denied the right of nominating their own senator just did not set right with the people. Newspaper editors throughout the state, and many politicians as well, were up in arms because the Executive Committee had denied voters the right to choose a nominee of the Democratic Party for the general election. It appeared at first that Brown would be elected without opposition, but the irritation of the people just would not calm down.

Among those disgruntled with the procedure was Governor James F. Byrnes, who was near the end of his four year term. Strom Thurmond had served as Governor from 1947 to 1951 and had in the summer of 1950 challenged Olin Johnston in a race for the United States Senate, but Senator Johnston, the incumbent, had won out.

Thurmond was back in Aiken practicing law with his friends Dorcey Lybrand and Charles E. Simons Jr., who later became a federal judge.

At that time my friend Alex McCullough of Spartanburg was serving as secretary to Governor Byrnes in Columbia. McCullough and his wife Birdie had been my loyal supporters over the years. He had covered the Legislature for the *Spartanburg Herald* while I was Speaker. Upon the expiration of Byrnes' term, McCullough served as administrative assistant to Senator Thurmond, who several years later had President Nixon appoint McCullough a director of the Import and Export Bank.

On the Monday after the nomination of Brown, while I was en route from Spartanburg to Conway to begin a term of court, I stopped by the governor's office to visit with McCullough. Brown's nomination by the Executive Committee was on everybody's mind, and it was the subject of conversation that day. I will never forget while I was sitting there talking to McCullough, he phoned President Donald Russell of the University of South Carolina, probably at Byrnes' suggestion, and urged Russell to mount a write-in campaign for the United States Senate. Congressman Bryan Dorn toyed with the idea but decided against it. At that time Thurmond had not publicly indicated an interest in running. Russell would not buy the idea. He seemed to be of the view that the furor which had been engendered would soon cool off and the Democrats would fall in line and vote for the man the Executive Committee had selected. Many think that if Russell had announced, Thurmond would not have run and Russell would have been elected, and history would have been different. Actually, I have always been of the view that quite a few people could have beat Brown that fall in a write-in campaign, but only Thurmond was willing to take the chance. I doubt that anyone else could have beat Brown as badly as Thurmond did, however. His majority was more than 60,000 votes.

Edgar Brown was for years a power in the Senate and the State of South Carolina. He was serving at the time of the election as Chairman of the Finance Committee of the Senate and was President Pro Tempore. A little history on that: In 1942, Senator R.M. Jefferies of Colleton County had been chairman of the Finance Committee and President Pro Tempore of the Senate. Lieutenant Governor Emile Harley was made governor when Maybank moved to the United States Senate, but Harley died after serving as governor for only a few months. This meant that Jefferies, as President Pro Tempore of the Senate, would become governor and would serve until a regular election (in November 1942) was held, at which time there would be a new governor. After serving as governor, Jefferies went back to the State Senate, but Brown had moved in and taken over; he was the senior Senator and Jefferies became the junior Senator.

Brown had been head of what is oftentimes referred to as the Barnwell Ring. The Barnwell Ring in the 1930s and early 1940s was composed of Senator Brown, Harley, Speaker Solomon Blatt and Winchester Smith. Smith and Blatt were members of the House, but in 1940 reapportionment took one House member away from Barnwell County and Smith did not run—which left the Ring, after Harley's death, composed of Edgar Brown and Solomon Blatt. Smith became a member of the Public Service Commission.

It will be recalled that Thurmond ran for Governor in 1946, campaigning against the Barnwell Ring. Brown was quite an issue in himself, and many people throughout South Carolina simply did not want him to be the United States Senator, so whoever was against him would have the benefit of their support.

It was a fact of life that if some two or three candidates ran against Brown in the general election of 1954, Brown would win. A plurality is all that is needed to win in a general election, and if the anti-Brown vote split up, then the old-line Democratic Party candidate would have gained a plurality. Fortunately for Thurmond, no other candidate announced and, accordingly, the two candidates came head-on down to the wire in November.

Over the years, Brown had developed a reputation for being able to get things done. He was a good financier, and I think the fiscal stability of the state had been largely attributable to the sound financial policies which he advocated as Chairman of the Finance Committee. Be that as it may, there were lots of people in South Carolina who looked upon Brown as a sort of shrewd operator and, although he could have been elected to any office in his area of the state, in the Pee Dee and the Piedmont sections there was less than full confidence in Brown.

Resentment throughout the state continued to rise. The voters simply did not like the idea of thirty-one members of the Executive Committee naming a senator to represent South Carolina for the next six years. Strom Thurmond always kept his ear to the ground and could (and still can and does at this time) evaluate public sentiment skillfully. Within a few days after Maybank's death, he announced that he would be a candidate for the United States Senate in a write-in campaign, with less than two months to get ready. Among the things his friends had to do was educate the people relative to a write-in candidacy. Most of us had never heard of such a thing and were certainly unfamiliar with the procedures for voting for a write-in candidate.

As a part of Thurmond's campaign, he pledged that if he were elected he would at the end of two years (actually it was only about eighteen months) resign from the Senate and leave the seat vacant so that the people would have a full, free choice of who would represent them in the United States Senate for the remaining four years of the six-year term. Senator Brown never made such an offer. We will never know just what part that played in the election, but I am sure that it got Thurmond a great many votes.

Sometimes an issue dies out. People talk it to death and forget, but this matter just would not die. The editors kept churning the facts over and over, and the people talked about it and the irritation seemed to escalate. Thurmond had a world of energy and campaigned vigorously throughout the state. He had friends who bought advertisements extolling his virtues and explaining how to vote for a write-in candidate. I recall that Thurmond's campaign headquarters gave away tens of thousands of short pencils. They were about as long as the pencils one gets at a golf course for marking a score card, and on those pencils was written "Write In Strom Thurmond for U.S. Senate." Today those pencils are quite a keepsake of the election.

One of the things that helped Thurmond considerably was the support of Governor James F. Byrnes. Byrnes had retired to South Carolina soon after serving as Secretary of State under the Truman administration. He had established his home in Spartanburg and run for governor in the summer of 1950; he was a popular Governor and a respected one. Although his term as governor was coming to an end, Byrnes was still a politically powerful person in South Carolina. Before Thurmond got into the race, he felt that he would have the support of Governor Byrnes if Russell did not run.

Actually, Byrnes and Brown had been chummy for some forty or fifty years. Byrnes had been in Senator Brown's wedding forty-five years earlier. But the two had come to a parting of political ways in 1952. Although Brown had left the national party and voted with the South Carolina Democratic Party for the States' Right candidates in 1948, he returned to the old-line Democratic Party in 1952 and supported Adlai Stevenson of Illinois. On the other hand, Byrnes, who was in the middle of his gubernatorial term, supported Republican Dwight Eisenhower. Thurmond also supported Eisenhower, his former Commander-in-Chief in Europe. And so the old bondage between Byrnes and Brown just was not what it had been, and this made it more feasible for Byrnes to oppose the Brown candidacy and vote for Thurmond.

Byrnes did not endorse Thurmond at first. He had been opposed to the way the Committee had handled the nomination, as a matter of principle. He believed a man to represent the State of South Carolina for a period of six years in Washington ought to have the backing of the people and ought not to be selected by a small group, such as a majority of the Executive Committee. It was near the end of the campaign when Governor Byrnes issued a statement which was beneficial to Thurmond. He said, and I quote:

> It took courage for Thurmond to lead this fight for the people. He is a man of courage. When World War II started, he was a circuit Judge in this State. As a Judge, he was exempt from military service. But with the announcement of our entering the war, Strom Thurmond resigned and volunteered. He asked for combat service. He got it. In that combat service he served his country so well that our government and the government of France decorated him for heroism on the field of battle.
>
> As Governor, on many occasions I have had to read the files as to transactions during Strom Thurmond's term of office. From the record of this office I know that as Governor he was honest, forthright and capable.
>
> Strom Thurmond is clean in his personal life, as well as in his public life.
>
> Not one of us is perfect. Certainly Strom Thurmond made mistakes. But there never has been even the breath of scandal as to his service either in the State Senate, on the bench or in the Office of Governor. There has never been the slightest suspicion of Strom Thurmond ever using public office for private gain.
>
> I followed his leadership in this fight with full realization of the difficulties. But in all our history South Carolinians have not let difficulties deter them from doing what they believed to be right.

In winning the election, Strom Thurmond made history.

The election of other candidates in November 1954 made little news. Ernest F. Hollings was nominated over Clator Arrants for lieutenant governor, and George Bell Timmerman Jr. defeated Lester L. Bates for governor. Hollings, at thirty-two, was one of the youngest to hold that office. Timmerman, at forty-two, was the first lieutenant governor to be elected governor in 169 years.

44

CAMPAIGN OF 1956

In 1956 Senator Strom Thurmond carried out the pledge he had made during his write-in candidacy in 1954 and resigned from the Senate. He then promptly announced his candidacy for re-election in the Democratic primary.

Having been elected by such an overwhelming vote just two years previously, Thurmond was a strong contender for the office, and no one announced against him. Accordingly, he was assured of serving the rest of the term. He was, however, out of office from April 1956 until the general election, during which time Thomas A. Wofford of Greenville served by appointment of Governor George Bell Timmerman Jr.

It will be recalled that Thurmond and Senator Olin D. Johnston had clashed in a vigorous campaign six years previously. As it developed, Senator Johnston was up for re-election in the primary of 1956 also. By this time the two had served in the Senate together for a total of two years, and it is my observation that senators working together usually come to be rather congenial or at least tolerant of each other. Johnston had at that time been in the Senate for twelve years and had kept his political fences mended. He too was unopposed in the primary.

It was an unusual quirk of fate that caused the people of South Carolina to be able to choose both of their United States Senators at one election. The terms are staggered so that a third of the Senate is elected every two years, and no state normally elects both of its senators at one time.

South Carolina came to have, after the 1956 election, two of its strongest political forces serving in the nation's capitol simultaneously. Johnston continued to serve until the time of his death in 1965, and Thurmond, as we write in 1989, continues to serve.

In 1956 there were no other statewide races. It was a good year for incumbents. Dwight Eisenhower was being re-elected as president, along with Vice President Richard M. Nixon. They defeated Adlai Stevenson and Estes Kefauver, the Democratic presidential and vice presidential nominees respectively.

173

Throughout South Carolina, those seeking re-election fared rather well. In Spartanburg, incumbents Senator Charles C. Moore, Sheriff B.B. Brockman, Supervisor J.B. Brockman and Clerk of Court E.W. Miller were re-elected.

In South Carolina's Fifth Congressional District, Robert W. Hemphill, a forty-one year old prosecuting attorney, defeated Tom R. Gettys, a Rock Hill lawyer. Hemphill was continuing a distinguished public service career commenced a decade before, when he served in the state House of Representatives before moving to the office of Solicitor of the Sixth Judicial Circuit. In Congress he would continue to serve until appointed by President Lyndon Johnson as a Federal District Court Judge in 1964, in which office he served until taking senior status, which is the equivalent of retirement.

President Eisenhower had little trouble being re-elected. He was the first Republican President to serve since Herbert Hoover left office in 1932. While Eisenhower was not a politician, he had a knack for making people want to vote for him. They just seemed to have confidence in him. Fortunately for him, business conditions were good. A big economic letdown was expected at the end of the war; however, it did not come according to expectations, and people were very well content to continue his administration because they were generally prospering.

In 1956 Ernest F. "Fritz" Hollings was serving as lieutenant governor and was definitely planning to enter the governor's race two years later. Donald Russell was making a distinguished record for himself as president of the University of South Carolina, and friends were urging him to seek the gubernatorial office too.

By 1956 people had begun paying sales taxes brought into being during the administration of Governor James F. Byrnes. The passage of that legislation was an issue in some areas, but most people were acclimated to the proposition that the state needed more money to carry on its functions, and especially to improve its schools. Few senators and house members were defeated by reason of helping to bring about this additional tax.

In 1956 D. Gordon Baker resigned as Chief Justice of the Supreme Court. Taylor H. Stukes was made Chief Justice to succeed him, and Joseph R. Moss of York moved from the circuit trial bench to Associate Justice of the Supreme Court, where he served as Associate Justice and later as Chief Justice until his retirement in 1975.

Two years prior to the campaign in 1956, the Supreme Court of the United States had issued its opinion in the *Brown v. Board of Education* case, outlawing segregation in public schools. People in the South were still irritated about the decision, and the issue was discussed in many campaigns. In several Southern states, there was considerable resistance on the part of the populace as well as on the part of public officials. Some violence was encountered.

In South Carolina, I cannot say that people received the Supreme Court ruling gleefully, but I think it a fair appraisal to say that it was received in South Carolina with more grace than in some nearby states. Along about that time, Harvey Gantt became the first black student admitted to Clemson College. Violence was expected but none occurred. It is my recollection that Gantt was the first black student admitted to any of the many all-white colleges in South Carolina. Before that time, black students seeking a college education attended Allen University or Benedict College in Columbia, State College or Claflin University in Orangeburg, Voorhees at Denmark or Morris at Sumter. In 1956 only a few blacks were voting, but every two years more of them voted than in the previous election. Soon their votes would become the balance of power in certain areas.

The results of the 1956 presidential election spoke a loud message throughout South Carolina. The people were in effect saying, "We are no longer wed to the Democratic party." While the Stevenson-Kefauver ticket won, more South Carolinians were against the ticket than were for it. A plurality prevails. Three sets of electors appeared on the November ballot: the Democratic electors, the Republican electors and the Independent electors (actually committed to Senator Harry Byrd of Virginia). The Democratic electors received 136,000 votes, the Republican electors 75,000 votes and the Independent electors 88,000 votes. Accordingly, approximately 27,000 more votes were cast against the Democratic nominees than had been cast for them.

More than fifty percent of the Democratic voters had left the party in 1948; nearly half of the Democratic voters had left the party in 1952; far more than half of the Democratic voters had left the party in 1954 when they wrote in "Strom Thurmond."

And now, in 1956, far more than half the Democratic voters had abandoned the party again. People were coming to openly admit more and more that they were Republicans. The time would soon come—in 1964, 1968, 1972, 1980 and 1984—when the Republican electors for President would receive a majority of the votes in South Carolina.

The state remained loyal to the John F. Kennedy ticket in 1960 and to the Jimmy Carter ticket in 1976. Simultaneously, in local elections the inclination was to support the Democratic nominees.

45

CAMPAIGN OF 1958

The race for governor in 1958 was quite a spirited one. Three well-known, highly respected candidates entered the race: Donald Russell of Spartanburg, who had previously been associated with Sam Nicholls, James F. Byrnes and Cecil Wyche in the practice of law; Ernest F. Hollings, who had served as Speaker Pro Tempore and lieutenant governor of the state; and William C. Johnston, who was a brother to United States Senator Olin D. Johnston.

Russell had, as of that time, already made for himself a distinguished career in several undertakings. In addition to enjoying a successful practice of the law in a firm of which James F. Byrnes was formerly a partner, he had served in several important offices in Washington and had been president of the University of South Carolina for several years.

Ernest Hollings came from Charleston, and it seems that Charleston people know a little bit more about politics than people who come from other areas of the state. He had a likable personality and had served well in the House of Representatives and as presiding officer of the state Senate.

William Johnston, in addition to having the political advantage of being brother to a United States Senator, had several terms as mayor of the city of Anderson.

Hollings received forty-one percent of the votes at the first balloting, while Russell was a close runner-up. Johnston fared rather poorly, and the run-off was between Hollings and Russell.

As the presiding officer of the Senate, Hollings had become closely allied with not only Edgar A. Brown, the senior state Senator, but also with Solomon Blatt, who for years had been Speaker of the House. These two at the time composed what came to be referred to as the "Barnwell Ring," which generally was not popular throughout the state. Russell attempted in the second race to tie the "Barnwell Ring" around Hollings' neck. He endeavored to make the "Barnwell Ring" an issue as Strom Thurmond did when he was elected governor in 1946. In the second voting Hollings was victorious, and with his election there came into being a strong political influence which was to last for many years. Russell and Hollings were to compete for a seat in the United States Senate eight years later.

Burnett R. Maybank Jr., an attorney, left his hometown of Charleston and moved to Greenville to pursue the practice of law there. He ran for the Legislature and was elected again and again. It seemed to be his thinking that his image and that of his father, who had served as mayor of Charleston and as governor of the state and as U.S. Senator, would stand him in well in the Low Country, and that simultaneously he would cultivate the Up Country from a Greenville base. In seeking the office of lieutenant governor in 1958, Maybank was obviously dreaming of running for governor four years later. In that race against him were Albert Watson, a member of the House from Richland County; and Hugo Sims, who had also experienced legislative service. Maybank had the advantage of the image that his father had created prior to his death in 1954 and was successful in defeating both his opponents in the first race.

Four years later Russell and Maybank were to contest for the office of governor. After the campaign of 1958 Russell returned to the practice of law in Spartanburg. Maybank returned to the practice of law in Greenville and presided over the Senate as lieutenant governor during the next four sessions.

It has been my observation over the years that people in small counties, of which there are about thirty-five in South Carolina, take their politics more seriously than do the people who live in the more urban areas. Candidates in small counties seem to be more eager to get elected and more disturbed upon defeat. They also are oftentimes disturbed when their enemies get elected.

On Tuesday night, June 11, 1958, in Bennettsville, my friend state Senator Paul A. Wallace was declared renominated in the Democratic primary. As circuit judge I had presided over the circuit courts at Bennettsville on at least one previous occasion. While there I came to know very pleasantly the clerk of court, who was Henry A. Rogers. In and about the courthouse people liked to bend the ear of the visiting presiding judge, and as a circuit judge I would oftentimes learn of the political conflicts in the county.

I came to know that the state senator and the clerk of court were at political odds. At that time the local senator controlled the purse strings of the whole county. Monies were allocated through the county supply bill which had to be passed by the General Assembly, and the local senator always controlled the appropriations.

On the night of his renomination, Senator Wallace was visiting with friends in the office of the sheriff. He had just defeated lawyer William A. Rogers for the senatorial office, winning by approximately fifty votes. The clerk of court walked into the sheriff's office and started shooting. Wallace was struck five times. He was rushed to a local hospital but died in the emergency room. It is to the credit of people everywhere that no one now seems to take their politics so seriously.

Rogers was charged with murder and committed to the state hospital for examination. While there he committed suicide by hanging himself with a belt. Thus the feud ended. My friend of many years William C. Goldberg was elected to succeed Senator Wallace.

Along about that time (the year I cannot recall) my law schoolmate William F. Stevenson was serving as judge of a court of limited jurisdiction in the same town where Wallace was shot. He was presiding over a hearing wherein the custody of a child was involved. The judge made the mistake of orally ordering a change of custody in open court by taking the child from the father and giving it to the mother. In a fit of rage, the father pulled a concealed weapon from his clothing and shot the judge dead; he then turned to the mother (his wife) and wounded her. The incident has prompted me on many occasions, when helping to orient family court judges who deal with domestic problems, to advise them not to make rulings in open court which might be expected to engender violence.

In 1958 T.C. Callison was retiring as Attorney General of South Carolina. In his office was a comparatively young assistant named Dan McLeod. McLeod was a relative of a former governor of the state and an excellent lawyer. He entered the primary to succeed his former boss and was elected. The name of McLeod has always been a prestigious one in South Carolina. Generally they have a Methodist background, and many of the sons have attended Wofford College in Spartanburg. Lawyers who bear the name are engaged in the practice in quite a few towns throughout South Carolina. Dan McLeod defeated Columbia attorney John A. Mason, who had served as legal assistant under Governor George Bell Timmerman Jr.

McLeod began a highly distinguished career in public service. His tenure extended over a period of twenty-four years until his voluntary retirement. Dan McLeod was one of the most highly respected public officials with whom I have been associated. He is due much credit for having provided state officials with sound advice during almost a quarter of a century when the state was adjusting to integration at the schoolhouses and at the voting precincts. Many friends urged the Attorney General to seek the office of governor, and I always felt he would probably have been elected; but he did not choose to run.

Good citizens deplore the fact that campaigning for public office has come to be so expensive. It has been said that one must be rich or beholden unto other people in order to wage a successful campaign. This is particularly true since campaigning from the stumps in various counties is no longer the way to seek votes. One must now reach the people by way of radio, television and through newspaper advertising—none of which is for poor people.

It is unfortunate that candidates elected and candidates defeated are normally saddled with debts that must be paid long after the voting is over. The day should never come when only the rich can get elected. The day should never come when elected officials owe allegiance to wealthy people who advance money to the candidate.

It would appear that the cost of campaigning is constantly escalating. The amounts spent by the three candidates for governor in 1958 contrast tremendously with the amounts spent by the various candidates for high office in 1986. On June 11, 1958 (the day after the first primary), *The Greenville News* reported that the three candidates for governor had spent a total of $35,525.22. It further recited that the three candidates for lieutenant governor spent a total of $20,000. It would not be unusual for candidates for these offices to spend such an amount in more modern times in any one of the larger urban counties.

The cost of campaigning has suffered the pangs of inflation just as the cost of all commodities has escalated. It prompted one of my friends to comment: "Inflation is so bad that you can no longer buy an honest election."

46

CAMPAIGN OF 1960

In 1960 South Carolina was still basically a one-party state. This was true in spite of the fact that there had been considerable erosion within the Democratic party in 1948, 1952, 1954 and 1956.

People had shown a willingness to leave the Democratic party in three presidential elections and in the write-in election of Strom Thurmond in 1954, all of which have been discussed heretofore. There had been, as of this time, little inclination, if any, to leave the Democratic party so far as local and statewide elections were concerned.

The term of junior Senator Strom Thurmond was coming to an end, and he was seeking his second term in the United States Senate. People envisioned that the strong showing he had made in 1954 and 1956 would entitle him to run unopposed for re-election, but R. Beverly Herbert, a Columbia attorney, at the last moment announced that he would challenge Thurmond for the office. Herbert had been an unsuccessful candidate for governor in 1930 and had served two terms in the House of Representatives some thirty years previously.

The state's voters were obviously satisfied with Thurmond's service and voted for him in the Democratic primary, giving to him 273,000 votes to Herbert's 32,000. Thurmond was victorious in every county in the state, receiving a total of almost ninety percent of the votes cast.

The great interest in the election of 1960 was in the contest for President of the United States. The Democrats had been in control of the White House from 1932 to 1952; then Eisenhower, a war hero, had captured the election for the Republicans in 1952 and 1956. His vice president was Richard M. Nixon of California, who was ambitious to win the election and retain the office of President for the Republicans.

The Republican National Convention selected Nixon and Senator Henry Cabot Lodge as their candidates.

John F. Kennedy had an admirable World War II record, had served in Congress from Massachusetts and was more recently serving as senator from that state. He was an attractive young fellow in his early forties, had an excellent personality and a knack for making people like him, especially voters. In 1956 Kennedy had, at the national convention, sought to be the vice presidential running mate of Adlai Stevenson.

Kennedy was the son of Joseph Kennedy, who was well known in political circles for his close connection with and his support, monetarily and otherwise, of President Franklin Delano Roosevelt. The elder Kennedy had served as Ambassador to Great Britain. The Kennedy family was fabulously wealthy and politically ambitious. They were among the few people who need not be concerned with monetary matters and could, and did, devote full time to politics. Estes Kefauver was the Senator from Tennessee. Traditionally a national party convention will give much consideration to the choice of the presidential nominee for his running mate. Kefauver prevailed over Kennedy, and the ticket for 1956 was Governor Adlai Stevenson of Illinois for president and Senator Estes Kefauver of Tennessee for vice president.

Senator Kennedy promptly began working at the chore of obtaining the Democratic nomination for President in 1960. There was one issue which greatly concerned the Democratic party: Kennedy was a Catholic, and before this time Catholicism was, if not a detriment, certainly not an asset in a national election. Al Smith had been the Democratic nominee in 1928, and the Democrats well remembered that his Catholicism had been a substantial issue in the campaign, especially in the Southland. Democrats were afraid that Kennedy's religion would keep him from being elected President in the fall of 1960.

Senator Lyndon Johnson of Texas had acquired much seniority. He was a Southerner and, generally speaking, delegates to the national convention from the South preferred him as the presidential candidate. Johnson sought the presidential nomination, denying all along that he would ever consent to run for vice president on Kennedy's ticket or anyone else's ticket. This was, of course, the only position he could take, because one cannot seek a higher office while simultaneously smiling upon the possibility of procuring a lesser office. When Kennedy succeeded in obtaining the nomination, there arose the important question: What running mate can help him carry the South? The obvious answer was Lyndon Johnson. Johnson promptly accepted Kennedy's invitation to join the campaign.

It is worthy of note that in actuality the Johnsons and the Kennedys were not great admirers of each other. Their working together both before 1960 and after was largely a marriage of convenience. They put up with each other because it was advantageous to all.

The center of political interest in 1960 was in the general election scheduled for November. People in South Carolina generally were not too happy with either the Republican nominees or the Democratic nominees. While they had been satisfied with Eisenhower's eight-year administration, they did not have the same admiration for his vice president (Nixon). Kennedy was considered rather liberal for the conservative Southern voter. In addition, there were many South Carolinians who were not yet ready to vote for a Catholic.

The Democrats were well aware of the fact that the Republicans had tasted blood in 1952 and especially in 1956, and if South Carolina was to be carried by the Democratic electors, unity was essential. It was decided that there should be no alternative and that the contest should be between the straight old-line Democratic party and the newly inspired straight-line Republican party.

The Democrats set up their own campaign headquarters in Columbia with Attorney Frank K. Sloan as campaign chairman.

The campaign developed into a genuine hard-fought contest. Prior to this time, presidential candidates had not devoted a great deal of time to procuring votes in South Carolina. Kennedy, Nixon and Johnson all came to the state in pursuit of votes.

James F. Byrnes added his prestige to the Republican effort by endorsing the Nixon-Lodge ticket. He had left the Democratic party in favor of Eisenhower in both 1952 and 1956. It was his contention that people should vote for the man and not for the label.

I do not think there is any doubt but that Kennedy would have lost except for having chosen Lyndon Johnson of Texas to be his running mate. There are years in which the running mate to a presidential candidate is unimportant, as in 1944, when Truman was designated to run with President Roosevelt. Roosevelt would have won regardless. But in 1960 a vice presidential candidate palatable to the Southland was essential to a Democratic victory.

Kennedy started a form of campaigning which I have always thought was bad. He challenged Richard Nixon to a public television debate. Having been challenged, Nixon felt compelled to accept. The people delighted in this approach; like enjoying a cockfight. They like confict. I think this method of reaching the voters is bad, because the questioners ask the debaters many questions which candidates ought not to answer without proper time for deliberation. Every candidate feels compelled to answer every question or be looked upon as ignorant. I do not recall hearing any candidate in a debate answer by saying: "I simply don't know." Once a candidate has "popped off" under the bright television lights, he feels compelled as a matter of honor to follow through and act in the future in keeping with the answers he has given under pressure. Were it within my power, I would abolish the debates as a method of reaching the voting public.

Once Kennedy was elected he began what I think is another bad habit. He began holding press conferences and subjected himself to questions by members of the media—some friendly and some unfriendly. Oftentimes a reporter likes nothing better than to embarrass the President, and the President feels compelled to respond. In actuality, a President isn't expected to know everything, and many of the questions which he answers in debate or at a press conference are questions that need considerable cogitation.

Many persons were of the view that Kennedy won the debates and his marginal victory could be attributed to the fact that he made a better appearance on the TV programs than did his adversary.

When the votes were counted in November, the South Carolina Democratic electors received 198,000 votes, while the Republican electors received 188,000 votes.

The Republicans had not won, but the taste of near-victory was sweet. The time had come when a tremendous portion, if not a majority, of South Carolina voters had abandoned the Democratic party long enough to cast at least one Republican vote. Having left the party, some of them again and again, it would be more palatable thereafter to openly declare allegiance to the Republican party and be active in its undertakings. Commenting in a Charleston newspaper in 1961, Senator Edgar A. Brown, who had for many years been labeled "Mr. Democrat," made the following statement:

> The future of good politics in South Carolina depends upon the establishment of Republican and Democratic parties along clear-cut lines. The people should line up with the party of their choice, and quit pussyfooting around between the two. A man ought to be either a Republican or Democrat. He cannot be both, like some politicians in this state are trying to do [obviously referring to Byrnes].

South Carolina could no longer be considered "in the bag." A new day in politics had arrived. One year later, the first Republican to serve in the General Assembly of South Carolina since 1901 would be elected. He was Charles Boineau of Columbia. Four years earlier a political unknown, L.P. Crawford of Clemson, had garnered 49,000 votes as a Republican in an effort to unseat the veteran Democratic United States Senator Olin D. Johnston. Four years later the state would choose Republican electors when Republican Senator Barry Goldwater and his running mate were contesting for the presidency and the vice presidency.

John F. Kennedy had proved that a Catholic can be elected President of the United States. He had proved that a Catholic can carry an election in South Carolina. It is in the scheme of things that people of all religions are coming to be more tolerant of persons of different faiths.

In 1974 Charles D. "Pug" Ravenel returned from New York to his native state of South Carolina and sought the Democratic nomination for governor. He prevailed at the polls but was declared ineligible to serve under the Constitution of South Carolina. The fact that he was a Catholic never came to my attention until a hearing relative to his eligibility was held in the Supreme Court of South Carolina some time after the primary election was over. This was one more evidence of the fact that one's religious leanings are not as important in politics now as in former years.

Kennedy proved to be a popular President throughout the United States. People in the South admired him and supported him in most of his programs, but many continued to feel that his leanings were too liberal. I have no doubt but that he could have been elected for an additional term in the fall of 1964 and would have been re-elected except for his assassination by Lee Harvey Oswald in Texas in the fall of 1963. After Kennedy's death, Lyndon Johnson became President and almost immediately became perhaps more liberal than Kennedy, getting ready to try to succeed himself in the 1964 election. Although Johnson had been the choice of the South in 1960, South Carolina did not support his candidacy in 1964.

47

CAMPAIGN OF 1962

By 1962, E.F. "Fritz" Hollings had served in the South Carolina House of Representatives, in the office of lieutenant governor and in the office of governor. He undertook to unseat United States Senator Olin D. Johnston, who had been a senator since 1944. It has never been easy for an outgoing governor to uproot a sitting United States Senator. Blease tried in 1914; Johnston tried in 1938; and Thurmond tried in 1950. All were unsuccessful. Hollings failed also. Johnston defeated him by a vote of 216,000 to 110,000. Johnston carried every county in the state except Calhoun, where he lost by 34 votes.

By this time the Democratic nomination was no longer the equivalent of election. After Johnston's victory in the primary, he was to encounter Republican W.D. Workman Jr., a popular and successful newspaperman from Columbia, in the general election. Workman received more votes on the Republican ticket than had outgoing Governor Hollings on the Democratic ticket. In the November general election the vote was Johnston 178,000 and Workman 133,000. It was the second time that Johnston had a Republican opponent, but in 1956 the opposition was not much of a challenge. L.P. Crawford, a Republican from Clemson, received a total of only 49,000 votes. Accordingly, Johnston was on the way back to Washington to continue his senatorial service with his colleague Strom Thurmand, who would switch to the Republican party two years later.

During Governor Hollings' administration from 1959 to 1963, Burnett R. Maybank Jr. had served as lieutenant governor. It had been well known for some time that he had an ambition to leave that office and become the state's chief executive. Maybank's father had served as governor from 1939 to 1941 and as United States Senator from 1941 to 1954. In the primary, Maybank's opponents included Donald Russell, who had distinguished himself as an attorney and as president of the University of South Carolina. He, too, would seek the office. Also announcing were A.W. "Red" Bethea, Dero Cook and Milton Dukes. Russell defeated all of them in the first Democratic primary voting. He received 199,000 votes to

Maybank's 103,000, Bethea's 17,000, Cook's 16,000 and Dukes' 2,000. Russell was not opposed in the general election. He had been associated with James F. Byrnes for many years and was highly respected for his intellect and credibility. He served as governor until the death of Senator Johnston, at which time he was appointed to the United States Senate.

While Johnston was being re-elected to the Senate and Russell was being sent to the office of governor, a spirited race developed for the office of lieutenant governor. Robert E. McNair had come from Berkeley County by way of Allendale and had served in the state House of Representatives as chairman of the Judiciary Committee. He announced for the office of lieutenant governor. Contending also for the Democratic nomination was Senator Marshall Parker of Oconee County who was serving his second term as a senator. Both were strong candidates, but McNair won out, beginning a statewide career that would carry him to the governor's office and later to a successful career at the practice of law with offices in Columbia, Hilton Head and Washington, D.C. McNair received 191,000 votes to Parker's 138,000. Later Parker would turn Republican and seek higher office as such.

That year in Charleston Fred Worsham was among the very few Republicans who sought a seat in the state House of Representatives. The previous year, Republican Charles Boineau of Columbia had become the first Republican to serve in the General Assembly of South Carolina in 60 years when he won an unexpired term. Worsham was the first Republican candidate for the House of Representatives to win a full term in the general election.

The time had come when more and more people took pride in advertising the fact that they were affiliated with the Republican party. Democrats were not a vanishing breed, but "yellow-dog Democrats" were.

48

CAMPAIGN OF 1964

So far as South Carolina state politics are concerned, 1964 is referred to as an "off year." It was not the year to elect a governor, a lieutenant governor or a member of the United States Senate. All Congressmen were running, and there were bitter contests of interest in the solicitorial races and in the many local county races.

The main center of interest that year was in the race for President of the United States. In 1960 Democrats John F. Kennedy of Massachusetts and Lyndon B. Johnson of Texas had defeated Republican Richard M. Nixon of California and his vice-presidential running mate by a comparatively narrow margin. Kennedy had been assassinated in November 1963, leaving the presidency to Johnson. Accordingly, in 1964 Johnson was the incumbent and chose for his running mate Senator Hubert Humphrey.

Barry Goldwater Jr., a conservative United States Senator from Arizona, was the choice of the Republican National Convention for President, and he chose for his running mate Congressman Bill Miller.

Before Johnson became President, his views on civil rights had not been greatly different from those of other Southern politicians. I think it would be a safe appraisal to say that he had, over the years, acquiesced reluctantly in the integration movements. Immediately upon being sworn in as President, he began changing his views in order to cultivate the votes of the minority groups. This was less than completely acceptable to a multitude of South Carolina voters. In addition, South Carolina voters were irritated with Johnson's choice of Hubert Humphrey as a running mate. Humphrey was one of the most outspoken advocates of integration and had oftentimes used the South as a whipping boy to get re-elected to the U.S. Senate in Minnesota and to promote civil rights legislation.

In years gone by, candidates for President had not devoted a great deal of time to cultivating Southern voters. The view was taken that the South was the "solid South" and that the Southern states would vote Democrat regardless of who the candidates were and regardless of what the platform said. This had been changing, beginning with Harry Truman's election in 1948 and continuing through Dwight Eisenhower's elections in 1952 and 1956.

In quest of votes, Lyndon Johnson came to South Carolina and spoke to a tremendous crowd on the steps of the State House prior to the November election. South Carolina voters were still reluctant to vote a Republican ticket and that was especially true in all elections other than for national offices. Our state broke away from the Democratic Party and supported Senator Goldwater and Bill Miller. The South was no longer the "solid South."

This was one more move in the direction of a genuine two-party system in South Carolina. The state was destined to support Republican Presidents in 1968, 1972, 1980, 1984 and 1988. It deviated in 1976 to vote for Democrat Jimmy Carter of our neighboring state of Georgia, and for Walter Mondale, his running mate.

I was a circuit court judge in 1964 and attended the Democratic national convention under circumstances which I describe in another chapter entitled "The Democratic Party." At that time, it was tolerated for members of the judiciary to participate a little bit in politics. This was before the day of the Unified Court System and before the inauguration of the Judicial Code of Ethics. Today, if a judge should take a similar part in a political activity, he would be promptly hauled before the Judicial Standards Commission, and I think this is as it should be.

Governor Donald S. Russell was chairman of the S.C. Delegation which went to Atlantic City for the Democratic National Convention. By this time black voters had become an important part of the election process in South Carolina. It was along about that time that all candidates wanted the support of blacks, but most candidates did not want the support of these voters publicized. All the 1964 delegates to the convention in Atlantic City were white. When two vacancies occurred, J. Arthur Brown of Charleston, President of the South Carolina branch of the National Association for the Advancement of Colored People, sought to have the vacancies filled by black delegates, but the request was not honored. That was probably the last year that South Carolina sent an all-white delegation to the Democratic National Convention.

It will be recalled that vacancies developing in the delegation after the initial state convention were filled by the remaining delegates. It was through this process that I came to serve, because Strom Thurmond, who had been elected as a delegate, was unable to attend. Soon thereafter Strom Thurmond would leave the Democratic Party and announce that he was joining the Republicans. He has since that time run and been re-elected as a Republican.

The fact that the Republican party was becoming more acceptable to South Carolina voters was emphasized soon after the 1964 election, when Congressman Albert Watson, who represented the Second Congressional District composed of counties in the middle section of South Carolina, did something unprecedented.

Watson had served in the South Carolina House of Representatives from 1955 to 1958 and from 1960 to 1962. In the summer of 1962 he won the congressional seat as a Democrat. In 1958 he sought to be lieutenant governor but was defeated. He was a skillful vote getter and went to Washington as part of the Democratic caucus. After his re-election in the fall of 1964 (in February of 1965), he switched parties and declared himself a Republican, simultaneously resigning the seat he had acquired three months previously as a Democrat and announcing that he would ask the people to send him back to Washington as a Republican. It took a lot of courage for one to leave the comforts of a congressional seat recently won and subject himself to possible defeat at the hands of a Democratic opponent. Attorney Preston Callison of Lexington and John Bolt Culbertson of Greenville, along with Oscar Fuller, announced for the Democratic nomination. Watson as a Republican bested them all and headed back to Washington to join the Republican caucus in the House of Representatives.

Perhaps Watson's courage was bolstered by the fact that in 1964 Senator Strom Thurmond had switched from the Democratic to the Republican party. Watson was the first Republican to be sent to Congress in South Carolina in many decades. He would be elected again and again until 1970. In that year he left Congress to run for governor of South Carolina as a Republican. His opponent was Lieutenant Governor John C. West. West was victorious and Watson never ran for public office again. Instead he accepted an assignment as a federally appointed administrative judge, in which capacity he served with distinction until his retirement.

The time had come when the conservative thinking of both Thurmond and Watson was more consistent with the ideals of the Republican party than with the ideals of the Democratic party. These two pioneered in converting South Carolina from a one-party to a two-party state. The time would soon come when the state would be represented by three Republican Congressmen and three Democratic Congressmen, by one Republican Senator and one Democratic Senator.

It is interesting to note that Watson in 1962 defeated Floyd Spence, both running as Democrats, for the Congressional seat. Spence was elected as a Republican to the State Senate in 1966 and in 1970 was elected as a Republican to succeed Watson. As we go to press in 1989, Spence continues to serve as Congressman for the Second District. Accordingly, Republicans have held that office for the last twenty-five years.

It is also interesting to note that John Bolt Culbertson sought the Democratic nomination to oppose Watson in a general election at a time when Culbertson lived in Greenville, some 100 miles away in another congressional district. Most people did not realize until that time that a member of Congress did not have to live in his district. As a practical matter, the voters take a dim view of one who lives in another district, and I do not recall in South Carolina any such candidate being successful.

49

CAMPAIGN OF 1966

In 1966 twenty-three Republicans were elected to membership in the General Assembly. Seventeen were House members and six were Senators; one Independent was also elected to the Senate.

While Democrats had been leaving the party in national elections, as shown by the presidential voting in 1948, 1952, 1956, 1960 and 1964, South Carolinians did not begin speaking out loud and clear at the state level until the elections of 1966. It will be recalled that in 1961 Charles Boineau was the first Republican elected to the House since 1901, and in 1962 Fred Worsham became the second. Worsham was re-elected in 1964.

Support of the Republican nominees for president had been substantial in 1952, 1956 and 1960, but it was not until 1964 that a Republican presidential candidate, Barry Goldwater, carried the state. (Nationally the Democrats prevailed.) The South was not generally pleased with the new views of its favorite son, Lyndon Baines Johnson of Texas, or with his running mate, Hubert Humphrey.

Other political activities paved the way for a strong Republican showing in 1966, including Strom Thurmond's write-in candidacy in 1954 and his switch to the Republican party in 1964. Thurmond's joining gave the Republican party the strong state leader they had needed for some time.

By 1966 a multitude of voters throughout the state had become accustomed to voting for Republicans, at least on the national level. This inspired many candidates to run as Republicans for seats in the General Assembly, and for a few county offices. Not all seats in the Assembly were contested by Republican candidates, but the overall result was that twenty-three moved into the two law-making bodies in Columbia, taking over offices traditionally held by Democrats.

For the election of 1966, the General Assembly had attempted statutorily to reapportion the Senate while increasing the number of senators from forty-six to fifty. In my home county of Spartanburg, Charles C. Moore, Horace C. Smith and Grady Ballard were elected among the fifty. Their tenure of office by that election would be short-lived. It was apparent that the success which the Republican party achieved in 1966 would inspire that party to field candidates in many statewide as well as county offices thereafter.

The strength of the Republican move in 1966 was reflected by the number of votes cast for the governor, the United States senator and the lieutenant governor.

In the November general election, Democrat Ernest F. Hollings received 223,000 votes for United States Senator. He was challenged by Republican Marshall Parker of Pickens, who had served in the General Assembly. Parker received 212,000 votes. Incumbent Senator Strom Thurmond, now a Republican, received 271,000 votes, while Democrat Bradley Morrah received 164,000 votes.

In the governor's race, Republican Joe Rogers challenged incumbent Robert McNair for the office of governor. McNair received 255,000 votes, while Rogers received 184,000 votes.

In the race for lieutenant governor, Democrat John C. West bested Republican Marshall Mays by a vote of 250,000 to 185,000.

If there remained any doubt as to whether South Carolina would or would not be a two-party state, that doubt was resolved by the voting in November 1966. Eight years later the people would elect the state's first Republican governor since Reconstruction days.

50

CAMPAIGN OF 1968

Inspired by the victories of 1966, many Republicans sought seats in the House of Representatives and the Senate of South Carolina two years later. All members of the Senate were up for re-election by reason of a ruling of the State Supreme Court referred to earlier. Whereas seventeen Republicans had been elected to the House in 1966, only five were elected in 1968. The number of Republicans in the Senate was reduced from six to three. Thomas Wofford, elected as an Independent in 1966, turned Republican in 1968.

Meanwhile, many of the senior members of the Senate and House were being returned without great difficulty. It was the last time Senator Edgar Brown of Barnwell, who had been in the Assembly nearly fifty years, would be elected. He retired in 1972. Veteran senators Rembert Dennis, John P. Mozingo III, Marion Gressette and Marshall Williams were elected again. These would continue for years to have great influence in Legislative matters in Columbia. Thomasine Mason, the only woman serving in the Senate, was defeated by James Morris, who would serve several years before taking a circuit court judgeship.

In the House of Representatives, Solomon Blatt of Barnwell and Rex Carter of Greenville were re-elected and resumed their important offices within the House, serving as Speaker and Speaker Pro Tempore respectively.

In the Fourth Congressional District where I resided, Robert Ashmore was retiring. The congressman from our district had been from Greenville since 1921. E.C. Burnett Jr. attempted to bring the office back to Spartanburg but was unsuccessful in the Democratic primary. James R. Mann bested Burnett, Leo Hill and Nick Theodore.

In the general election Charlie Bradshaw, a Republican of Spartanburg, contested with Mann, but Mann was victorious. Greenville was to retain the congressional seat until 1986, when Elizabeth J. Patterson, a Democrat from Spartanburg, beat out Republican Mayor W.D. Workman Jr. of Greenville after Republican Carroll Campbell left Congress and was elected governor.

At the national level, the Republicans were faring better in South Carolina. The Republican Nixon-Agnew electors received 254,000 votes; the Humphrey-Muskie Democratic ticket received 197,000 votes; and Wallace-Griffin ticket (by petition) received 215,000 votes. Since a plurality prevails in a general election, those electors chosen by the Republicans cast the South Carolina votes.

The victory of Senator Hollings in 1966 was for an unexpired term only and he was up for re-election in 1968. Republican Marshall Parker opposed him again and received 248,000 votes, but Hollings won, receiving 404,000 votes. There was no governor's race in 1968.

Back home in Spartanburg, House member James B. Stephen unseated Grady Ballard, who had been elected to the Senate in 1966. Paul Moore defeated Raymond Eubanks and Horace Smith ran unopposed. Veteran Senator Charles C. Moore retired. It was Paul Moore, along with Wade Weatherford Jr., who as attorneys brought the action in the federal court forcing the Senate to reapportion. Both Moore and Weatherford came to serve in the Senate, and both were later made circuit court judges. After 1966 no longer could each of the forty-six counties have its own senator. Under a 1968 reapportionment plan, the Senate again would be composed of forty-six senators. By the new plan a senator might represent a county or several counties. Single-member districts for senators were yet to come.

In 1968 neither the office of governor nor the office of lieutenant governor was open. Governor Robert E. McNair would not be eligible for re-election in 1970 and Lieutenant Governor John C. West was preparing to run.

51

CAMPAIGN OF 1970

By 1970 the Republican Party had made many inroads in many political areas. This was not a year for the election of a President or of United States Senators representing South Carolina, but it was a year to fill other important offices. Governor Robert E. McNair was bringing to an end his one and a half terms as governor. McNair was a popular governor and could probably have been elected again if the Constitution had permitted.

Lieutenant Governor John C. West was ending a four-year term. He had been preparing to seek the chief executive's office during all that time. The acceptability of the Republican party was emphasized by the fact that Congressman Watson was willing to leave a seat in Congress and gamble, as a Republican, on the possibility of election as governor in contest with a seasoned Democratic vote-getter, the lieutenant governor.

The contest was reasonably close, with West receiving 251,000 to Watson's 224,000 votes.

The office of lieutenant governor was also up for grabs. Earle Morris, who had served with distinction as state senator from Pickens County, was the Democratic nominee. Running against him was a newcomer to politics, Jim Henderson, a Republican of Greenville. The votes in the races for governor and for lieutenant governor were approximately the same, with Morris receiving 254,000 to 216,000 for Henderson.

The strength of the Republican party was further emphasized by the fact that four of South Carolina's six congressmen had Republican opponents in 1970. Only one Republican candidate, Floyd Spence, was elected—to succeed Republican Congressman Watson—but the time would soon come when South Carolina would have as many Republican congressmen as Democratic congressmen.

Attorney General Dan McLeod was chosen again to serve in the office he had held for some time. McLeod was a very popular vote-getter and many people were of the view that he could have been elected governor, had he chosen to run.

52

CAMPAIGN OF 1972

In 1968 the Richard Nixon/Spiro Agnew ticket for President prevailed in South Carolina with a plurality rather than a majority. To vote Republican, especially in a national election, was becoming more palatable. Nixon and Agnew had, up to 1972, served with reasonable satisfaction, and the public generally was fairly well pleased with that administration.

In 1972 the Democrats chose George McGovern and Thomas Eagleton, a Senator from Missouri. That ticket appeared at first to be reasonably strong. It developed after the convention that Eagleton, sometime previously, had received shock treatments. Although he had apparently recovered, people quickly took a dim view of electing someone with such a history to serve in an office one heartbeat away from the presidency. Overnight Eagleton became a burden to McGovern and to the Democratic party. He left the campaign and Sargent Shriver, who had married one of President John F. Kennedy's sisters, was substituted for Eagleton and became McGovern's running mate.

Today the news media is perhaps more investigative; the personal, political, financial and social activities of candidates for political office come under close scrutiny. Today the media would probably have discovered Eagleton's malady much earlier in the game and saved the Democrats much embarrassment.

In actuality, with or without Eagleton, McGovern could not have been elected. He fared very poorly throughout the United States and especially in South Carolina. In South Carolina, McGovern's electors received a total of only 168,000 votes, while the electors for Nixon and Agnew received 478,000 votes.

Senator Strom Thurmond, after turning Republican in 1964, had been re-elected as a Republican in 1966, and 1972 was his year to run again. Democratic former state Senator E.N. "Nick" Zeigler, a very capable lawyer from Florence, carried the Democratic banner. Zeigler had great potential as a statewide officeholder, but his timing was not good. In the general election in November, Senator Thurmond prevailed by a vote of 428,000 to 246,000.

Nixon and Agnew were inaugurated again in January 1973. It was a gala affair. Little did the public know what fate had in store for the two of them. Agnew would soon plead guilty to tax fraud in the courts of Maryland, resign and be given a probationary sentence by my good friend Walter Hoffman, who was a United States District Court Judge serving in senior status retirement.

Nixon would soon become involved in the well-known Watergate fiasco and would resign rather than suffer the danger of impeachment. After Agnew resigned, Nixon designated Congressman Gerald Ford Vice President. Ford filled Nixon's unexpired term, serving until 1976, when he was defeated by Georgia's former governor, Jimmy Carter.

53

CAMPAIGN OF 1974

The principal interest in the campaign of 1974 was in the governor's election. Earle Morris had served four years as lieutenant governor and desired to follow in the footsteps of former lieutenant governors George Bell Timmerman Jr., Ernest F. Hollings, Robert McNair and John West, who all had used the same office as a stepping stone to the governorship. As Morris announced his candidacy for the Democratic nomination, he was joined by six others who had the same ambition. They were: William Jennings Bryan Dorn, who had served for a quarter of a century in Congress; Charles D. "Pug" Ravenel, a Charleston banker who was a newcomer to South Carolina politics; Maurice Bessenger; John Bolt "Cotton" Culbertson; Milton J. Dukes; and E.N. "Nick" Zeigler.

By this time the traditional stump meetings in the respective forty-six county seats were vanishing. Radio and television were coming to be the best way to reach the great mass of voters. Ravenel used television to a maximum advantage and surprised everyone by leading in the first Democratic primary held in July. He received a total of 107,000 votes in the first primary, besting Dorn, who received 105,000 votes, and Morris, who received 83,000. The others got a total of about 25,000.

In the second Democratic primary Ravenel again bested Dorn, this time 180,000 to 154,000, but his victory was short lived. The Supreme Court declared Ravenel ineligible to serve and the Democratic Executive Committee designated Dorn to carry the party's banner in the general election. Ravenel's plight in court is told in the next chapter.

While the Democrats were holding their primary and choosing candidates, the Republican party was, for the first time, holding a statewide primary to determine its candidates for governor and lieutenant governor. The Republican primary attracted only some 35,000 voters, while the Democratic primary had attracted well over 300,000 voters. State Senator and oral surgeon James Edwards of Charleston bested retired General William Childs Westmoreland by a vote of about 20,000 against 14,000. Simultaneously,

Carroll Campbell of Greenville was defeating Welsh Morrisette for lieutenant governor by a vote of about 23,000 to 10,000.

In 1974 William Wilkins of Greenville was getting elected Solicitor of the Thirteenth Judicial Circuit as a Republican candidate. He is, according to recollection, the first Republican to hold the office of a state prosecuting attorney for at least a half century.

In the November general election of 1974, Edwards defeated Dorn 266,000 to 248,000 and Edwards became the first Republican Governor of South Carolina for more than a century. He was not eligible for re-election under the Constitution as written at that time.

There was considerable interest that year in the Democratic primary contest for lieutenant governor of South Carolina. There were three strong contenders, Brantley Harvey of Beaufort, Alexander Sanders of Columbia and Horace Smith of Spartanburg. This was one of the closer contests with Harvey receiving 105,300 votes, Sanders receiving 97,900 votes and Smith receiving 105,500 votes in the first primary. In the run-off, Harvey bested Smith and later the Republican nominee Carroll Campbell and served until 1978, at which time he ran for governor and was defeated.

In the general election, Republican Campbell did not fare quite as well as Republican Edwards but received a highly respectable 239,000 votes to Democrat Harvey's 272,000.

Senator Ernest F. Hollings had little little trouble in the general election defeating the Republican candidate, Gwen Rush, more than two to one.

In January 1975 the new Republican governor was sworn in. There were comparatively few Republicans in the House and Senate, but Governor Edwards got along well with the Democrats and his administration as governor of the state was a highly successful one. He was not eligible for re-election and has not entered politics again but did serve in the early 1980s as Secretary of Energy by appointment of President Ronald Reagan. More recently, after leaving the cabinet, he has been serving as president of the Medical University of South Carolina in Charleston.

54

MORE ABOUT PUG RAVENEL'S ELIGIBILITY

A great portion of the work of the Supreme Court is routine. Normally, the Court is asked to determine whether a litigant, civil or criminal, received a fair trial at the courthouse. Occasionally, however, there arises an unusual situation with which the Court must become involved. Such a matter arose incident to the election of governor in 1974.

Charles D. "Pug" Ravenel was born in Charleston in 1938. He resided there with his parents until he graduated from high school in 1956. Thereafter he was away from South Carolina, in college at Harvard and employed in New York and/or Washington for a period of seventeen years. He returned to take up residency again in Charleston on March 20, 1972. In 1974 he entered the race for governor seeking the Democratic nomination.

The Constitution of South Carolina, Article IV, Section 2, provides as follows:

> No person shall be eligible to the office of governor who . . . shall not have been . . . a citizen and resident of this state for five years next preceding the day of election.

As the Democratic party primary campaign waxed along, it came to be rumored that Ravenel was not eligible to serve. In order to combat the rumor, he commenced an action in the Court of Common Pleas for Richland County in March 1974, wherein the Democratic party was his adversary, and procured an order of the trial court, which was not appealed, permitting him to participate in the Democratic primary. The action was for all practical purposes uncontested.

Pug Ravenel was a tremendous salesman. He was particularly effective on television, and to the surprise of a multitude of people, he was victorious in the primary and was named the Democratic candidate to oppose all comers in the November general election.

The issue of his eligibility then became crucial, because under the basic law one may not, even if elected, serve if ineligible under the terms of the Constitution. Attorney Eugene Griffith of Newberry brought a class action on behalf of Ben K. Dekle and Milton J.

Dukes against the Democratic party and the Election Commission, asking the Court of Common Pleas to declare Mr. Ravenel ineligible. Soon thereafter, Ravenel petitioned the Supreme Court to assume original jurisdiction to decide the issue. The two actions were consolidated. They came to be heard in the Supreme Court after Circuit Court Judge J.B. Ness by assignment took testimony and made an evidentiary record.

The evidence revealed that Ravenel had been away from South Carolina for seventeen years prior to 1972. This was documented by his New York income tax returns, his voting in New York and his resident club memberships. It was basically his contention that only a temporary absence was involved and that he intended in the last analysis to return to South Carolina.

The Court held that Ravenel was not eligible to serve, and this caused pandemonium within the Democratic party. The party was left without a candidate with the November general election approaching. Another primary was not practical or possible. That's when the executive committee of the party designated William Jennings Bryan Dorn as their candidate. Dorn had served in the South Carolina House and Senate and Congress many years and had sought the United States Senate nomination in 1948. He was the logical candidate.

The problem created by Ravenel left the Democratic party frustrated. Ravenel did not lend great support to Dorn's candidacy. Edwards got the benefit of the fact that no unity was left in the party.

Democrats will tell you that the problems created by the Ravenel candidacy left the party in disarray and permitted a Republican governor to move in. On the other hand, Republicans will tell you that they simply had the best candidate. Jim Edwards served with distinction.

The impact of television on vote-getting has often been debated. Ravenel used it to perfection, and it was his main selling instrument. He did not do the things candidates had traditionally done to get votes. His success at the ballot box proves beyond doubt that the way to reach the people in modern times is through television.

Ravenel has succeeded in business in South Carolina. In 1978 he ran for the United States Senate against Senator Strom Thurmond and in a subsequent election he ran against Congressman Thomas Hartnett of the Charleston Congressional District. Both candidacies were unsuccessful. Thurmond and Hartnett beat Ravenel at the TV game.

55

CAMPAIGN OF 1976

Nineteen Hundred and Seventy-Six was the year to elect a President and Vice President of the United States. Since the previous election in 1972, Vice President Spiro Agnew had plead guilty to income tax fraud in the courts of Maryland, resigned and been replaced under the succession law, as it then existed, by Gerald Ford, who was the Republican leader in the House of Representatives. Thereafter, Nixon resigned in order to avoid the likelihood of impeachment. This made Ford President, and as the 1972 election approached, Ford was the incumbent President seeking a four-year term in his own right.

Ford had never previously sought the office through the usual process of election. He was a well liked individual, oftentimes accused of being clumsy, but there was never any breath of scandal about Gerald Ford; and he was without question the logical choice in 1976 of the Republican National Convention. In traditional fashion, the convention permitted Ford to choose his vice presidential running mate, and he selected Senator Robert Dole of Kansas.

The history of the happenings during the previous four years when Nixon and Agnew left office in disgrace did not enhance the possibility of Ford and Dole getting elected. People in general were disgusted with national politics, especially as related to the election of the two highest officers in the land.

After Nixon's resignation there appeared to be a high likelihood that he might be indicted for violation of criminal laws. The very fact that he had resigned to avoid impeachment did not give great weight to his presumption of innocence. In order to put the matter at rest, President Ford announced that he was granting a pardon to Nixon for any laws he may have violated for which he might be indicted at the time or thereafter. History was made. Certainly no other pardon of a President had ever been issued. Ford and the Republican party suffered the brunt of this action.

In retrospect, I am of the opinion that the action was wise, not because Nixon was necessarily innocent but because of the turmoil and disruption an indictment and trial would have brought about. The country would have suffered. Ford's decision was one of judgment. The wisdom of his judgment can never be proved or disproved.

Down in the state of Georgia there was a peanut farmer named Jimmy Carter. He was a very capable person in many respects and had graduated from the Naval Academy at Annapolis, had served in the Navy and later as governor of Georgia. Carter became the selection of the Democratic National Convention. He chose as his vice presidential running mate Senator Walter Mondale, who was a protégé of Hubert Humphrey (both were from the state of Minnesota). Carter took full advantage of the fact that Americans were unhappy with what had been taking place in Washington, and the gist of his campaign was to run against Washington and the establishment.

When Carter announced his candidacy for President, no one took him seriously. It has been extremely difficult for a Southerner to muster enough votes to be chosen chief executive. Also, it was pretty generally accepted as a fact that Carter had not been a popular or successful governor of his state. Be that as it may, in several of the early Democratic advisory primaries, held in the spring of 1976, he made an excellent showing and ended up carrying enough states to win the nomination.

In recent years there has been a joke going around relative to the election of John F. Kennedy, Jimmy Carter and Ronald Reagan. There was a time when a Catholic simply couldn't get elected to a national office. There was a time when a divorced man could not overcome the stigma of having a divorce and be elected. The joke went like this: Kennedy proved that a Catholic could be elected President; Reagan proved that a divorced man can be elected President; and Carter proved that anybody can be elected President.

South Carolinians voting for President in 1964, 1968 and 1972 had left the Democratic Party to support Goldwater once and Nixon twice. In 1976 South Carolina reverted to its former custom of voting for Democratic electors and supported the Carter/Mondale ticket by 450,000 votes, while giving to the Ford/Dole Republican ticket 346,000 votes. In support of the Democratic nominees, the Democratic hierarchy made much of the fact that the Republican President and Vice President since 1972 had not done a very good job and of the fact that the South now had an opportunity to select one of its own to serve in the high office.

Mondale was not a good choice so far as South Carolinians were concerned. Obviously Carter chose him in hopes of attracting

Northern liberal votes. The Democrats prevailed in South Carolina not because of Mondale but in spite of him. Four years later, in 1980, the Carter/Mondale Democratic ticket would be repudiated by South Carolina voters and eight years later the Democrats' Mondale/Ferraro ticket would be repudiated. Among those things South Carolinians simply could not stomach about Mondale was the fact that he was a protégé of Hubert Humphrey.

In South Carolina the Republicans were continuing to field acceptable candidates. Five of the Congressmen had Republican opponents and sixteen state Senators had Republican opponents.

Floyd Spence, a Republican from the Second Congressional District, was re-elected, but the other four Republican challengers did not fare as well. The five other congressional seats remained with Democrats.

Carter came from Plains, Georgia, a very small town in the southern part of the state. He was apparently a successful peanut farmer. It was during the middle of the campaign that I visited with my brother in Columbus, Georgia and we rode over to Plains just to look around. It was obvious that the town was in substantial support of their native son. His campaign headquarters were in an abandoned railroad station. His brother Billy, of "Billy Beer" fame, had a filling station across the street. Several souvenir shops had been opened up to serve the tourists who were coming by to visit the town solely because Jimmy had put Plains, Georgia, on the map.

56

CAMPAIGN OF 1978

In 1978 there were no national elections, but there was more than usual interest in the statewide campaigns. A governor and lieutenant governor and a United States Senator were to be elected.

It will be recalled that four years previously William Jennings Bryan Dorn had attempted to salvage the governor's office for the Democratic Party. He was unsuccessful but continued his ambition to serve as chief executive of the state. In 1974 he had made a credible showing, and it was logical for him to undertake the campaign again.

Joining him in the Democratic primary were Lieutenant Governor Brantley Harvey Jr. and state Senator Dick Riley. From the backgrounds of the three, it is easy to understand that the campaign would be hotly contested. All had substantial political strength and sagacity.

Dorn brought to the campaign experience gained from some twelve to fifteen successful elections to the state House of Representatives, to the state Senate and to the Congress of the United States. In addition, he had the advantage of having campaigned four years previously and accordingly had many good recent contacts throughout the state.

Brantley Harvey Jr. had served in the House of Representatives. His father had served in the Senate before him. During his four years as lieutenant governor he had had the advantage of much political exposure. He brought to the campaign much experience and substantial support which he had cultivated while serving as lieutenant governor.

Dick Riley had served in both the state House of Representatives and the state Senate. He was the son of a distinguished lawyer, E.P. "Ted" Riley, from Greenville who had rendered substantial public service in different capacities, including that of President of the South Carolina Bar Association.

In the June primary, Harvey led the ticket with 142,000 votes; Riley got 125,000; and Dorn ran third with only 112,000. In the Democratic primary run-off, Riley overcame the lead which

Harvey had experienced and won the Democratic nomination by a vote of 180,000 to 158,000.

In the meantime the Republicans were holding their second statewide primary. The vote was even smaller than in 1974, when some 34,000 Republicans participated. The two Republican contenders for governor were Raymon Finch and Ed Young. Young barely won out by a vote of 12,000 to Finch's 11,000.

For lieutenant governor, Senator Horace Smith of Spartanburg and Senator Thomas Smith of Florence were contesting for the Democratic nomination along with Nancy Stevenson, a member of the House of Representatives from Charleston. Stevenson led in the first primary, receiving 149,000 votes to Horace Smith's 122,000 and Thomas Smith's 107,000. In the run-off, Stevenson surprised everybody by defeating Horace Smith by a vote of 179,000 to 155,000.

In the general election Stevenson defeated the Republican nominee, John Strong, almost two to one. She became the first woman lieutenant governor of the state. She was to be presiding over the Senate for four years, and it was rumored that she had an ambition to be the first woman governor of South Carolina.

The Democrats had to choose a candidate to oppose Republican Senator Strom Thurmond. Charles D. "Pug" Ravenel was the strongest contender, defeating John Bolt Culbertson, Thomas McElveen and Tom Triplett. Although Ravenel was the winner in the Democratic primary on the first ballot, he never had the enthusiastic support of the Democratic Party because of his having "messed up" the election in 1974, causing South Carolina to have its first Republican governor in more than 100 years.

In the November general election, the Democrats were successful except for Ravenel. Riley beat Ed Young, and Nancy Stevenson beat Republican John Strong, but Thurmond bested Ravenel by some 75,000 votes.

For the first time in modern history, the Republicans claimed two of the state's Congressional seats in Washington. Carroll Campbell Jr. defeated all the Democratic oldtimers and joined Republican Floyd Spence to give to the Republicans two seats as against the Democrats' four. The four Democratic Congressmen in route to Washington along with these two Republicans were Mendel Davis, Butler Derrick, Ken Holland and John Jenrette. Two years later the Republicans would gain two additional seats giving, to that party a majority of the delegates from South Carolina.

57

CAMPAIGN OF 1980

Nineteen eighty was an interesting political year—at least at the national level. In South Carolina many local officeholders were up for re-election, but it was an "off year" for the governor and lieutenant governor and only the contest for a United States Senator to succeed Ernest F. Hollings was of statewide interest. By this time Hollings had been a member of the United States Senate nearly fifteen years and his political roots ran deep in South Carolina. He came from Charleston, and Charleston politicians are normally more sagacious than politicians emanating from other sections of the state. While he had Democratic primary opponents, they were not of significant strength, and Hollings prevailed over Nettie Durant Dickerson and William P. Kremal, who together received only a total of 61,000 votes. Hollings enjoyed a little landslide during the primary and received 266,000 votes, winning on the first ballot.

While Hollings was securing the Democratic nomination, the Republicans were again holding a statewide primary. It is significant that these Republican primaries mustered only a handful of voters. Marshall Mays, an attorney of Greenwood, was the front runner, but he received only 14,000 votes while Robert Carley got 7,000 and Charles Rhodes received 11,000 votes. So it is seen that the Democratic primary mustered well over 300,000 ballots, while the Republican primary was mustering only some 32,000—not quite as many as were cast in 1974.

The fact that few Republicans participated in their own primary did not deter them from voting Republican in substantial numbers when the general election came to be held in November. Whereas Mays had only received 14,000 votes in the primary, he garnered 257,000 in the general election. Simultaneously, Hollings was receiving 612,000 to win.

By 1980 the time had come when people were no longer greatly concerned with party labels. Through television and otherwise the great mass of voters were coming to size up the candidates without considering a party label. They were gradually adopting Strom Thurmond's theory; he always preached that one should vote for the man based on his character, credibility and other qualifications.

That year, in the First Congressional District, Charles D. "Pug" Ravenel was trying one more time to win an election. His candidacy of 1974 had been aborted by the Supreme Court; his candidacy of 1978 had been rebuffed by incumbent Strom Thurmond, who was returned to the United States Senate. In 1980 Ravenel undertook a campaign to represent the people of the First Congressional District, composed of Charleston and adjoining counties. He procured the Democratic nomination, but Republican Thomas Hartnett bested him in November, and Hartnett, for the first time, gave that district Republican representation. The office had been held by Mendel Rivers for more than two decades and by his namesake Mendel Davis in more recent years.

It has often been said that timing is important in politics. Ravenel was a rather capable investment banker and, had he not alienated the Democratic hierarchy in 1974, he might easily have gained some statewide or regional office. Having failed in his attempt to serve as governor, as United States senator and as congressman, it is not likely that he will return to campaigning. However, he is a good salesman, and it is conceivable that he might successfully come to render public service of some kind in the future.

The main interest in politics of 1980 was not at the state level. It was at the national level. Jimmy Carter and Walter Mondale were completing their four-year terms of office and seeking to serve four more years. Their administration had not been a truly successful and satisfactory one, but a national political convention is hard put to deny its incumbents another chance, and so the Democratic National Convention chose incumbent Carter and incumbent Mondale as its candidates.

Out west there was a very attractive disc jockey, movie star and former Governor of California named Ronald Reagan. He was well known throughout the country because of having a successful administration as governor of one of the largest states and by reason of the many motion pictures which he had made. Reagan had for some time had an ambition to serve as President of the United States and had sought to be the nominee on at least one former occasion. In 1980 the Republican Party and the United States were ready for Reagan.

It might be said that Reagan had been in training for campaigning for some forty years. All campaigners, all politicians and, for that matter, all public speakers are actors. Reagan had been an actor for several decades and knew all the tricks of the trade so far as persuasion is concerned. He was, and is, one of the most attractive public speakers who has come to my attention. He was certainly equal to President Franklin Roosevelt (who persuaded by way of the "fireside chat") and has become known as the "Great Communicator."

The timing was right for Reagan. In addition to the fact that he was an excellent salesman, his opposition was not strong. People were ready for a change and had, since 1952, elected Republican presidents on four occasions. Reagan had the happy faculty of making people like him; whether one respected his judgment or not, one could not help but like Ronald Reagan. Into every election is blended an element of popularity. People delight in voting for candidates that they like—whether they are the best for the office or not.

Some twenty years previously, Democrat nominee John F. Kennedy and Republican nominee Richard Nixon had engaged in public television debates. The custom was continued during the campaign of 1980. The Reagan/Carter debates were well advertised and probably attracted one of the largest television audiences ever experienced in the United States. Reagan "ran circles around" Carter and gained much advantage from the televised events. We can never prove the benefit to Reagan and the detriment to Carter growing out of participation in these public appearances, but it is generally accepted that Reagan gained a tremendous advantage.

In the general election in November, Reagan and his vice presidential running mate, George Bush, scored a landslide. In South Carolina there was no landslide, but the Reagan/Bush ticket defeated the Carter/Mondale ticket by a vote of 441,000 to 427,000.

Reagan became a Republican president saddled with a House and Senate of the opposing party. He worked with them well under the circumstance. Two years later the Republicans would barely gain control of the Senate. The House remained, and still remains, Democratic. Reagan rapidly became a very popular President. He was destined to serve the entire eight years permitted under the Constitution.

This was a good year for the Republicans in South Carolina. State Senators and House members had the advantage of riding in on Reagan's coattail. A few county offices also went to Republican candidates, but the tendency of the people to elect Democrats to the offices in the respective courthouses continued.

For the first time, South Carolina Republicans came to occupy a majority of the South Carolina seats in Congress. Joining Hartnett, Spence and Campbell was Republican John Napier, who prevailed in the Sixth Congressional District where Democrats had heretofore been elected by substantial majorities.

58

CAMPAIGN OF 1982

The elections of 1982 centered upon the state offices of governor and lieutenant governor. Prior to 1926 the Constitution provided that the governor be elected for two years. That year the Constitution was amended so that the governor could serve for four years and be ineligible for re-election.

When Dick Riley was elected governor in 1978, it became well known that he favored amending the Constitution so as to allow a governor to succeed himself and serve a total of two terms. He persuaded the Legislature to propose an amendment to the Constitution to be voted on in the fall of 1980 and ratified in 1981, so that when his term expired in 1982 he would be eligible for re-election. It is to the Governor's credit that the members of the House and the Senate agreed. A resolution proposing any amendment required the approval of 82 House members and 32 Senate members. Both agreed by the required vote and the people voted to amend the Constitution. It was ratified routinely when the Assembly convened. Accordingly, Governor Riley was eligible to seek the office for another term, which he did and was unopposed in the Democratic primary.

W.D. Workman Jr., the Republican mayor of Greenville, secured the Republican nomination, defeating Rodney Thomas Martin by a vote of 17,000 to 3,000. This pitted two Greenvillians against each other in contest for governor in November 1982. Riley had performed well as governor and his administration was generally approved. He had served ably as both a House member and a Senator. He had been a leader in the judicial reform movement of 1972. The people gave to him 468,000 votes while Workman received 202,000.

Mike Daniel was a member of the House of Representatives from Cherokee County. He came to serve with distinction as Speaker Pro Tempore of the House. Nancy Stevenson was leaving the office of lieutenant governor and abandoning politics, at least for the moment. Among those seeking the Democratic nomination for the office of lieutenant governor were Daniel and Tom Turnipseed. Turnipseed had served as a member of the Senate from Lexington

County simultaneously with his brother David, who was serving in the same body from Spartanburg County. Seldom have two brothers served at the same time in the Senate. Daniel prevailed and came to represent the Democratic Party in the November election.

Republican Norma Russell had served in the House and the Senate from Lexington County, and she hoped to be the second lady to preside over the Senate of South Carolina. In the November election, Daniel won out, defeating Russell by a vote of 440,000 to 219,000.

This was one of the less eventful election years.

59

CAMPAIGN OF 1984

By 1984 Strom Thurmond had served five full terms as a member of the United States Senate. Few have served longer than thirty years. In 1954 Thurmond became the first and only United States Senator to be elected in a write-in campaign. By the 1980s he was among the senior Republican Senators, and during the time that a majority of the Senators were Republicans, from 1982 to 1986, he served as chairman of the important Senate Judiciary Committee. It is a prestigious assignment, because this committee passes on the qualifications of all federal judges who are appointed by the President and who must be confirmed by the entire Senate.

Most persons who had served as long as Thurmond and were in his age bracket would have chosen to retire, but Strom was robust in health and continued through the years to do all the things a much younger politician does in order to assure re-election. Republican Thurmond could always muster a multitude of Democratic votes. There were many Democrats who wouldn't vote for any Republican except Thurmond.

And there were always enough "dyed in the wool" or "yellow-dog" Democrats to inspire opposition to his candidacy. In the Republican primary, Thurmond had an opponent named Robert Cunningham. In the primary voting, Cunningham received 2,000 votes to Thurmond's 44,000. It is worthy of note that this represents far more Republican voters than had cast ballots in any previous Republican primary election. The Thurmondites came out en masse to make sure that their candidate would be the one carrying the Republican banner in the general election in November.

A man named Melvin Purvis Jr., as well as Cecil J. Williams, sought the Democratic nomination to contest with Thurmond in the general election in November. Neither of these had appreciable political experience, but Purvis was somewhat well known, in name at least, because it was his father (an FBI agent) who had apprehended John Dillenger some three or four decades previously.

That year 149,000 people voted for Purvis in the primary election and 148,000 voted for Williams, making a total of some 300,000 people participating in the Democratic primary. Accordingly, Purvis was to carry the banner in November against incumbent Senator Thurmond. When the votes were counted, Thurmond got 644,000 to Purvis' 306,000. Accordingly, Thurmond was entering his sixth term in the United States Senate, which would make him up for re-election in 1990.

Since leaving the office of lieutenant governor in 1981, Nancy Stevenson had moved to Columbia. She sought the Democratic nomination for the Second Congressional District. Ken Mosley beat her out by a vote of 21,000 to 19,000, and accordingly Mosley had to attempt to defeat the well-entrenched Republican Floyd Spence, who by this time had twelve or fourteen years' seniority in the House of Representatives in Washington. Since that time the former lieutenant governor has not sought political office. Spence continues to serve.

We pointed out in a previous chapter that South Carolina sent four Republicans to Congress in Washington in the election of 1980. The majority control of the House delegation was short-lived because John Napier of the Sixth Congressional District lost the election to Robin Tallon in 1982. This left three Republicans and three Democrats in Congress and one Republican and one Democrat in the United States Senate. In 1984 the balance remained the same, with equal numbers of Republicans serving in each house of Congress.

This was the year for candidates to run for president and vice president of the United States. Ronald Reagan had served for four years and continued to be a very popular president. There was no real debate but that the Republican National Convention would, and did, nominate him for re-election for president, with George Bush as his vice presidential running mate.

The Democratic National Convention chose Walter Mondale to run for president on the Democratic ticket. He had served as vice president from 1976 to 1980 and was defeated along with Jimmy Carter in 1980. No one considered the advisability of nominating Carter again. Mondale was a rather clever politician and ended up as the "sweetheart" of the Democratic convention. It was well recognized that the Democrats had an uphill battle. Mondale appreciated the fact that he had to do something different to defeat a candidate as popular as Reagan. The Democratic convention permitted him to select his vice presidential running mate, and he broke tradition by selecting a congresswoman from upstate New York. She was said to be the protégé of the Speaker of the House of Representatives, Tip O'Neil. Her name was Geraldine Ferraro. She was somewhat of an actress and a showgirl but had a very minimal voter appeal, particularly in the South. The time will likely soon come when a woman will be elected vice president or president, but it will be a politician with more voter appeal than the choice of Mondale and O'Neil. It was obviously the thinking of Mondale that he would combine the black vote, which normally goes Democrat, with the female vote, which normally goes both Democrat and Republican, to the end that a majority vote would be attracted. In the 1984 election, Jimmy Carter gave his support to the Mondale/ Ferraro ticket, but by this time his influence had become almost nil.

When the votes were counted, Reagan and Bush enjoyed one of the biggest landslides known to a presidential election. In South Carolina the vote was overwhelming, with Reagan and Bush receiving 615,000 votes while Mondale and Ferraro received 344,000.

There was a day when the candidates for president of the United States paid little attention to the South. Our section of the country was known as the "Solid South," and it was generally conceded that the Republicans could not prevail in the area. This school of thought has been dying out over the years, and the tremendous votes which the Republicans received in both 1980 and 1984 proved that the South must now be courted for its support in national elections.

Two years later, the second Republican governor of the state would assume office. The time had long gone when people hesitated to admit that they were voting Republican. Actually, the time had come when a substantial part of the people were proud to advertise that they were Republicans. Few people remain who have not at some time or other cast at least one Republican vote.

60

CAMPAIGN OF 1986

In the mid-1960s, E.F. "Fritz" Hollings was first elected to the United States Senate to fill an unexpired term. He prevailed again in 1968, 1974 and 1980. During most, if not all, of these times the Republican party had nominated a candidate to run against him in the general election. Nineteen eighty-six was no exception.

It was in 1984 that Hollings sought the Democratic nomination as president of the United States. He had developed some substantial national stature because of his seniority and by reason of the fact that he accepted quite a few speaking engagements throughout the country. He made a good impression wherever he went. He was a good public speaker and was, and is, sagacious in political matters.

Many of the columnists and people throughout the country were of the opinion that Hollings was actually more qualified to serve as president of the United States than any of the Democratic nominees. This can never be proved or disproved, but in spite of his ability and knowedge of governmental affairs, he was not able to muster enough financial resources to carry on an effective campaign throughout the fifty states. In several advisory primaries he made a good showing, but somewhere along the line he withdrew before the nominating convention.

Just eight years earlier, the voters had selected a Southern politician from Georgia. He did not pan out to the liking of the people, and the very fact that Hollings was also a Southerner made vote-getting difficult in other areas of the country. Had Jimmy Carter not been president, Hollings' chances of winning would have been substantially improved.

As the 1986 campaign began, no Democrat chose to oppose Senator Hollings, but there were two Republicans who contested for the right to challenge him in November. They were Henry McMaster, who had served as District Attorney by appointment of President Reagan, and Dr. Henry Jordan, who was also without substantial political background. McMaster bested Jordan by a vote of 27,000 to 24,000 in the Republican primary, and by so doing won the right to be the Republican candidate against Hollings in

November. Hollings showed his strength by carrying all the counties in the state except Lexington, which has been, for many years, predominantly Republican. Hollings received 465,000 votes while McMaster received 262,000 votes.

Dick Riley was completing eight years as governor of the state. His tenure in office was perhaps longer than any other governor who has served. There were four Democratic candidates seeking the nomination to succeed the outgoing governor. They were: Mike Daniel, who was ending his four-year term as lieutenant governor; retired Circuit Court Judge Frank Eppes, who had left the bench for the purpose of entering the race; Phil Lader, former president of Winthrop College; and Senator Hugh Leatherman of Florence.

Daniel proved to be the best vote-getter and came so near to defeating all others in the first race that the others withdrew from the second race. Daniel had 156,000, Lader 86,000, Eppes 59,000 and Leatherman 28,000 votes. This gave Daniel the right to contest the Republican nominee for governor in the November election.

The Republican nominee was Congressman Carroll Campbell of Greenville. The Republicans had enjoyed the prestige of having their candidate (James B. Edwards) serve as governor from 1975 to 1979, and they were especially anxious to control the office again.

Both Campbell and Daniel were young, energetic and ambitious. Their race was one of the most hotly contested within my memory. The vote was close in a substantial portion of the counties, but in the last analysis, Campbell received 384,000 votes to 361,000 for Daniel; and accordingly, Campbell became the second Republican governor to serve in South Carolina in more than a century.

While Hollings was being sent back to the Senate and Campbell was being sent to the governor's office, Barber and Nick Theodore were contesting for the Democratic nomination of lieutenant governor. Theodore won the right to run against Republican Congressman Thomas Hartnett who had for several years represented the Second Congressional District, composed of Charleston and surrounding counties. Theodore beat Hartnett by some 15,000 votes and gained the right to preside over the Senate and to pursue the office of governor four years hence as lieutenant governor candidates normally do.

By 1986 the Republicans were beginning to field more and more candidates in all races both local and statewide. A few Republican candidates were coming to serve in the various offices within the courthouses, but these officeholders remained predominantly Democrats.

This year the Democrats retained a majority of the seats in Congress. Elected Democrats were Butler Derrick, Liz Patterson, Robin Tallon and John Spratt. The Republicans continued to send their representatives back to Congress for the First and Second Districts. They were Arthur Ravenel, a newcomer and Floyd Spence, who had served for fifteen years already.

The South Carolina Election Commission reported that 1,300,000 people were registered and qualified to vote in 1986, while 770,000 actually cast ballots. This represented approximately sixty percent of all those who were qualified to vote. The Commission reported that of those voting, 572,000 were white and 197,000 were black; 347,000 were male and 422,000 were female.

Voters in South Carolina have never been required to register by party. Any qualified voter can vote in either primary but not both. A split ticket in the primary is not permitted, but in the general election a split ticket is, of course, allowed.

61
CAMPAIGN OF 1988

While the nation was voting for Republican presidents in recent years, more often the voters in the respective states were leaving both the national House of Representatives and the United States Senate in the hands of the Democrats. Rare have been the times in recent years when the Republicans controlled either of these two legislative bodies.

In South Carolina, Republicans have constantly gained strength at the state and local levels. Senator Strom Thurmond has been elected repeatedly as a Republican since 1964. Several Republicans have served in Congress, and by 1987 thirty-four House members and twelve Senators had come to serve after being elected on a Republican ticket to the General Assembly.

And so it might be said that there is a new day in South Carolina politics as will be reflected by the following story concerning the elections of 1988.

To the amazement of many, Jimmy Carter of Georgia, a Democrat, was elected President in 1976, but his administration was repudiated vigorously when he sought re-election in 1980. Ronald Reagan was elected in 1980 and 1984 with George Bush as his vice presidential running mate, but Reagan was not eligible for re-election and the presidential office was up for grabs in 1988. Both parties had quite a few candidates who were willing to serve.

Among the Republican Presidential candidates was Vice President George Bush, who had served in Congress and held many prestigious assignments by appointment but had been defeated in Texas in 1972 by Lloyd Bentsen in a contest for the Senate. Senator Robert Dole of Kansas, who was the vice presidential running mate of Gerald Ford in 1976, sought the nomination along with Pat Robertson, a television evangelist, and Jack Kemp, a conservative Congressman from New York.

The Democrats were blessed with eight people who were willing to serve: Michael Dukakis, Governor of Massachusetts; Richard Gephardt, Senator from Missouri; Albert Gore Jr., Senator from Tennessee; Paul Simon, Senator from Illinois; Jesse Jackson, who had no political background and was the only black candidate in pursuit of the office; Bruce Babbitt, Governor of Arizona; Gary Hart, Senator from Colorado; and Joe Biden, Senator from Delaware.

Gone are the days when nominees for President were chosen by high-powered political people in smoke-filled rooms. In recent years a new custom of selecting candidates has come into being. The new system has made the conventions almost meaningless. Under the new plan, advisory primaries are held in a substantial portion of the states. These advisory primaries may be either by popular vote or by precinct caucus. This is good and bad. It is good because it allows the great mass of people to have a voice in selecting the nominee. It is bad because, in my opinion, it results too often in an incompetent nominee—or at least a highly undesirable one. As these advisory primaries were held, candidates were, one by one, for all intents and purposes eliminated. The system gives to the first states holding primaries more prestige and influence than is due. In other words, whoever runs well in the first few states, as did Jimmy Carter in 1976, creates a psychology in his favor and gains substantial advantage in those states which hold primaries later on.

Nineteen eighty-eight was the first year in which we had what was referred to as "Super Tuesday." The Southeastern states agreed to hold their primaries simultaneously, hoping that a unified showing would give them substantial influence and an advantage. It can be forcefully argued that no such advantage was forthcoming.

Primaries demand prolonged campaigning time and they are expensive. For these reasons, many persons who might serve well as president simply will not take on the chore.

Several weeks before the Democratic convention in July in Atlanta, it had been definitely determined that Michael Dukakis would be the Democratic nominee. Several weeks before the Republican convention in New Orleans in August, it had been determined that Bush would be the nominee. All candidates for the nominations of the two parties had withdrawn well in advance, except for Jesse Jackson, who continued to campaign until the time of the Democratic convention.

Two candidates withdrew and by so doing made history. One was Senator Gary Hart from Colorado. In the spring of 1988 he was considered to be the leading candidate. He had sought the office before, not successfully but with respectability, and it was conceded that he was probably the strongest of all the eight Democratic nominees. Hart had been accused of being a womanizer and made the mistake of challenging the press to prove that allegation. A Miami newspaper took the challenge and publicized a meeting he had with the "wrong woman," resulting in such tremendous unfavorable publicity that he withdrew from the race. My brother Boyd, has often said, and I do not think it original with him, that the doors of destiny often swing on small hinges. Except for the bad judgment which Gary Hart exhibited on this occasion, it is quite conceivable that he might have been president of the United States.

Senator Joe Biden of Delaware was faring reasonably well in the campaign also, when it was discovered that he was plagiarizing other speakers without giving those speakers credit for the things he was saying. He too received much unfavorable press and was forced to "voluntarily" leave the campaign.

And so as the Democrats came to convene in Atlanta, it was well understood that Dukakis would be the nominee. He had been elected Governor of Massachusetts on more than one occasion and was a capable, hard-working individual but one who had little personality appeal and made less than good television appearances. Be that as it may, immediately after the Atlanta convention adjourned, six of seven respected national polls indicated that Dukakis would, by a good margin, win the election against George Bush.

As the New Orleans convention came into being, it was well conceded that Dole, Robertson and Kemp were no longer to be considered. The big question was: Who will Bush choose as his vice presidential running mate? Many were of the view that he should choose either Senator Dole or Congressman Kemp. To the surprise of almost everyone he designated Senator Dan Quayle of Indiana.

Quayle had made a name for himself when he defeated extreme left-wing Senator Birch Bayh in 1980 for a seat in the Senate. This pleased South Carolinians because of the important part Bayh had played in defeating Fourth Circuit Court of Appeals Judge Clement Haynesworth for a seat on the United States Supreme Court some fifteen years previously.

It developed, however, that Quayle was not a popular choice. He promptly came under fire, being accused of using family political influence to get in the National Guard some twenty years before in lieu of going to Vietnam during hostilities there. He had not had a good academic record and had not made for himself an enviable record as a United States Senator. His lack of voter appeal caused the Republicans to put him on the back burner during the campaign, and, in the last analysis, Bush was elected not because of Quayle but in spite of him.

In the meantime, Dukakis had chosen as his running mate Senator Lloyd Bentsen, who had served in the Senate from Texas for eighteen years. And so from late summer until November, the campaign for president and vice president was well under way. It is unfortunate that the time has come when money plays such an important part in these elections. It is now well recognized that television is the way to reach the voters, and television is expensive. As the campaign waxed along in September and October, the polls to which I have referred began to change. Bush developed rather skillful campaigning tactics. Dukakis failed in this area. The people had been reasonably well satisfied with the Reagan conservative administration. Bush labeled Dukakis a "liberal," and the people were simply in no mood to elect a liberal president of the United States. They wanted someone who advocated less government rather than more government.

In the last analysis, candidate Bush carried forty-one states. Dukakis carried nine states and the District of Columbia. Until 1988, no vice president had been elevated to the presidency for approximately 150 years, since President Van Buren was so elevated.

No presidential campaign in the history of the country created as much interest and demanded as much attention as the November 8, 1988 election. There was a time when members of a political party voted for the candidate of the party because he had been chosen by the party bigwigs. That day has changed, and television has been largely responsible for bringing this about. In modern times candidates for president are in the television news every night and oftentimes throughout the day. Individuals at home see them and hear them and make up their own minds, in effect saying, "To heck with the party, I know who I want to vote for."

Endorsements are no longer of great importance. In South Carolina, the very popular Strom Thurmond endorsed Senator Dole. The very popular former Governors Robert E. McNair and Dick Riley endorsed Gephardt. Neither candidate prevailed in South Carolina. All of which is another way of saying that there is, in the South today and throughout the country, an independence of thought where political matters are concerned.

While South Carolina was voting Republican in the president's race for the third time in a row, interesting situations were developing at the state and local level. Republican primaries are now held, and oftentimes the contest within the Republican Party is intense. No longer do candidates go on vacation after the primary is over, unless perhaps they are unopposed in the general election.

In South Carolina some eight or ten Republican sheriffs were elected in 1988. The percentage of Republicans serving in the General Assembly remained about the same as in the previous year. In 1988, thirty-seven Republican House members were elected along with eleven state Senators.

It had always been considered that Spartanburg was one of the stronger Democratic counties. Perhaps this comes from the fact that Spartanburg was one of only two counties out of forty-six which remained with the Democratic Party in 1948, when Governor Strom Thurmond ran for president on a States' Rights ticket. Of the eight House members elected in November 1988 in Spartanburg County, six were Republicans. Of the three Senators, two were Republicans. For the first time this century, a Republican, Bill Coffey, was elected sheriff.

Once more it has been emphasized that the South is no longer solidly Democratic, and Spartanburg County, as well as all of South Carolina, is now truly two party.

The cost of campaigning in either a Republican primary or a Democratic primary has been escalating in recent years. When a candidate selected by either party's primary must meet an opponent in the general election, the cost becomes correspondingly more high.

Candidates are required to report their expenditures. These expenses may be paid by the candidate or raised through friends and committees. The cost of campaigning tends to prohibit people of moderate means from seeking office. A recent news story, appearing after the November 8 election, indicated that six candidates for the State Senate in South Carolina spent more than $100,000 each. Two of these six were defeated in spite of the money spent. One candidate, who was defeated, commented that the time had come when one must spend $75,000 to get defeated.

In races for the House of Representatives, seven candidates spent more than $25,000 each. Four of them were defeated. Expenditures by other candidates for the Senate and the House were also staggeringly large, but not as great as the figures recited above.

It is unfortunate that the cost of campaigning has become so tremendous. There are a few people who make contributions to a candidate because they are interested in good government and have no axe to grind, but one need not be bit by Solomon's dog to come to the realization that most people who contribute to the candidate will call upon the candidate, if elected, for some favors or advantages. The time may come when the government will finance all campaigning and the law will forbid that candidates accept contributions.

The power of incumbency was emphasized again in 1988 in both the election of House members and Senators to Washington and House members and Senate members to the General Assembly in South Carolina. Elsewhere reference has been made to the fact that it is almost impossible to defeat a Congressman. In actuality, it is almost impossible to defeat any incumbent legislator in either the Congress of the United States or the General Assembly of South Carolina. Even though the great mass of people are traditionally unhappy with what goes on in Congress and in the General Assembly, they admire and respect their own representatives and vote for them to continue to serve.

It is routine that a few do not seek re-election, but of those who do seek re-election, well over ninety percent are returned to office. Public officeholders develop a knack of cultivating friendships. In all elections, voters tend to support people they like, oftentimes disregarding competency. If presidents were permitted to run for office again and again, it is likely that they too would serve over long periods of time. There is substantial thinking to the effect that members of Congress and the Legislature should be limited as to the duration of their service. It is a concept which will not take hold rapidly.

A large book could be, and doubtless will be, written about the elections of 1988. In this brief chapter I have merely attempted to touch the highlights.

62

CONCLUSION

In 1987 I published a book entitled *Littlejohn's Half Century at the Bench and Bar—1936-1986*. In that book I attempted to record for history many of the changes which took place during that era, at the bench and bar, in the administration of justice and in the court system of South Carolina. It might be said the book contained my "legal memoirs."

My reason for writing my political memoirs is to record for history some of the tremendous changes which have taken place in South Carolina's political world and government from 1934 to 1988. It is by no means an all-inclusive history. The matters about which I have written come largely from my memory and from a few political files which I have accumulated over the years. By this time it must be apparent to the reader that the politics of 1934 and the politics of 1988 are as different as night and day.

The United States celebrated its 200th anniversary in 1986. I have lived more than a third of this country's 200 years and have been either a participant in, or at least intensely interested in, political matters in South Carolina during more than one-fourth of this time. One in a position to write about the first fifty years of the life of the United States (1786-1836) could report many changes. One writing about the second fifty years (1836-1886) or the third fifty years (1886-1936) could also tell of many changes which have come about. The fourth fifty years of the life of the United States (1936-1986), about which I write, involve more changes than any other similar period of time. It is difficult to envision the changes which may take place during the next fifty years. Is it conceivable that there will in the future be just as many changes—or perhaps even more.

My political memories bring to mind the seventeen inaugurations of governors of South Carolina which I have attended in some official capacity or as a spectator. These include the inauguration of Olin D. Johnston (first term) in 1935, when I was a student at the University. Thereafter as a member of the Legislature and/or as Speaker, I attended the inaugurations of Burnett R. Maybank (1939), Emile Harley (1941), Richard M. Jefferies (1942), Olin D.

Johnston (second term, 1943) and Strom Thurmond (1947). I missed the inauguration of Ransom Williams, who in 1945 was elevated to the governorship while I was away in the United States Army. As a circuit judge or a member of the Supreme Court, I attended the inaugurations of James F. Byrnes (1951), George Bell Timmerman Jr. (1955), Ernest F. Hollings (1959), Donald S. Russell (1963), Robert E. McNair (unexpired term, 1965), Robert E. McNair (full term, 1967), John C. West (1971), James Edwards (1975) and Richard Riley (twice, in 1979 and 1983). In retirement I was invited by Chief Justice J.B. Ness to sit with the Supreme Court, substituting for absent Associate Justice David W. Harwell, and attended the inauguration of Carroll Campbell in January 1987. If any other South Carolinian, except perhaps Strom Thurmond or Rembert Dennis, has attended as many inaugurations, I am not aware of it.

During the era about which I have written, South Carolina has changed from a largely agricultural state to an industrial state. During that time there have come into being social security, worker's compensation, minimum wage and unemployment insurance.

The growth of the government has been gigantic. The State Appropriation Bill in 1937 was $13 million dollars. Today it is more than three billion dollars. The devaluation of the dollar is emphasized by the fact that the salaries of the governor and of the members of the Supreme Court were approximately $6,000 in the mid-thirties. Today each receives nearly $100,000. A hotdog could be bought for a nickel; by contrast one now costs almost a dollar.

During this time we have seen the maturing of radio (first station in South Carolina in 1930) and the coming of TV. This state now has sixteen television stations, 214 AM radio stations and 88 FM radio stations. These have changed appreciably the complexion of political campaigning. They have brought about a virtual abolition of the campaign stump meetings we used to know.

Among those things which have changed greatly is the activity of the state and federal courts. Not until the tenure of office of President Franklin D. Roosevelt did the Supreme Court of the United States come to affect lives of the great mass of people. Simultaneously, the state courts too have come to affect the lives of all citizens.

Integration of the schools came about by edicts of the Supreme Court of the United States in the mid-1950s. Not all states in the South accepted the new regulation gracefully. Harvey Gantt was the first student admitted to a higher school of learning in South

Carolina (Clemson). It is to the credit of South Carolina people that our state experienced less violence and fewer disruptions than any other Southern state. While some integration problems still exist, as a whole South Carolina has made more progress in this area than most Southern States.

Some fifty years ago, fourteen circuit court judges worked about half-time and disposed of the criminal and civil cases expeditiously. The Supreme Court of South Carolina operated at a leisurely pace. There came into being in South Carolina in 1973 the unified court system, followed by the creation of the family court system, the Court of Appeals and the expansion of the circuit court system. All courts, both state and federal, are now operating under a strain. It is difficult for courts to keep abreast of the case load. More and more people are now engaged in the trial and disposition of cases, in law enforcement and in penal affairs as well as the administration of justice in general. It is inescapable that society as it has come to be developed has required, and will continue to require, more regulation.

As I came to practice law in the mid-1930s, a few implements of law and other offices were not available. These included such things as the ball point pen, the electric typewriter, the word processor, the copying machine, air conditioning and dial telephones. All of these are now accepted as routine necessities in any modern business office.

The return of the Republican Party to great activity came into being about 1960 and has constantly increased since that time. From the beginning of my political activities in 1934 until the late 1950s, nomination by the Democratic Party was the equivalent of election. Several times in recent years the state has voted for a Republican president. In increasing numbers Republicans are coming to serve in Congress from South Carolina and in the General Assembly as well as in local offices. Truly South Carolina has become a two-party state.

Among those things which the United States Supreme Court has come to require of all states is reapportionment of their representation in legislative bodies periodically. The single-member district is now required in many regions. Home rule is now the order of the day. Until a few years ago, the local legislative delegation controlled courthouse activity through legislation at the General Assembly level.

At the beginning of my political career, just about everything governmental was controlled by white, male Democrats. Blacks did not vote, and women indicated little interest in participating in political functions; this is not true today.

In 1934 there were few paved and hard-surfaced roads in South Carolina. The network of excellent roads, including interstate highways, now appear on a South Carolina road map like a spider web. I would estimate that in 1934 there were registered in South Carolina 100,000 automobiles. Today there must be a million and a half.

All of the things which I summarize in this chapter have helped to bring about a new day. The South Carolina of 1934 is not the South Carolina of 1988. Hopefully, it is better.

Looking down the road I predict that the great mass of citizens and taxpayers will be more demanding of those who serve in political office. The Freedom of Information Act which makes most public records available to the citizenry, and the tendency of the media to investigate and report have caused public officials to live in a fishbowl. There was a time when people would select an outstanding member of the community to serve in Congress or in the State Legislature. Work in both bodies was largely part-time, and officeholders did not make a career of the chore. Today, at the national level and to some degree at the state level, legislators are required to devote their full time to this effort. Campaign money has become too important a part of political activities. The honor of serving still remains high, but the desirability of serving has been considerably lessened because of the tremendous demands on one's time, energies and other activities.

I am to some degree acquainted with political activities in other states. By comparison, I conclude that government in South Carolina is as efficient and as trouble-free as any state in the country.

APPENDIX

BLACKS WHO HAVE SERVED RECENTLY
IN THE HOUSE OF REPRESENTATIVES

Name	County
Barksdale, Hudson L.	Spartanburg
Goggins, Juanita W.	York
Matthews, John W., Jr.	Orangeburg
Middleton, Earl M.	Orangeburg
Mitchell, Theo W.	Greenville
Murray, Joseph R.	Charleston
Patterson, Kay	Richland
Washington, McKinley, Jr.	Charleston
Wilson, George	Richland
Blanding, Larry	Sumter
Murray, Julius	Richland
Broadwater, Thomas D.	Richland
Foster, Samuel R.	York
Gadson, Tobias, Sr.	Charleston
Joe, Isaac C.	Lee-Kershaw
White, Juanita M.	Jaster-Beaufort
Ferguson, Tee	Spartanburg
Gilbert, Frank	Florence-Darlington
Martin, Daniel E., Sr.	Charleston
Miles, Mary P.	Calhoun-Orangeburg-Lexington
Williams, Dewitt	Berkeley
Bailey, Kenneth E.	Orangeburg
Brown, Joe E.	Richland
Faber, James	Richland
McBride, Frank E.	Richland
Mitchell, H. Larry	Orangeburg
Shelton, Sara V.	Greenville
Whipper, Lucille S.	Charleston

WOMEN WHO HAVE SERVED RECENTLY IN THE HOUSE OF REPRESENTATIVES

Name/Party	County
Shealy, Sherry (R)	Lexington
Baskin, Jewel Senn Breland (R)	Richland
Frederick, Carolyn E. (R)	Greenville
Goggins, Juanita W. (D)	York
Rudnick, Irene Krugman (D)	Aiken
Russell, Norma Caldwell (R)	Lexington
Stevenson, Ferdinan Backer (D)	Charleston
Toal, Jean Hoefer (D)	Richland
Dreyfus, Sylvia K. (D)	Greenville
Eargle, Martha Lois (D)	Horry
Hearn, Joyce C. (R)	Richland
Keyserling, Harriet H. (D)	Beaufort
Meyers, Jean Brewer (D)	Horry
Crocker, Virginia Leaman (D)	Laurens
Harris, Jean Laney (D)	Chesterfield
White, Juanita Mitchell (D)	Jasper-Beaufort
Miles, Mary Pondexter (D)	Calhoun-Orangeburg-Lexington
Moss, Donna Anderson (D)	Cherokee
Nelson, Denny Woodall (D)	Darlington
Shelton, Sara Valena (D)	Greenville
Wells, Carole C. (R)	Spartanburg
Whipper, Lucille Simmons (D)	Charleston

REPUBLICANS WHO HAVE SERVED RECENTLY IN THE HOUSE OF REPRESENTATIVES

Name	County
Cain, Marshall C.	Aiken
Atkinson III, R.O.	Chester
Rowell, J. Victor	Williamsburg
Dunbar, C. Julian	Aiken
Limehouse, Julian Sidi	Charleston
Campbell, Carroll A., Jr.	Greenville

* Johnson, George Dean, Jr. .... Spartanburg
Adams, Weston .... Richland
Baskin, Jewell Senn Breland .... Richland
Baskin, Weems Oliver, III .... Richland
Collins, Cecil Lennis .... Aiken
Ebert, Michael Preston .... Richland
Hines, Richard Towill .... Spartanburg
Kirk, Lewis Roger, Jr. .... Richland
LaFitte, John Hancock, Jr. .... Richland
Marchant, Thomas Mood, III .... Greenville
Russell, Norma Caldwell .... Lexington
Sanders, W.T. .... Richland
Shealy, Sherry Lynn .... Lexington
Stroud, William H. .... Greenville
Bradley, John Daniel, III .... Charleston
Earle, John Kern .... Greenville
Evatt, H. Parker .... Richland
Ham, Harold Ray .... Lexington
Koon, Larry Labruce .... Lexington
Lister, Toney J. .... Spartanburg
Simpson, Edward Whitson, Jr. .... Pickens
Burriss, Thomas Moffatt .... Richland
Hearn, John C. .... Richland
Kohn, Robert Alfred .... Charleston
Bradley, Philip Tibbs .... Greenville
Brinker, Lawrence Hamner .... Charleston
Hardy, Archibald .... Richland
Rigdon, Richard Levi .... Greenville
Winstead, Daniel Edward .... Charleston
Aydlette, Derwood Lorraine, Jr. ...... Charleston
Gonzales, James Elliott .... Charleston
Sheppard, Dalton, Jr. .... Lexington
Wilkins, David Horton .... Greenville
Brett, Timothy Andrew .... Greenville
Cork, William Neville .... Beaufort
Derrick, Paul Wayne .... Lexington
Russell, John R. .... Spartanburg

---

* George Dean Johnson Jr. has the distinction of having been elected as a Democrat
at the head of the ticket. He was later elected as a Republican, again heading the
ticket.

Thrailkill, Benjamin Edward, Jr. ..... Horry
Burriss, John Hay .... Lexington
Burriss, Mildord Deal .... Richland
Davenport, Ralph Guy, Jr. .... Spartanburg
Fair, Michael L. .... Greenville
Foxworth, Eugene D., Jr. .... Charleston
Sharpe, Charles Ray .... Aiken-Lexington
Sturkie, Charlie Lenoir .... Lexington
Woodruff, Tom Griffin, Jr. .... Aiken
Baker, Boyd Odell .... Greenville
Brown, Henry Edward, Jr. .... Berkeley
Clyborne, Harry Howell, Jr. .... Greenville
Corning, Roland Shelton .... Richland
Haskins, Terry Edward .... Greenville
Limehouse, Thomas A. .... Dorchester
Mappus, Theodore Tobias, Jr. .... Charleston
McCain, William Simonton .... Orangeburg
Wells, Carole C. .... Spartanburg
Cole, J. Derham .... Spartanburg
Lanford, Steve .... Spartanburg

REPUBLICANS WHO HAVE SERVED RECENTLY IN THE SENATE

Name	*County*
McMillan, Gilbert E.	Aiken
Wofford, Thomas A.	Greenville
Edwards, James B.	Charleston
Hartnett, Thomas F.	Charleston
Dooley, A.J.	Lexington
Laughlin, Michael L.	Aiken
Richardson, Jeff Roland	Greenville
McConnell, Glenn F.	Charleston
Ravenel, Arthur, Jr.	Charleston
Russell, Norma C.	Lexington
Ellis, Ralph H.	Horry
Shealy, Ryan C.	Aiken-Bamberg-Barnwell-Edgefield-Lexington
Applegate, William Edward, III (Sam) ..	Charleston
Branton, William Strobel, Jr.	Dorchester-Berkeley

Courson, John Edward .... Richland
Giese, Warren Kenneth .... Richland
Lee, William Richard .... Spartanburg
Thomas, David L. .... Greenville
Wilson, Addison (Joe) Graves .... Lexington
Russell, John R...................... Spartanburg

INDEX